LIFE OF LORD DENMAN

Eng^d by Geo. E. Perine, New York.

LORD CHIEF JUSTICE DENMAN.

JAMES COCKCROFT & Co

LIFE

OF

THOMAS, FIRST LORD DENMAN

FORMERLY

LORD CHIEF JUSTICE OF ENGLAND

BY

SIR JOSEPH ARNOULD

LATE JUDGE OF THE HIGH COURT OF BOMBAY

IN TWO VOLUMES

VOL. II.

BOSTON:

ESTES & LAURIAT,

143 WASHINGTON STREET.

1874.

CONTENTS.

CHAPTER XXIV.

CHAPTER XXV

CHAPTER XXVI.

CHAPTER XXVII.

CHAPTER XXVIII.

CHAPTER XXIX

CHAPTER XXX.

CHAPTER XXXI.

CHAPTER XXXII.

CHAPTER XXXIII.

CHAPTER XXXIV.

CHAPTER XXXV.

CHAPTER XXXVI.

CHAPTER XXXVII.

CHAPTER XXXVIII.

LIFE

OF

LORD DENMAN.

CHAPTER XXIV.

PEERAGE—BARON DENMAN OF DOVEDALE.

A. D. 1834. ÆT. 55.

IN the Spring Assizes of 1834 Denman presided on the Norfolk Circuit, his companion being Sir John Vaughan, then one of the Barons of the Exchequer, but shortly after removed to the Common Pleas.[1]

It was while on this circuit that the Chief Justice was raised to the Peerage by the title of Baron Denman of Dovedale.

The immediate moving cause of this elevation to the Peerage was the urgent want felt by Brougham of additional legal assistance in the House of Lords. Early in the spring of this year Brougham had twice written on the subject to Lord Grey,[2] pressing the appointment very strongly, intimating that Denman would not decline it, stating even the title, Denman of Dovedale, that he wished to take, and winding up by the assurance, "My

[1] Sir John Vaughan, long famous at the Bar as Mr. Sergeant Vaughan; born 1768; called to the Bar, 1781; Sergeant, 1799; Baron of Exchequer, 1827; Common Pleas, Easter Term, 1834; died 1839, æt. 71. Foss's "Lives of the Judges," vol. ix. p. 288.

[2] See the two letters in Brougham's "Memoirs," vol. iii. pp. 337, 340.

belief is that it will be one of the most popular things that you ever did.'

Lord Grey in consequence wrote to Denman in the following terms:

"Downing Street: March 19, 1834.

"My dear Lord Chief Justice,—The Chancellor has expressed to me his anxious desire to obtain your assistance in the House of Lords, where he is indeed much in want of it; and I feel myself of how much benefit it would generally be to the Government. He states to me also your consent to the immediate adoption of the necessary measures for this purpose.

"I am therefore prepared to propose to the King your elevation to the Peerage, and shall have the greatest pleasure in doing so both from personal and public motives.

"But before I speak to His Majesty on the subject I feel it to be necessary that I should have your personal sanction, and shall hope to receive it by the return of the post; I say by the return of the post because the King goes out of town on Friday, and I should wish to make the proposal to him that morning before he leaves St. James's.

"I am, with the truest regard,
"Ever yours most faithfully,
"GREY."

Denman's answer was immediate, and ran as follows:

"Bury St. Edmunds: March 20, 1834.

"My dear Lord,—Allow me to express my warmest acknowledgments for the honor which you tender me, and which I accept in the hope of rendering some public service in the House of Lords.

"The engagements of my own court will hardly allow of my rendering much assistance in the judicial business there; but I will be happy to contribute to the extent of my power.

"You will excuse my requesting that if the proposal should be unacceptable to the highest quarter [the King], you may not be prevented from withdrawing it by the communication you have made to me. Nothing could give me more pain than to cause any difficulty in conducting the administration.

"I must also assure you (though I am writing in a narrow corner of time) that the highest satisfaction I derive, not only from your present kindness, but from that which led you to place me in my present office, arises from the evidence of your esteem and confidence.

"I have the honor to be, my dear Lord,

"Your most obliged and faithful,

"THOMAS DENMAN."

Denman having thus given the required sanction, the Prime Minister lost no time in submitting the matter to the King, with what result appears from the following letter:

"Downing Street: March 21, 1834.

"Dear Lord Chief Justice,—I am just returned from St. James's. The King did not make an objection, but at once assented in the most gracious manner, expressing himself in terms of great approbation of your conduct since you have been Chief Justice, which, he said, he felt more bound to do from having been originally opposed to your appointment.

"I make this communication with increased pleasure, as it is most gratifying to the sincere feelings of friendship which I entertain for you.

"I cannot conclude without thanking you for the kind expressions contained in your letter, which I received this morning.

"I remain, dear Lord Chief Justice,

"Yours very faithfully,

"GREY.

"P.S. Orders are given at the Home Office for the immediate preparation of your patent."[1]

Denman's answer followed immediately:

"Bury St. Edmunds: March 22, 1834.

"My dear Lord,—I must trouble you with my thanks for your prompt communication. The generous approval of His Majesty enhances my satisfaction, as much as his

[1] Extract from "London Gazette," March 22, 1834: "The King has been pleased to direct letters patent to be passed under the Great Seal, granting the dignity of a Baron of the United Kingdom of Great Britain and Ireland to the Right Hon. Sir Thomas Denman, Knight, Chief Justice of the Court of King's Bench, and the heirs male of his body lawfully begotten, by the name, style, and title of Baron Denman of Dovedale, in the county of Derby."

former reluctance does my sense of gratitude to yourself.

"Most faithfully, my dear Lord, yours,
"T. DENMAN."

On the same day, Saturday, March 22, Brougham communicated the intelligence to Lady Denman in the following note:

"Dear Lady D.,—I ought to have let you know yesterday that H. M. has been graciously pleased to make the C. J. a peer, and he will be accordingly created in the course of to-day.

"Yours truly,
"H. BROUGHAM."

The answer of the new peeress, which, as Mrs. Baillie remarks, is "a striking instance of her perfect simplicity of character," ran thus:

"My dear Lord Brougham,—I was never so much surprised in my life as when I received your note. Thank you for breaking the news to me, and pray tell me whether my husband is coming to town.

"Believe me, very sincerely yours,
"THEODOSIA DENMAN."

Brougham answered:

"Dear Lady D.,—I see the Ch. J. is well worthy of promotion to be an hereditary councillor, for he can keep a secret. He will not, I suppose, be in town any the sooner for being a Lord.

"Yours very truly,
"H. BROUGHAM."

Denman in the meanwhile, on the same day, directly the appointment was rendered certain, had written to his wife from Bury St. Edmunds the following letter, which she of course did not receive till the 23rd, the day after Brougham's communication:

"Bury: March 22, 1834.

"My dearest love,—The enclosed papers [Lord Grey's letters and copies of his own replies] will, I think, interest you. I have marked them in the order in which they should be read.

"Most likely you have already heard some reports on the subject, and you may feel a little angry that I did not consult you. But the strictest secresy was enjoined, and I, not feeling quite sure that the *Principal* [the King] would acquiesce, insisted upon it that the matter should be dropped rather than at all pressed upon him.

"His handsome, generous conduct enhances my satisfaction, as much as his former reluctance [about the Chief Justiceship] does my gratitude to Lord Grey.

"I most sincerely hope this elevation will give you pleasure; nobody ever deserved honor or prosperity better.

"I don't suppose the young ladies will require any apology or consolation. I think my sister [Mrs. Baillie] will like to hear of this, and you to tell her.

"I am, my dearest love,

"Your most affectionate and faithful husband.

"I hope you approve of our taking our old names of Dovedale, in the county of Derby."

Lady Denman's letter to her husband after first receiving Brougham's communication has not been preserved: on Sunday 23, Denman writes to her from Norwich, acknowledging it:

"A thousand thanks for your letter: in the course of the day you will receive a more formal announcement of our change of condition, which I am very glad you do not dislike. I shall have the power of franking on Wednesday."

On the Wednesday accordingly, the 26th, he writes again from Norwich:

"I will not address you as I had intended, 'my peer-less peeress,' because that might look as though you had lost your new-made peer. What a strange state of things! but it will soon be as familiar as any other of our numerous changes of condition.

"This [the Norfolk] is reckoned the easiest of the circuits, and generally lasts the shortest time; but somehow or other, there is a dragging tendency in these times, which keeps one a monstrous long while on the judgment-seat. I have done my criminal work, but Vaughan's list is very heavy, and I must give some aid.

"Coke[1] has been here—the greatest of all compliments—and I must keep my promise of spending a short time at Holkham. You would wonder at his spirits. The day

[1] Coke of Holkham, then in his eighty-second year.

before yesterday he dined here; I was unluckily kept in court. Yesterday, he sent word that he would take coffee with us; I was again in court till past ten. He came at eleven, and kept us gossiping till near one; then he went and made the under-sheriff, his host, sit up till near two. His boys came from school to-day, and he has taken them home. Pretty well for 82 years of age."

To his third daughter, Fanny (Lady Baynes), then at Stony Middleton, Denman wrote as follows, immediately after his return to town and while awaiting his first introduction to the House of Lords.

"Dear and Honorable Fanny,—Did you ever read Pepys' Memoirs? He describes his own dignity by saying that when he went to church in his native village the minister addressed his congregation, at the opening of the service, as 'Right Honorable and Dearly Beloved,' &c.

"Being now in a remarkably bad humor, and you being the person in the world I should select to vent it on, I take you in hand, sitting in the Chancellor's room, waiting for two Barons to arrive to introduce me into this noble House, there to take oaths and my seat.

"Your mother was so much in love with you for your letter on this subject of elevation, that she copied it out for me while on the circuit. You view things in their true light, and must be acknowledged (spite of my ill-temper) to be a sensible as well as a good girl.

"Not only will I send you the newspaper which relates the trial of the mineral murder (if to be found), but I shall enclose the learned judge's report of the same trial. you will like his letter for other reasons, and, indeed, the mode in which the news has been received by my brother judges is a most agreeable feature in the case.[1]

"Some of the peers, too, are very civil, the Duke of Norfolk having remained in London on purpose to officiate as Earl Marshal. Do not infer from *some* being

[1] The only communication of this kind that has been preserved, is one written from Warwick on April 6, 1834, by his excellent colleague, Sir Nicolas Conyngham Tindal, Chief Justice of the Common Pleas: "No one of your friends," says the Chief Justice, "can look at your recent and deserved elevation to the Peerage with more satisfaction than myself." Denman had always the most sincere esteem and regard for the high and endearing qualities of his brother Chief.

civil that others are the contrary; I have seen and heard from but few, but *all* were civil.

"Dick [his son Richard, who had been on circuit with him as Judge's Marshal] came up with me from Holkham yesterday, having left his heart with Margery Coke, an affectionate little beauty, just two years old.[1] He and the Honorable Miss Denman [Elizabeth, then his eldest unmarried daughter] both bear their honors meekly.

"Do you approve keeping the name? Do you like the place? [Denman of Dovedale.]

"As to your balustrades [this refers to some improvement in the grounds at Stony Middleton], I think we had better see how things look when we get there, and then choose our pattern. Yours is pretty, but I am disposed to prefer open work, with something of the trefoil, perhaps, within it. I know you like Frost's [head-gardener] style. I sent him some Canada poplars from Holkham yesterday.

"Ever your affectionate father,

"DENMAN."

From the tone of these letters it will be seen that Denman, with his usual sanguine cheerfulness, looking principally if not exclusively to the brighter side of things, was unaffectedly gratified at his elevation to the Peerage. But, as his sister, Mrs. Baillie, observes in her biographical sketch, "to some of those who loved him best this accession of rank did not afford the same unmingled satisfaction as they had felt at his former elevation, partly because they felt his want of fortune to support a Peerage, and his want of power to save anything considerable in his present situation; but still more because they feared that the additional duties thus required of him might have a prejudicial effect on his health, notwithstanding the still unimpaired and vigorous state both of his bodily and mental powers."

Neither of these apprehensions were unfounded. Denman's professional emoluments while at the Bar, though lately considerable, had never been on the same scale as those of Scarlett, Sugden, and several others of his leading contemporaries, and they were more than absorbed

[1] Born, therefore, when her father was eighty.

by the expenses incident to a numerous family, and a style of living which, without being profuse, was generous and liberal. He had never been economical, was frequently embarrassed, saved nothing, and died poor.[1] His case was one of several which seem to afford a strong if not an irresistible argument for the expediency of vesting in the Crown a power of conferring peerages for life.

Nor can it be doubted that his exertions in the House of Lords, added to the onerous and ever increasing labors of the judgment seat, proved in the end too much for his strength, and greatly contributed to bring on that prostration of mind and body which compelled his retirement from judicial and public life at an earlier period than might otherwise have been necessary.

Shortly after his accession to the Peerage, Denman removed from his former house in Russell Square to another in a more expensive and fashionable neighborhood, having purchased the lease of No. 38 Portland Place, a large and stately mansion of the mid-Georgian æra, well fitted to be the residence of a Chief Justice of England.[2]

The following is an extract from a letter to his daughter, the Honorable Mrs. Wright, the accomplished wife of the translator of Dante, which was written from the library of the House of Lords, not long after his elevation. The earlier passages refer to some popular publication of the day which his daughter had brought to his notice as containing a panegyric on his public and professional career.

"I am always delighted with your remembrances, and have a few moments in the library of the House of Lords to thank you for your affectionate letter. I rejoice to accompany you in your drives along the road in your open carriage with the merry group following. These are more agreeable circumstances than the panegyrics in the book you name, which is so very ignorant and daring in the statement of facts that its authority is of no high

[1] Denman, as appears from a letter written to his man of business, March 22, 1834, was obliged to borrow the sum (£550) payable for the expenses of the patent conferring his peerage.

[2] This house was not given up till after the death of Lady Denman in 18[illegible]2; it was the last of Denman's London residences.

value in any respect. It is, however, far pleasanter to me to receive the praise even of such a writer than to encounter his abuse, and I ought to be thankful to him, if not for his praises, at least for the feelings to which he has given birth in your mind.

"My lot has, indeed, been fortunate, far above my talents or merits of any kind. But there is one merit of a kind entirely within one's own command, to which no man could ever more boldly lay claim—*the determination to do what is right, whenever that can be discovered.* It is satisfactory to obtain credit for precisely the quality on which I pride myself most. Another happy circumstance is the cordial concurrence, and, I believe, full confidence and respect of my brother judges, all, (except Williams)[1] nearly strangers to me when I was made Chief Justice.

"I must conclude, not because I have no more to say, but because the Duke of Wellington and Lord Ellenborough are in full discussion of the revenues of the Duchy of Cornwall, which, it seems, are collected at a cost of 44 per cent.—a good illustration of the old proverb, that 'the King's cheese goes in parings.'"

In the summer and autumn of 1834 a succession of ministerial changes took place which must have led Denman to congratulate himself that his post was no longer planted on the shifting quicksands of party, but on the firm resting-ground of a permanent appointment. Lord Grey's resignation, on July 9, was followed by that of Lord Melbourne and the whole Whig Ministry on November 15, and a few days after the Duke of Wellington assumed the temporary supervision of all the affairs of the realm, a charge which he continued to exercise till the return from the Continent, on December 9, of Sir Robert Peel,—"the great man in a great position, summoned from Rome to govern England."[2]

During the interregnum, Denman, by virtue of his office as Chief Justice of the King's Bench, was called upon to hold provisionally the seal of the Chancellorship of the Exchequer; and he held it accordingly from November 28 till December 10, when Peel, the day after

[1] Williams had succeeded Parke as a Judge of the King's Bench in Easter Term, 1834.

[2] Coningsby.

his arrival in England, was appointed to the office, in conjunction with that of First Lord of the Treasury.[1]

The following note from the Duke of Wellington to the Chief Justice relates to and explains this matter:

"Downing Street: November 27, 1834.

"My Lord,—The King has just informed me that Lord Spencer will resign into His Majesty's hands to-morrow the seal of the Chancellor of the Exchequer, at 3 P.M.

"The practice has been to give the custody of the seal to the Lord Chief Justice of the King's Bench till a Chancellor of the Exchequer should be appointed.

"I request your Lordship, therefore, will be so kind as to attend the King at 3 P.M. to-morrow, in order to receive the seal of the Exchequer.

"I have the honor to be, my lord,

"Your lordship's most obedient, humble servant.

"WELLINGTON."

Just before Lord Melbourne's first administration went out of office Lord Auckland, then first Lord of the Admiralty, had, greatly to Denman's delight, appointed his second son, Joseph, then a young Lieutenant in his 24th year, to the command of the "*Curlew*," a 10-gun brig, which for so young an officer was a very good appointment.

The first reformed Parliament was dissolved on December 20, 1834, and the new Parliament met on February 19, 1835. The swearing-in of members occupied till Tuesday, the 24th, on which day the King went in state to the House of Lords and delivered the royal speech. Two days later Denman, who was then presiding at the London sittings after Hilary Term, wrote from Court as follows, to his daughter, Mrs. Wright:

"Guildhall: Thursday, February 26, 1835.

"Dearest Doe,—As you say that my advice is so useful and is always the same, I must refer you in case of need 'to my last-esteemed favor,' as the mercantile correspondence runs, where I have no doubt you will find it

[1] Peel, soon after the meeting of the new Parliament, found the struggle to carry on the administration against an adverse majority a hopeless task, and after a little less than four months continuance in office resigned on April 8, 1835.

written, 'I am glad you are very well and very happy, only take care not to be too well or too happy,' or words to the like tenor and effect. But I take the opportunity of the Solicitor-General[1] giving the jury a long history of a case not very entertaining to repeat my good advice and exhortations.

"I have a very heavy entry at Guildhall, and some fear that some of the causes may not be tried in the time appointed. This would grieve me, as I have completely destroyed that gigantic monster called 'Arrear,' who was always obstructing and defeating justice, and tearing out the bowels of unhappy plaintiffs and defendants by accumulated expense and long solicitude. I have intimated my resolution to sit late both to-day and to-morrow, to the no small dismay of the M.P.'s of the Bar, who are groaning under their double duties.

"I suppose you see the Parliamentary Debates, and observe that His Majesty was well received in passing through the streets,[2] as were his ministers in the House of Lords, but rather differently, it appears, in the Commons. The only question is how large the majority will be against them: the 'shabbies' are a large section; so also are the 'poor creatures,' to which latter party Holland seems likely to give in his adhesion

"I suspended my epistle while the evidence was being given: now it is over, and Mr. Attorney-General[3] is stating his defense with not a little fierceness. He is clearly right, and I have tried to stop the cause in his favor; but the jury still doubt. He bestows tediousness in a spirit of lavish prodigality: *Sed fugit interea fugit irrevocabile tempus.*

"Brougham was very good in the House of Lords on Tuesday night.[4] The Chancellor [Lyndhurst] evidently seeks to recommend himself to the Duke of Cumberland and the Ultras by his personal rudeness to the man

[1] Sir William Follett, appointed Solicitor-General December 17, 1834.

[2] To open the new Parliament on February 24, 1835.

[3] Sir F. Pollock, appointed Attorney-General, December 17, 1834; what follows is a very graphic picture of the late admirable and excellent Chief Baron as a Nisi Prius advocate.

[4] February 24, first night, in the Lords, of debate on the Address.

[Brougham] who in his utmost need, made him Chief Baron:

> Ejectum littore, egentem
> Excepi, et regni *demens* in parte locavi.

At the same time he seeks to recommend himself to the country by following with feeble steps and at a humble distance, Brougham's great principles of Legal Reform. I don't thing he will lead a quiet and happy life for it.

"I have not yet taken my seat this Session; had I done so on the first night I could not have helped taking some part in the debate—probably much better not.

"The jury have, at length, concurred in my view, and the Solicitor-General gives up the point.

"We start with another cause at ten minutes after four.[1]

"Ever your affectionate father."

[1] This, if the cause were of the average duration of London special jury cases, might imply a sitting protracted till nine or ten at night, or even later.

CHAPTER XXV.

JUDICIAL CIRCUITS—HOUSE OF LORDS.

A. D. 1834 TO 1837. ÆT. 55 TO 58.

IN the years 1834 and 1835 two changes took place among the Judges of the Court of King's Bench which rendered Lord Denman's position as Chief of that Court still more agreeable.

The first was the transfer from the Exchequer to the King's Bench, in Easter Term, 1834, of his old friend Williams, in the place of Sir James Parke, who went to the Exchequer.[1] Williams was an admirable scholar, a Fellow of Trinity, renowned for his Greek epigrams, for his translations of Demosthenes, and for some first-rate articles on the Greek orators in the "Edinburgh Review." He had fought side by side with Brougham and Denman on the Queen's trial, and had described in classic Greek how from behind the broad shield of his leaders he had harried with the fiery arrows of cross-examination the profligate and mendacious Italian witnesses, especially the female ones (*τὰς κυνὰς 'Ιταλικὰς*).[2] He had also gone hand in hand with Denman in those vigorous and persevering attacks in the House of Commons on old Eldon's

[1] Sir John Williams, born 1777; fellow of Trinity College, Cambridge, 1798; called to the Bar, 1804; M. P. for Lincoln, 1822; King's Counsel, 1827; Baron of Exchequer, February, 1834, on retirement of Mr. Baron Bayley; removed to King's Bench, Easter Term, 1834, and continued a Judge of that Court till his death, September 14, 1846, æt. 69. Foss's "Lives of the Judges," vol. ix. p. 313.

[2] The epigram:

Προύγαμ'! (Brougham) ἀρΐφιλ', ἐσθλ' ἐχθροξυλε, πο..μὲν 'Ανάσσης
Νῦν μὲν ἀριστεύων ἐν προδομοισι μαχου,
Μοί δ' 'Αἰαντείην πρόβαλ' ἀσπίδα παμφανοωσαν
Κἀγὼ ἔνερθεν ἕλω τὰς κυνὰς 'Ιταλικάς.

procrastinations as Chancellor, which were among the first efficient causes of Chancery reform.

Sir John Williams, though so ripe a Grecian, was by no means a bad lawyer, and ultimately became a competent judge. His manner and appearance were indeed eccentric. On the Bench he had a little the look of Punch in ermine. He had also a considerable spice of Welsh irritability, and a very strong and decided way of expressing his opinions; but with all this, from the genuine cordiality and kindness of his nature, he was a great favorite both with his brethren and the Bar.[1]

Sir John Taylor Coleridge, promoted by Lord Lyndhurst, in January, 1835, to fill the vacancy in the King's Bench occasioned by the sudden death of Mr. Justice Taunton, was one of the most superior and highly cultivated persons who ever adorned that famous tribunal. His career at Eaton and Oxford was extremely briliant: at the Oxford examination for honors in Easter Term, 1812, he enjoyed the distinction, unexampled in the annals of the University, of being placed alone in the first class in Classics; and, in 1813, he carried off in one and the same year the Chancellor's prizes for both the English and Latin Essays, an academical feat which has only thrice been accomplished since the first establishment of these prizes in 1768—the two other instances being those of Keble in 1812, and of Milman in 1816.

His academical successes did not prevent his working hard at law in London. He became an accomplished jurist, and a successful practitioner; but he never abandoned literature, and so well was he known as an able periodical writer, that when Gifford retired from the editorship of the "Quarterly," Coleridge succeeded him in that ardous and distinguished post, and held it for a year (the year 1824), at the close of which he resigned it as incompatible with the claims of his rapidly increasing practice. After his promotion to the King's Bench in 1835, he continued to act as Judge of that Court foi more than twenty-three years (till June 28, 1858). How well he demeaned himself in his high office may be learned from the impressive and eloquent farewell address pronounced by the then Attorney-General (now

[1] See his life in Foss's "Judges of England," vol. ix. p. 315.

Chief Baron) Sir Fitzroy Kelly, on the occasion of his retirement.

"Three-and-twenty years have now elapsed since your Lordship was raised by the well-deserved favor of the Crown to a seat on that Bench. Throughout that eventful period your public life has been distinguished by that dignified and sustained exercise of high judicial conduct which has rendered so many of your predecessors illustrious, and has won for the administration of law in this Court the respect and confidence of the people. But, my Lord, it is more especially to the members of the Bar that your long and eminent judicial career has exhibited a bright example of the display of all those attributes which best become a judge in the discharge of his many duties. To a clear and powerful intellect, to legal and constitutional learning at once acute and profound, to a patient and unwearied assiduity and attention, your Lordship has ever added the estimable and scarcely less important qualities of unvarying courtesy of demeanor, evenness of temper, and kindliness of heart."[1]

Sir John Coleridge, immediately on his retirement from the Bench, was sworn in of the Privy Council, and, as a member of the Judicial Committee, has for many years given the public the benefit of his high judicial ability, unimpaired by age, and mellowed by experience.

For Coleridge Denman at once felt the elective affinity which generally is entertained by one superior mind for another, however various and unlike the order of their superiority. They became very intimate, and frequently corresponded. Several of Denman's letters to his brother judge, which, by his courtesy, have been placed at the disposal of the family for the use of this Memoir, will appear in the course of the following pages.

In the Summer Assizes of 1834 Lord Denman presided on the Western Circuit:

"The circuit [he writes to Mrs. Baillie] has been entirely satisfactory. Very hard work came, indeed, more than once in very hot weather, and I was almost knocked up at Exeter: but I rallied, and am now remarkably

[1] Foss's "Lives of the Judges," vol. ix, p. 175. The biographical sketch of Mr. Justice Coleridge is *very* ably executed.

well. Tom [present Lord Denman] told you of the happy hours we spent at Winterslow [Rev. W. Brodie's]. I could hardly escape for a single night at Merivale's, at Barton Place, but I carried Merivale himself off on the box of the carriage along the south coast of Devon to Plymouth and Liskeard—an excellent guide, lovely weather—a delightful tour. I had several leisure days after concluding the business at Bodmin, enjoyed the magnificent land and sea views at Clovelly: but was visited by the only foul weather in the fairest district, and prevented from approaching Linton and Linmouth. Combe Flory, where I dined and slept at Sydney Smith's, is one of the loveliest valleys that can be seen. Our host was severely attacked with gout, and could not dine with his guests, but I had a most delightful morning with him the next day, and he was in excellent spirits."

A letter written to Lady Denman from Bristol (the last place on the Western Circuit), on August 19, 1834, gives an account of his difficulties on the road between Wells and Bristol, and of his reception in the great trading city, which he had not visited since he appeared there as Attorney-General, in the winter of 1832, to prosecute the rioters under the special commission.

"I have tried four long causes to-day, and have still eight to try, how long or short I can not guess. I am eagerly watching for the opportunity to take wing, and may, perhaps, fly faster than this letter to its destination; but in case this should be otherwise I give you a little notice of my goings on.

"After finishing the business at Wells, I found myself at liberty on Saturday morning to start for Banwell—the Bishop's cottage—where some of those extraordinary caves full of antedeluvian bones have been discovered. The Bishop called and took me; I ordered my own carriage to follow instantly. The carriage came not, for want of horses. I had to walk to the adjoining town; still neither carriage nor horses. Then came the Bristol javelin man.[1] I borrowed his horse and rode on five

[1] Javelin men are an escort of men, carrying light (and harmless) spears, provided by the Sheriffs to meet the Judges on their entrance into the assize town; they are now a "sham," but were once a reality, having formed the armed force by which the Sheriff safeguarded the Judge from his en-

miles across country to the nearest place on the high road where horses were kept. But one mare was blind, the other had staked herself, and the postboy was ill. I prevailed with the landlord to the extent of sending a boy over with the blind mare, to carry my apology to the Sheriffs, who had to meet me at Tillenden Hill (the place where Wetherell was so shockingly maltreated in the riots of 1831). At length the landlord's heart relented on my declaring the real meaning of the case, and he undertook to drive me himself. While the long divided materials of the chaise were putting together, my carriage at length came up, and finally brought me to the appointed place, not long after the appointed time.

"A very curious sensation entering Bristol, after I had prosecuted the Mayor and all the Aldermen,[1] and they place the Judge by himself in a chariot with six horses, which proceeds at a funeral pace to the Court House and the Mansion House.

"The Mayor is a very gentlemanly man, married to a Nottinghamshire lady. I am lodged and entertained by them with great good humor and hospitality. Miles [the member] dined here, which made everything pass off pleasantly. Yesterday I went with the Mayor to see old Mr. Miles' pictures—a splendid collection, and the country, too, very beautiful.

"To-day, after sitting in court till half-past eight, I dined with the Sheriffs—a great Tory party. My health was splendidly received, and I proposed that of Sir Charles Wetherell, the Recorder. The utmost good humor has prevailed.

"When I began this it was past midnight, and, as I must be in court by 9 to-morrow, I will now wish your Ladyship good-night.

"Your ever affectionate and faithful husband."

The next day, August 20, he writes again:

"I hope the sight of my handwriting instead of myself is as hateful to you as the task of writing instead of

trance into the county, to the assize town, during his stay there, and again on his departure, as far as the borders of the county.

[1] For criminal laches in not earlier suppressing the great Bristol riots of 1831; tried at Bar, before Lord Tenterden and other Judges, in November, 1832; see vol. i. chap. xxii.

coming is to me; yet it would be even worse for you to receive neither husband nor letter. Twelve hours of yesterday (from 9 A.M. to 9 P.M.) were given to two causes full of difficulty and without the least interest or value. Six causes still remain, and I have the comfortable assurance that they are likely to be equally long, equally insignificant, and equally tiresome. I can only promise to work at them like a dragon, and lose no chance of knocking them on the head."

At the Summer Assizes of the next year, Denman went the Oxford Circuit with his friend Williams. Writing from Oxford, to Lady Denman, on July 21, 1835, he says:

"I have had a light calendar, which I fully dispatched before one to-day. Williams will not be liberated till to-morrow, by reason of the everlasting speeches in civil cases on this circuit. A curious scene took place in court yesterday. The Marquis of Blandford acted as foreman of the grand jury, and brought in all the bills found for *felony*. Then came another foreman with a bill for an assault (*misdemeanor*), in which the defendant was the former foreman—the aforesaid Marquis. It seems he was served with a writ for a debt, and thought proper to tear the writ, and grievously beat the bailiff. He has been wise enough to make up the matter this morning, and saved me the trouble of fining him, by paying a sum of money to the prosecutor.

"The dons dined here (Judge's lodgings) yesterday—nine in number. The University is very empty, but Dr Buckland has been offering the exhibition of his museum, and Dick Croft[1] feeds the judicial suite to-day. We had a delightful walk, and dinner at the Archbishop's [Harcourt, of York] beautiful park of Nuneham, on Sunday: they are a very good-humored family. Tom [the present Lord Denman] is quite well, and rides every morning with my brother Williams."

From Worcester he writes, some days later:

"At Oxford I saw many of the major lions, among the rest, Magdalen, which has the finest walks and gardens; and we dined in state with Richard Croft, in Exeter

[1] Sister's son to Lord Denman. The dinner referred to was given in the hall of his College—Exeter.

Hall. No bachelors' dinner could be better appointed, or more agreeable. Next day I breakfasted again with Dr. Buckland, who introduced me to his famous geological museum, and gave me, in a condensed form, the subject of his whole course of lectures. I found much more entertainment than I expected, and was highly delighted with the lecture. Tom brought Bessy[1] from Bisham, and she saw several of the most striking things in Oxford. We then went on to Blenheim, and went through that magnificent mansion. The Duke politely tendered us leave to walk through his gardens and pleasure grounds, which are about a mile in length, beautifully laid out, and full of rare plants. We then proceeded to a most comfortable lone inn—'Chapel House'—where we had a family, but rather late, dinner, under Bessy's presidency, at 10. Next day Tom and I rode about seventeen miles, to Colonel Davies' beautiful place—Elmley Park. We slept in that sweet air, then came into Worcester, and attended cathedral service. Afterwards, I sate for five hours in a pretty hot court, and, by way of a pleasing change, dined [at the Sheriff's] in wig and gown, in presence of about thirty magistrates, almost all strangers. The rest of my work I finished to-day by 4 o'clock. Williams is still enjoying the luxury of *nisi prius*, and leaves me to play the host to about fifty barristers, but without canonicals. We dine with the Bishop to-morrow; the next day I may take a little of my learned brother's work off his hands, but I am anxious to get off in good time to Lord Lyttelton, who has sent us the kindest invitation to Hagley—a visit to which I look forward with peculiar pleasure.

From Gloucester, still on the same circuit, he writes, on August 16, 1835:

"This week has been cut up between hard work and long and delightful journeys. The former was over at Hereford about noon on Wednesday, and Tom, Archer,[2] and I proceeded without delay, along the bank of the Wye, to the beautiful town of Ross, visited the house

[1] The Hon. Mrs. Hodgson, who went round the rest of this circuit with him.

[2] Sir Archer Croft, Bart., eldest son of Denman's sister Margaret, one of the Masters in the Court of Queen's Bench.

and gardens of the benevolent John Kyrle, so celebrated for his good deeds as the 'Man of Ross,' and rode the next morning to Goodrich Castle, a fine ruin on the banks of the same river. We got to Monmouth in good time for church and court, and the remainder of that day and the whole of Friday till nightfall I gave to the criminal business. Yesterday (Saturday) morning we again mounted our horses and rode to breakfast at the village of Abbey Tinterne, graced by the splendid ruins of Tinterne Abbey. At a small but very comfortable inn there my brother Williams and his Marshal joined us. We then proceeded to those walks of the highest beauty on the top of the lofty hill called Wyndcliff, which look down on the curving rocks and woods above the Wye. These are of the most picturesque character, on the grandest scale, and of the finest forms—the eye follows the basin they compose all along the banks of the river right away to the Bristol Channel. One object is disappointing to the eye, but that is no less than the river itself, which gives its name to the scene. We had the ill luck to see it only at low water, shrunk to a thread, and yellow with thick mud. We dined at Chepstow, famous for its noble castle. I came here (Gloucester) to open the commission about 9 at night, in a large and busy town on a market day and a Saturday. Such a contrast to our peaceful wanderings! and such a drunken attendance while the foolish forms were going through! As soon as a few moments' silence was obtained, a gruff voice halloaed out, 'Silence in the gallery, I can't hear the gentleman for the noise!' but all were civil enough, and one man kept pretty close, crying 'God bless Lord Denman!'"

These letters have been transcribed, and others similar to them will be so, not, certainly, for their literary merit, for they possess little or none, but principally for their simple and unadorned presentment of an English Judge's life on circuit, in those days before railways, with its curious alternations of hard work in court, hard dining at formal banquets, agreeable visits at great houses, and, perhaps pleasanter than all the rest, quiet sojourns at wayside inns in the neighborhood of famous sights or beautiful scenery.

This Oxford Summer Circuit of 1835 was an exceptionally idle one; and Denman, in writing to his wife during one of his many intervals of enforced leisure, says:

"I must acknowledge that these intermediate holidays are not quite so welcome as they ought to be, because they suggest the reflection, 'What a pity to be detained here doing nothing, when I might have been enjoying myself at home.' However, they give some pleasure, and are really sometimes desirable as an interruption to severer labors."[1]

Of the mode in which he occasionally amused these leisure intervals a sample is afforded by the following *jeu d'esprit* in Maccaronic Latin, which Denman, a ripe scholar, who always kept up his scholarship, wrote while on the present Oxford Circuit in reference to a somewhat whimsical adventure which, on the Oxford Circuit of the previous year, had befallen his learned brother the Chief Justice of the Common Pleas, Sir Nicolas Conyngham Tindal, one of the most benevolent and good-natured men that ever breathed, with a vein of grave, sly humor which made him vastly relish telling the story himself.

It is here given as communicated by Lord Denman's fourth son, the present Mr. Justice Denman, himself well known in the world of scholarship for his choice translations of the first book of the "Iliad" into Latin Elegiacs, and of Gray's "Elegy" into Greek Hexameters.

The Lord Chief Justice of the Common Pleas, on his way from Shrewsbury to Hereford (on the Oxford Circuit) ran over and killed a pig. An ancient crone to whom the pig belonged came out and abused him vehemently. Sir N. C. Tindal, who was the very personification of good humor, asked the enraged matron what the pig was worth. On her naming £2 he at once handed her the amount (not depriving her of the pork and bacon) and said, "There, my good lady, is 40*s*. for you, and that, you know, carries costs."

Denman's version runs thus, slightly varying the facts:

[1] Since the general introduction of railways, the Judges, especially on the less remote circuits, can frequently contrive to steal home for a day or two between the close of the work at one assize town and its commencement at another.

I.

Judex Capitalis,
  Habens odio porcum,
Vi et armis malis
  Tradidit in Orcum.

II.

Porcum amans anus,
  Tanquam Vitrea Circe,
Huic injecit manus,
  Ut penderet furcæ.

III.

"Facinus cefandum!"—
  Ut piaret necem
Solvit Deo-dandum
  Solidis quater-decem.

IV.

Ne vocato stolidos,
  Qui habitant villagia;
"Quadraginta solidos!
  Ubi sunt castagia?"

V.

Addidit Communium,
  Placitorum Pater
Solidos (quam pecuniam!)
  Quadraginta quater.

MORAL.

Interest clientibus,
  Ut sit finis litium,—
Bene jus scientibus,
  Melius est initium.

In the Session of 1835, Denman, as Chief Justice of England, acted for some months, *ex-officio*, as Speaker of the House of Lords while the Great Seal was in commission. On Brougham's presenting his celebrated Fourteen Resolutions of the 21st May, for the establishment of an Education Board, the Chief Justice addressed the House in a few impressive sentences, which, coming from such a quarter, carried great weight with them, on the connection between ignorance and crime, and on the duty of Government as a mere measure of precaution, and with a view to the preservation of Society, to bestir themselves for the education of the masses. In the course of his observations he touched upon a point of still deeper and graver significance. "He had," he confessed "after reflecting on the question, not as a subject for rhetorical declamation, but as one demanding grave attention, doubted *how far the State was justified in inflicting punishment for offenses against which it had taken no means to guard.*"[1]

On June 19, 1835, Denman expressed his entire approval of the principle of the Execution of Wills Act, declaring the opinion, the correctness of which time has shown, that the attestation of two persons was quite a sufficient guarantee in cases of wills.

On August 27, 1835, in the course of one of the long and angry debates that took place on the Municipal Corporations Reform Bill, there arose one of those personal discussions which generally, and naturally, succeed better in fixing the attention of deliberative assemblies than solemn arguments on matters of much higher import.

Lord Lyndhurst, in the course of a vehement attack on the ministerial measure, had made some very disparaging remarks on the alleged extreme political opinions of almost all the gentlemen selected by Government to act as Municipal Commissioners. This called up Denman, who said that,

"These observations had given him the greatest pain; they were entirely unfounded. These gentlemen had been described as entertaining extreme opinions on political subjects. Such an imputation was more applicable to the noble and learned person by whom it was made. For that noble and learned Lord he had a great respect; he was indebted to him personally for a long series of kindnesses. If it was a calumny to declare that that noble and learned Lord had changed his opinions on such subjects, he could only declare that he uttered it with perfect good faith, and he believed also it was the perfect conviction of all who knew that noble and learned Lord."[2]

Lord Lyndhurst said he had certainly stated it as a matter of charge against His Majesty's Government that they had selected as Commissioners gentlemen of one

[1] Hansard, Parl. Deb., third series, vol. xxvii., p. 1335, sqq. It is curious to see the chief of the English criminal law giving, in 1835, a certain sanction to the argument which the French man of genius long afterwards worked out in "Les Miserables."

[2] Hansard, Parl. Deb., third series, vol. xxx. p. 1042.

class of political opinions, and of one class only. As to the reference to his own political life Lord Lyndhurst said:

"I have been on terms of intimacy with my noble and learned friend (Denman) for a long period; I went the same circuit with him; I have been engaged in long and varied conversations with him at different times; and, if he speaks of a period of twenty years past, I can only say *that I am unable to recall to my recollection the particular opinions which I might then have entertained or expressed with regard to political measures* (!): but I can assert that I never belonged to any party or political society whatever; I never embarked in politics, and I never wrote a political article on either side of any question which might have been agitated. This was my conduct till I came in the House of Parliament, now nearly twenty years ago. From that period my life has been before the public; my course has been direct and straightforward; I have always belonged to the same party, and I have always entertained the same opinions from that time to the present."[1]

Denman's reply was short and incisive, with a certain tone of high-bred irony about it, which must have made it additionally unpleasant to *Mephistopheles*.

"If my noble and learned friend has understood me as alluding to certain opinions which he was supposed to entertain, with a view of conveying an imputation against him, I can only say it is an imputation which has often been repeated, which I stated, believing it to be true, and which I should now believe to be true, were it not for the assertion of the noble and learned Lord.

"And, I must say, I feel somewhat astonished, that, when the question is, what were the political sentiments of my noble and learned friend, he should plead forgetfulness with reference to the opinions he entertained twenty years ago, undoubtedly, but still when he had attained, nay, passed, the mature age of forty.[2]

"Up to the period when he came into Parliament, the

[1] Hansard, Parl. Deb., third series, vol. xxx. p. 1050.

[2] Lord Lyndhurst was born in 1772; he would, therefore, have been forty-three in 1815, and sixty-three in 1835.

universal impression of those who lived on terms of close intimacy with my noble and learned friend, undoubtedly was this: that his opinions were—not with reference to any one particular measure, or any one occasion, but generally and unequivocally—what would be now called Liberal. Those opinions were not uttered merely in the presence of those who were intimate with him, or in the course of private conversation; but they were avowed as if my learned and noble friend felt a pride in entertaining and avowing them.

"I beg to be understood as standing corrected in the opinion I had expressed as to the former political sentiments of my noble and learned friend, and I shall only, therefore, remind him that stronger proof of his having been a Whig, and something more than a Whig, could be adduced with respect to himself, than as to these Commissioners against whom my noble and learned friend has really been 'scattering his arrows in the dark.'"

The prolonged and embittered discussion on the Municipal Reform Bill, not finally closed till after more than one conference between the Lords and Commons, kept Parliament sitting till September 10.

Denman, who, from his position as *ex-officio* Speaker of the House of Lords, was, of course, unable to leave London till the adjournment, lost no time, after the conclusion of the session, in establishing himself at Stony Middleton, whence, on September 19, he wrote, as follows, to his sister, Mrs. Baillie, who had, it seems, been communicating to him her alarm at some reports of his riding too spirited a horse:

"Thank you for your good advice, but my horse and his rider have been greatly misrepresented; nothing can be more prudent, careful, or slow. Fanny rides with me, and we all flatter ourselves that her health and looks are much improved. I think she is never long without writing to Sophie. We are a very reduced family—the two old folks, Fanny, and Margaret, though the latter can hardly be said to be of our party, as most of her time is spent at Stoke [the Arkwrights]. For the last week Miss Adelaide Kemble, the divine singer, has been there, with her mother [Mrs. Charles Kemble], the idol of my play-going youth. The Duke is also at Chatsworth. There is, therefore, plenty of society within reach. But you can hardly imagine how quiet a life we lead. The weather is magnificent: if the showers are rather more than necessary to preserve the various verdure, they are just right for our transplantations. The face of things is a good deal changed; the number of trees being now rather excessive. I fancy we are making a very pretty, and, for its size, rather a handsome place; but I shall not feel thoroughly attached to it till both my sister [Lady Croft] and you have become acquainted with it, and suggested your improvements."

On January 6, 1836, while at Stony Middleton for his Christmas vacation, he writes to Mrs. Baillie respecting the dramas of her gifted sister-in-law, Joanna, which had then recently been published in a collected form:

"I may challenge you to have bewept the 'Bride' more than I did; reading it in the carriage with no one but Richard, even his presence was at the time an annoyance to me. That play and 'Henriquez' stand out to me far prominent before all the rest, many of which, however, possess a high order of excellence; the 'Homicide,' for example, in which I greatly prefer the substituted scene to that originally written, thinking the effect of heroic resolution on a young and generous mind far more dramatic than any scenic exhibition. Empson [editor of *The Edinburgh*] tells me he has been performing some of the plays in his brother's family circle with great applause. Merivale mentions those which he has read as delightful, and they do not include either of my two prime favorites. The early notices in reviews, &c., are likely to be useful in attracting readers; and it seems probable that a new edition will soon be called for, in which event I should be glad to tender my services.

"Tempted by Coleridge's 'Table Talk,' which ranks the story of Ben Jonson's 'Alchemist' with the two which I ever thought the most interesting, 'Tom Jones' and the 'Œdipus' of Sophocles, I have been studying that play and others of Ben's in your two volumes. It turns out that the 'Alchemist' has no story at all,[1] only a magic lantern of knaveries conducted by rogues and

[1] A most strange extra-judicial dictum! The plot of the 'Alchemist' is a

trulls. The language, indeed, is vigorous and rich, and some of the pictures of the time amusing; but how different from those which please from their truth to general nature, and appeal directly to the human heart! I am happy to say my sons all enjoy Joanna's volumes. The young ladies are preparing for a splendid entertainment for this evening—Twelfth Night—and are all but absorbed in it."

Denman, who had returned to town for the first day of Hilary Term (January 19), writes thence to Lady Denman, who had remained for a time in the country, communicating some of the legal gossip of the day respecting the then recent elevation of Lord Cottenham to the Woolsack, and of Lady Campbell to the Peerage as Lady Stratheden.

"You will see the end of our law changes in to-day's paper. I do not admire any of the new titles. There is much talk of the Attorney-General's [Campbell] being passed over, his indecent boast that he had resigned, and the oddity of his subsequent reconciliation. Littledale just now at a meeting of the judges complimented Lord Abinger on his daughter's elevation.[1] He said, rather abruptly, 'It was not matter of congratulation to him.' I have seen the new Chancellor [Lord Cottenham][2] a good deal touching the new arrangements, and shall call on the other parties to-morrow."

The next day, January 20, he writes again:

"I give myself a little holiday from law papers, that I may have the pleasure of again writing to you. I told you this morning [in a letter not preserved] how gay we had been, but not that I called on Jekyll on Sunday, who is either eighty-two or eighty-three, extremely deaf, and entirely helpless, carried by servants to and from his carriage, but as lively as a bird, in raptures at my calling, with a voice deeper than mine, and peals of laughter

marvel of constructive ingenuity, only equaled in the English drama by those of Ben's two other masterpieces, the 'Fox' and the 'Silent Woman.'

[1] Lady Campbell, raised to the Peerage in 1836 as Baroness Stratheden, was daughter of Lord Abinger (Sir James Scarlett.)

[2] Sir Charles Christopher Pepys, who, since April, 1835, had been Chief Commissioner of the Great Seal, was appointed Lord Chancellor on January 16, 1836, and created Lord Cottenham on the 20th of the same month.

louder than Lewis's.[1] He kept me more than an hour, saying odd things. The Attorney-General's reconciliation with Government he called the *Camel* (Campbell) going through the eye of a needle. He desired, most particular, remembrance to you, and said you two understood one another; he is not likely ever to dine out again, but hopes you will call on him.

"Afterwards, I met both Mr. Attorney-General and Lady Stratheden (for that is to be her title) at Lord Holland's, as well as the Speaker [Abercrombie, afterwards Lord Dunfermline] and his lady, and others, a very pleasant party, and many inquiries after you. Yesterday we met Rogers at Cavendish Square [Mrs. Baillie's], and had a very amusing day, though not anything worth reporting.

"Have you seen that 'Henriquez' [play of Joanna Baillie's] is advertised for Covent Garden, and a popular new actress to take the principal part? I don't think Joanna has been consulted, or is at all in communication with the theater at present. Your continuing to enjoy the country is delightful to me. Pray have your eye on the form of the sloping ground beyond that which is to be leveled—much care and taste will be required—easy, graceful, and natural slopes must be aimed at.

"I have generally walked down to Westminster [from Portland Place], not liking the carriage, unless it rains, and being deprived of Gamester (alas!) by his lameness; but I am flattered with hopes of its being only a corn or defect of shoeing: this morning I rode the chestnut, but we shall never like one another. Tell your father [Rev. R. Vevers] you will see him in three weeks; much sooner, I hope. Your ball is this day fortnight!"

His attached sister, Mrs. Baillie, was always in the habit of making her brother a present on his birthday (February 21). The following graceful lines, on receiving this annual gift, hastily scribbled off while he was sitting in Guildhall, will serve to show the unaltered warmth and steadfastness of the affection which united the brother and sister:

"Another graceful memorial of good taste and affec-

[1] Lord Denman's youngest son, then about fifteen.

tion assumes its destined station, shedding lustre on my official labors. The gift resembles the giver, whose early kindness cultivated every quality that could have a chance of being ripened into fitness for such a station, and whose constant friendship is one of my best encouragements."

Parliament met on February 4; but Denman's name does not appear as a speaker, except on two occasions in the course of the Session—on June 10, 1836, when he intimated a very strong opinion in favor of abolishing the Palatinate Courts of Durham;[1] and again on June 23, 1836, when he assisted at the last discussion that took place in Parliament on the Prisoners' Counsel Bill, the second reading of which was, on this occasion, moved by Lord Lyndhurst.

In the course of his observations on this long-pending question, Denman, after paying some deserved compliments to Lyndhurst, on the ability with which he had stated the case, declared, emphatically, "that it was essential to carry the principles of the Bill into practical execution for the *honor of the laws, for the due administration of justice, for the realization of truth, and for the protection of innocence.*"

He added, that the only difficulty he had ever felt on the subject was this, that he could never meet with any serious argument against the principle of allowing counsel to prisoners.[2]

In the summer of 1836, Lord Denman chose the South Wales Circuit, of which the two following letters to his wife furnish some pleasant reminiscences:

"Haverford West: July 29, 1836.

"Dearest Love,—I must send you a little letter to tell you that we are all well, and have enjoyed a most delightful holiday at Mirehouse's,[3] going round the most wild and romantic coast of craggy cliffs that can be imagined. We (that is Tom[4] and I) were both made un-

[1] Hansard, Par. Deb., third series, vol. xxxiv. p. 299.

[2] Hansard, Parl. Deb., third series, vol. xxxiv. pp. 760–778. The Prisoners' Counsel Bill received the Royal Assent on August 20, 1836, and became law as the 6 & 7 Will. IV. c. 114.

[3] The Hall, Angle, Pembrokeshire.

[4] The present Lord Denman, who accompanied his father as associate.

comfortable by Georgiana's[1] adventurous style of courting danger on the edges of tremendous precipices, and it might not be amiss if you gave her a hint on the subject. Our host and hostess were perfectly kind, and their children are extremely amiable. We finished [at Milford Haven] with seeing old George III.'s favorite yacht, the 'Royal Sovereign:' they are building an enormous steamer and an eighty-gun ship. This scrap is written because I don't know when I may be able to write again, with a heavy crop of causes to be mown. I wish I could give you a notion of 'Elligoy Stack.' It stands a great rock perpendicularly out of the sea, stuck all over, as a garden wall with flints or bottles, with millions of the Elligoy—a kind of sea duck, with about equal parts of black and white, in stripes. Millions are also floating on the waves; when disturbed they fly around, with such a shrill, rattling scream. The rock is much in layers, where they stand (for want of sitting room), and are said to hatch their eggs with their feet. The sight is never to be forgotten."

From Brecon, a little later, August 7, he writes:

"As the post goes out early to-morrow morning, I shall just send you a few lines. We arrived here soon after seven, having performed a most delightful journey through a most rich and cultivated, yet bold and picturesque, country. We are quite well—have charming apartments and fine prospects here, with plenty of old churches and ruined castles. The sheriff is the same gentleman who entertained Shadwell and me in 1797;[2] we are going to dine with him to-morrow. The criminal cases here are very trifling, and not much to be done in the civil line; then there is only the little county of Radnor, before we get to Chester, the last place on the circuit, but with more than twice as much crime as all Wales put together. Having a beech tree struck by lightning on one's grounds [Lady Denman had reported this from Stony Middleton] has a very grand effect. You do not say which beech it is; I shall make it out in a moment by description."

From Chester Denman wrote to his brother judge, Sir

[1] First wife of present Lord Denman.

[2] In their walking tour. See vol. i. pp. 17, 18.

John Taylor Coleridge (then on the Northern Circuit with Mr. Baron Parke), the first of the series of letters which that eminent and learned person has preserved, and kindly placed at the disposal of his old friend's family for the purposes of the present memoir. It relates, amongst other things, to the appointment of his third son, Richard, to the Clerkship of the Assize, which had just been vacated on the South Wales Circuit, by the sudden death of its former incumbent, and is a proof of Denman's scrupulous care in the exercise of patronage.

"My dear Coleridge,—I can not return your visit by proxy, because my marshal left me at Presteign [assize town of Radnorshire] on his way to Ireland. I have seen your cause list [at Liverpool], and wish you a good deliverance. Vaughan [Mr. Baron Vaughan, who, after taking the North Wales Circuit, had joined the Chief Justice at Chester] will have twenty causes here; and I have near fifty prisoners, some for very bad offenses."

"Alderson[1] wrote me a letter from Wells, with a much better account of Williams and with this P. S.: 'Williams has respited one of the convicts at Exeter, and I am clear he is innocent. God be praised that he was not hanged on Saturday week.' What does Parke say of the confessions at Shrewsbury respecting the man tried before him in '35, and before me in '36? I am not over confident in the truth of scapegoat confessions, yet that statement must produce its effect. These things make me more anxious for the Bill [Prisoners' Counsel Bill] passing, which will give every fair advantage to a prisoner; but I fear there will be no alteration of the law this Session, and we must go on another year trying in a manner pronounced unsatisfactory by both Houses of Parliament.[2]

"Poor Caliban[3] died of apoplexy at Brecon. I wish you and Parke would tell me whether it would be *quite*

[1] Mr. Baron Alderson, born 1787, senior wrangler, first Smith's prizeman and senior medalist, 1809; Judge of Common Pleas, 1830; Baron of Exchequer, 1834; died 1857, æt. 70; more than twenty-seven years on the Bench.

[2] It received the Royal assent on August 20 of this year (1836).

[3] Nickname of Mr. Jones, Clerk of Assize on the South Wales Circuit.

right that I should give the office to my son Richard, who can, I doubt not, do the work very well. The place is said to be worth £800 a year. How is that possible? £500 would be enormous for such a circuit. I knew you would like the Northern. Remember me kindly to Parke and the sheriff."

After his return from the circuit, Denman, on August 23, 1836, again wrote from Middleton to his brother judge, announcing that, acting on the advice of himself Parke, and Vaughan, he had given his son Richard the appointment.[1] He then proceeds as follows with reference to the unusually heavy cause list that Mr. Justice Coleridge had before him at Liverpool:

"Now for yourself: the task imposed upon you I verily believe to be the heaviest that ever judge underwent. This would give me no uneasiness (for in my sincere opinion none ever possessed more perfectly all the mental qualities required), but that I know you sometimes complain on the score of health. Let me then remind you that your first duty in every point of view is to pay constant attention to that prime object, and religiously avoid all extra exertions on, whatever pretense. Let everything take its own course as much as possible, and flow in its accustomed channel. I hope you may dispense with the modern practice of summing up—so much at variance with the meaning of the word —and merely recapitulate the great points of the evidence. Another commonplace counsel I venture to throw in, 'Discard all anxiety.' This demands a great effort, which, however, may be successfully made, and will fully repay the trouble.

"I have now another suggestion to offer. Whether you finish at Lancaster or Liverpool you are within a day's journey of this place [Stony Middleton]; and, as I understand Lady Coleridge is at Scarborough, I don't think you could have a more convenient point of reunion. We have plenty of room for all your party, can find beautiful rides at a short distance for any time you can stay, and shall be delighted to receive you. Lady

[1] The Hon. Richard Denman held this appointment till 1839, when, on the death of Mr. Gould, he was made Clerk of Assize to the Home Circuit, an office he still holds. He is now the senior of all the Clerks of Assize.

Coleridge had better come rather earlier than the expected period of your release, and, if you will tell me her present address, my wife will immediately write to her. I really should hope to provide no disagreeable relaxation from your labors, and it seems to me that no arrangement could be more convenient."

Denman always took a great interest in the jurisprudence and legal literature of the United States, and never failed to pay every attention in his power to any members of the American Bar who brought letters to him from the other side of the Atlantic. Mr. Benjamin Rand, an eminent advocate in Boston, who, in 1835, had been in London, and was there received by the Chief Justice with his usual courtesy, sent him, on his return to the United States, a series of the most recent reports then published of the Supreme Courts of the respective States of Maine and Massachusetts. Denman, while on the South Wales Circuit, acknowledged the gift in a letter, from which the following are extracts:

"South Wales Circuit: July 17, 1836.

"Dear Sir,—Your great kindness imposes on me no light task, which is rendered more difficult by my delay in performing it. I had earnestly desired to become, in some degree, acquainted with the contents of your valuable present before answering your letter; but the Terms and Nisi Prius have been too strong for me, and I find myself among the mountains of Wales, at the seat of my friend, Sir John Nichol, traveling an easy circuit, before I have been able to tell you how much I am flattered by your remembrance.

"Englishmen must always regard with pride and satisfaction the share their country has had in forming the legal institutions of your enlightened community; and I am satisfied that we may, in return, derive great benefit from studying the system adopted by you, and canvassing the alterations you have made. Our municipal law will thus be always improving; and it is essential for uniformity of decision throughout the civilized world, that we should be apprised of your proceedings on international and commercial questions. Even in the application of those general principles of law on which all believe themselves to be agreed, our errors may be corrected by watching the conduct of our neighbors, and our deficiencies supplied by what they have effected.

"Do me the favor, dear Sir, to place on your shelves a copy of the decisions of my illustrious friend, Brougham, when Chancellor.

"I am your obliged and faithful servant,

"T. DENMAN."

In the course of September of this vacation, Denman, with his wife and several members of his family, passed some days at the Duke of Devonshire's, at Chatsworth, whence he wrote the following to his sister, Mrs. Baillie:

"Chatsworth: Monday, September 11, 1836.
"Quarter before seven, P. M.

"My dear Sister,—I have not had an idle moment till now, when I am waiting till Theodosia [Lady Denman] is dressed, to take her down to dinner. She and I, Joseph and Margaret, are the party here, Bessie and Richard being unavoidably left behind to entertain Mr. and Mrs. R. Vevers [his brother and sister-in-law], who unluckily fixed for their visit the very day of our invitation here. I hope you have enjoyed your stay in the country as much as I have; mine will be interrupted next week, when I shall have to sit at the Old Bailey. I fear you will not return to town during my stay there; if you do, and the autumn smiles, I shall certainly recommend you to come back with me and look at our verdant valley. If the Brodies give you any account of us before that time, I am confident it will be an encouraging one. They certainly enjoyed themselves with us, and it was most delightful to me to talk over all existing things with Ben [Sir Benjamin Brodie] and become a little acquainted with his family."

"Tuesday morning. Half-past nine.

"I had intended to give you a kind of 'Morning Post' account of our last night's party, but the servants did not call me till a late hour; and I must soon conclude—not on account of breakfast (for that lasts from nine till twelve), but that my letter may be in time for the post. We have great people here—the Duke of Rutland and his three sons, and Lady Adeliza, the Duke and Duchess of Sutherland, Lord and Lady Tavistock, some Cavendishes, and many others. The weather has been dismal, chilly, and rainy. I must leave off. Do offer my kind remembrances to all your party, and believe me always your truly affectionate brother."

CHAPTER XXVI.

THE CASE OF STOCKDALE *v.* HANSARD—PRIVILEGE.

A. D. 1837 TO 1840. ÆT. 58 TO 61.

FROM the spring of 1837 to the spring of 1840 Lord Denman was, from time to time, engaged in a conflict, not sought by him, but forced upon him, with the Commons House of Parliament on the question of privilege arising out of the well-known case of *Stockdale* v. *Hansard*.

In a fragment—unfortunately only a very brief fragment—which he has left behind him, written in his own hand, relating to this memorable struggle, and which will be found in the Appendix, he speaks of it as "the most important event of my life, and that on which my future reputation must mainly depend." [1]

No attempt will here be made to weigh the authorities adduced on either side in this ably and exhaustively debated question. Those specially interested in legal and constitutional studies will find ready access to the authentic materials of inquiry in the published Reports of Parliament and of the Court of Queen's Bench.[2] A concise statement of the principal facts, illustrated by occasional reference to Denman's own judgments, speeches, and writings on the subject, is all that seems required

[1] This MS. fragment was written in June, 1851, the year after his retirement from the office of Chief Justice. It is given entire in the Appendix III.

[2] "Ad. and Ellis," vol. ix. p. 1, and for the Sheriff's case, vol. xi. p. 273 The "Annual Register" for 1840, chap. ii., "the Privilege Question," gives, at large, the facts, dates, and summary of the Parliamentary proceeding; and Sir Thomas Erskine May in his "Constitutional History of England," vol. i. chap. vii. pp. 459-462, states clearly and in very brief compass the salient points and principal stages of the controversy. See also Denman's article in the Quarterly Review for March, 1840, art. ix. vol. lxv.

in a record of his life designed rather for general readers than for special students of constitutional law.

The House of Commons in the session of 1835 had resolved that the Parliamentary Papers and Reports printed for the use of the House, should be rendered accessible to the public by purchase at the lowest price at which they could be sold (a price afterwards fixed at one halfpenny a sheet); that a sufficient number of extra copies should be printed for the purpose; and that Messrs. Hansard, the printers of the House, should be appointed to conduct the sale thereof.

In March, 1836, a report of the Inspectors of Prisons for the Home District was laid before the House, in the course of which the Inspectors stated that they had found in Newgate Gaol some copies of a work "On the Generative System," published by Stockdale, which they described as a book of a most disgusting nature, containing plates indecent and obscene in the extreme. The Court of Aldermen, to whom it was referred to consider the report of the prison inspectors so far as it referred to the prison of Newgate, defended the work as rather scientific than prurient. The Inspectors, in reply, denied "that the book was a scientific work, or that the plates were purely anatomical, calculated only to excite the attention of persons connected with surgical science;" and they added: "We adhere to the terms we have already employed as those only by which to characterize such a book." They further stated, "We have also applied to several medical booksellers, who all gave it the same character, and described it as one of Stockdale's obscene books. They said it never was considered as a medical work; that it never was written for or bought by members of the profession as such; but was intended to take young men in by inducing them to give an exorbitant price for an indecent work."

The Report and Reply of the Inspectors were printed and published by Messrs. Hansard, by order of the House, and in pursuance of the resolutions of 1835 and 1836.

On November 7, 1836, Stockdale brought an action against Messrs. Hansard for publishing the report containing the above passages, which he complained of as libelous and defamatory. Messrs. Hansard, wno were very ably defended, their leading counsel being Lord Campbell, then Sir John Campbell, Attorney-General, put two pleas on the record—1, not guilty (under which it was open to the defendants to contend that the publication, under the circumstances of the case, was privileged, and therefore not a libel); 2, a justification on the ground of the truth of the alleged libel.

The cause came on to be tried before Lord Denman at the Middlesex sittings, after Hilary Term, on February 7, 1837.

On the first issue the Chief Justice at the trial expressed a strong opinion that the publication of the Report of the prison inspectors, considering the circumstances under which that report had been made, was, in law, a privileged publication, and could not be made the subject of an action for libel; and he offered to reserve this question for the opinion of the full Court—an offer which the Attorney-General declined. On the second issue—that, namely, whether the alleged libel was not justified by the indecent and objectionable character of Stockdale's book—Lord Denman, after a pretty clear intimation of his own opinion on the point, left it to the jury to say whether, in their judgment, the defendants would not, on this second issue, be entitled to a verdict. The jury, after attentively examining the book, which had been produced in court and commented on with deserved severity by the defendants' counsel, took this view, and, on the second issue, *which in effect decided the case*, found a verdict for the defendants.

The Attorney-General, however, pressed strongly for a direction in favor of the defendants on the ground of privilege; on the ground, namely, that the publication was justified by reason of having taken place under the authority of the House of Commons' resolutions.

Pressed upon this point, the Chief Justice, in vigorous and emphatic language, denied both the power in the House of creating such privilege, and also the operation of such supposed privilege to suspend, alter, or supersede any legal remedy to which an Englishman was entitled by the known laws of his cuntry.

The substance of what fell from the Chief Justice on

this point, is thus given in the report of the trial, published in *The Times* of February 8, 1837:

"On the third point that has been submitted to you, namely, that this is a privileged publication, I am bound to say (as it comes before me as a point of law for my direction) that I entirely dissent from the law laid down by the learned counsel for the defendants. I am not aware of the existence, in this country, of any body whatever, which can privilege any servant of theirs to publish libels on any individual. Whatever arrangements may be made between the House of Commons and any publishers whom they may employ, I am of opinion that the person who publishes that in his public shop, and especially for money, which can be injurious and possibly ruinous to any one of His Majesty's subjects, must answer in a court of justice to that subject, if he challenges him for that libel. *I wish to say so emphatically and distinctly, because I think, if on the first opportunity that arose in a court of justice on such a question, that point were to be left unsatisfactorily explained, the judge who sat there might become an accomplice in the destruction of the liberties of his country, and expose every individual who lived in it to a tyranny no man ought to submit to.* Therefore, on this issue, my direction to you, subject to question hereafter, is, that the fact of the House of Commons having directed Messrs. Hansard to publish all their Parliamentary Reports and Papers, is no justification for them, or any bookseller, in publishing a Parliamentary Report containing a libel against any man."

Lord Denman, in the MS. fragment already referred to, thus states the position assumed by the Attorney-General at the trial, and his own mode of dealing with it:

"Ultimately, this position was maintained—that the paper, admitting it to be both libelous and untrue, might yet, under order of the House of Commons, be published to the plaintiff's injury without his having any legal redress.

"The doctrine on which this audacious proposition was founded, was soon averred and maintained—that the House of Commons is the sole judge of its own privileges—in other words, that it has power, by the Constitution of England, to make anything lawful which it declares to be done in virtue of its privilege; or, in still more general language, that we in England live under an absolute despotism, wielded by the majority of the knights, citizens, and burgesses in parliament assembled for the time being.

"Brought face to face with this alarming doctrine, I did not hesitate to denounce it in strong terms."

In his admirable speech in the House of Lords, delivered on April 6, 1840, in the course of the discussion that immediately preceded the close of the controversy by the passing of the Printed Papers Act (3 and 4 Vic. c. 9),[1] Lord Denman said, in reference to what had fallen from him at the trial:

"I felt it to be my duty, on the part of the people of England, to take the ground I had taken, and to say that I did not admit the claim of privilege as asserted, and would not give it the name of law. I may have expressed my opinion too warmly and too largely; but that the doctrine I asserted was right, I was, my Lords, at that moment, as I am still, convinced; and I felt that if I had thrown a doubt by any delay in declaring my opinion on a question of this importance, and which was so clear to myself, I should have betrayed that duty which I was placed in the Court over which I preside principally to discharge."

Elsewhere, in the same speech he states the nature of the defense set up in the House of Commons in this short and pointed form:

"It amounts to this, my Lords, that they *must have a right to sell all that they printed, because they had a right to do all that they pleased.* My lords (he added), I do not understand that to be the law of England. If it be so (he says in another part of the same speech), the people of this country have been mistaken for years and centuries in thinking that they lived in a land of freedom."

In the MS. fragment of 1851 Lord Denman says, with reference to what passed on the first trial, after he had been forced by the persistence of the Attorney-General to declare his view of the law on the third issue, "I was

[1] This speech is reprinted in the Appendix, No. IV.

informed and believe that the Attorney-General, turning to his neighbors in Court, expressed his concurrence with the law as I laid it down."

Lord Denman never forgave Lord Campbell for the part that he afterwards took in reference to these proceedings; not, indeed, for laboring to establish (as he was no doubt obliged to do as leading counsel for the Messrs. Hansard, in other words, for the House of Commons) that the exposition of law with which he had thus in conversation expressed his concurrence, was erroneous, but also and still more for repeatedly insinuating, both orally and in well-considered written publications,[1] that Lord Denman, in denouncing as he did the claim to privilege set up by the House, was actuated by a vain desire of putting himself forward as a champion of, the people's rights with a view of obtaining popular applause; and this, when none knew better than Lord Campbell himself that the expression of the Chief Justice's opinion on the question of privilege was not in any sense volunteered by him, but was forced from him by the part taken by the leading counsel for the defendant in insisting on a decision upon it.

The House was very indignant at the strong and decided terms in which the Chief Justice had denounced the claim of privilege which their leading counsel, the Attorney-General, had set up.

"There are always (continues Lord Denman in the fragment already cited), some zealots of privilege in the House of Commons, and none of its members are more averse than other people to the possession of absolute power. A committee was speedily appointed to consider my proceeding. My nephew, Sir Archer Croft,[2] attended with the record in Stockdale *v.* Hansard, and expressed in private to the Attorney-General his pleasure at hearing that the doctrine I had laid down had his approbation. The Attorney-General did not deny it, but said that considerable doubts were entertained about it by eminent legal members of the House, whom he named."

The committee,[3] on May 8, 1837, after six weeks of

[1] Such as his Lives of the Chancellors, and of the Chief Justices.

[2] One of the Master's of the Court of Queen's Bench.

[3] Among the members of this committee were Lord John Russell, Sir Robert Peel, Sir William Follett, Sir Robert Inglis, and Mr. O'Connell.

deliberation, reported in favor of the exclusive right of the House of Commons to judge of its own privileges, fortifying their conclusion by a lengthened and elaborate reference to cases and precedents.[1]

In consequence of this Report, the House, on May 31, 1837, passed the three following resolutions:

"1. That the power of publishing such of its Reports, Votes, and Proceedings, as it shall deem necessary or conducive to the public interests, is an essential incident to the constitutional functions of Parliament, more especially of this House, as the representative portion of it.

"2. That, by the law and privilege of Parliament, this House has the sole and exclusive jurisdiction to determine upon the existence and extent of its privileges, and that the institution or prosecution of any action, suit, or other proceeding, for the purpose of bringing them into discussion before any Court or Tribunal elsewhere than in Parliament, is a high breach of such privilege, and renders all parties concerned therein amenable to its just displeasure, and to the punishment consequent thereon.

"3. That for any Court or Tribunal to decide upon matters of privilege, is inconsistent with the determination of either House of Parliament, and is a breach and contempt of the privileges of Parliament."

On these resolutions Denman thus remarks, in the "*Observations*" he drew up and printed soon after their publication:

"Were it not better to drop the name of *privilege*—which holds out the semblance of peculiar rights adapted to the proper and unquestioned functions of Parliament—and substitute the name of *power*? The Lords came to a resolution that neither House of Parliament can, by its vote, change the law of the land; but the Commons have now resolved that either House has the exclusive power to judge of the existence and extent of its own powers, without any human control. Consider, then, for a mo-

[1] Soon after the appearance of this Report, Denman drew up and printed, but without his name, a very able paper, entitled "Observations on the Report of the Committee of the House of Commons on the publication of Printed Papers," dated May 8, 1837.

ment, if this theory should become practice, what effect it would have on the mixed constitution of England—Kings, Lords, and Commons?

"The head of the State, acting through the agency of responsible officers, can do no act whatever without the full sanction of law. He claims no right to obstruct the access of his meanest subject to the temple of Justice, interposes no shield between his most favored servant and the law, and wields no weapon for the annoyance of those ministers by whom its behests are declared. Sheridan once happily said of the King of England, 'In the Legislative branches he sees his equals, and in the law his superior.' But we are now told that his superior, even in executive proceedings, is to be found in either of the legislative branches. Let the Lords or Commons declare the most ordinary act of any servant of the Crown a breach of privilege, and the service may be thwarted, the agent lodged in Newgate, or exposed to any other punishment, without appeal or remedy. And, as in the daily disputes between man and man, either House may supersede the law, and give its award in favor of either party, so, in the highest concerns of the State, the interposition of either may hand over the power of acting from responsible Ministers of the Crown to the uncontrollable hands of what is now called privilege."[1]

Stockdale, meanwhile, shortly before the passing of these resolutions, having purchased a second copy of the Report, had brought a second action of defamation (as he was entitled to do on the proof of any fresh instance of sale of the Report), and to this action the sole defense put on the record by the Attorney-General was a plea of privilege, justifying the publication under the order and resolution of the House. This plea was demurred to on the grounds, "1. That the established laws of the land can not be superseded, suspended, or altered, by any resolution or order of the House of Commons. 2. That the Commons in Parliament assembled, can not, by any resolution or order, create any new privilege inconsistent with the known laws of the land."

The demurrer came on for argument early in Trinity

[1] "Observations on Resolutions of May 8, 1837," pp. 47, 48.

Term, 1839. It was most ably and exhaustively argued on both sides (Mr. Curwood for Stockdale and Sir J. Campbell for the Messrs. Hansard).[1] At the close of the argument the Court of Queen's Bench was unanimous, and Denham and Littledale were prepared to deliver judgment immediately. Patterson and Coleridge, however (and very properly, considering the importance of the question and the vast mass of authorities brought before the Court), thought it better that time should be taken for the preparation of well-considered written judgments, which having accordingly been drawn up, were read *seriatim* by the various members of the Court on May 31, 1839.[2]

The judgment of Lord Denman alone, which is very able, occupies 54 pages (from p. 107 to 161) of Messrs. Adolphus and Ellis's reports; fortunately, however, from its great clearness and method, it will be possible, without any material omissions, to state the substance of it—principally in Lord Denman's own language—in much smaller compass.

After stating the terms of the Plea of Privilege, Lord Denman said:

"This plea it is contended establishes a good defense to the action on various grounds:

"I. The grievance complained of is an act done by order of the House of Commons, a Court superior to any Court of Law, and none of whose proceedings are to be questioned in any way.

"This is a claim for an arbitrary power to authorize the commission of any act whatever on behalf of a body, which, in the same argument is admitted *not* to be the supreme power in the State.

"The supremacy of Parliament, the foundation on which the claim is made to rest, appears to me completely to overturn it, *because the House of Commons is not the Parliament, but only a co-ordinate and component part of the Parliament.*

[1] Campbell, who was thoroughly convinced he was in the right, took immense pains with his speech, which extended over sixteen hours—of course not consecutive.

[2] See Lord Denman's statement on March 28, 1843, in the House of Lords. Hansard, Parl. Deb., third Series, vol. lxvi. pp. 1102, 1103.

"That sovereign power [the Parliament] can make and unmake laws, but for that the concurrence of the three legislative estates is necessary: *the resolution of any one of them can not alter the law, or place any one beyond its control.* This proposition, therefore, is absolutely untenable and abhorrent to the first principles of the Constitution of England.[1]

"II. The next defense involved in the plea is, that the defendants committed the grievance by order of the House of Commons *in a case of privilege; and that each House of Parliament is the sole judge of its own privileges.*

"This last proposition requires to be first considered; for if the Attorney-General was right in contending, as he did more than once, in express terms, that the House of Commons, by *claiming anything as its privilege, thereby makes it matter of privilege; and also that its own decision on its own claim is binding* and conclusive, then plainly this Court can not proceed to any inquiry into the matter, and has nothing else to do but to declare the claim well founded because it has been made."[2]

After stating that this was the form in which he understood the Committee of the House of Commons to have asserted its privilege, and the House, by a large majority, to have adopted that assertion, the Chief Justice proceeded as follows:

"It is not without the utmost respect and deference that I proceed to examine what has been promulgated by so high an authority. Most willingly would I decline to enter on an inquiry which may lead to differing from that great and powerful assembly. But, when one of my fellow-subjects presents himself before me, in these Courts, demanding justice for an injury, it is not at my option to grant or to withhold redress. I am bound to afford it, if the law declares him entitled to it."

The Chief Justice then proceeds, by the light of precedents, to examine the proposition that the opinion either House may entertain of its own privileges is necessarily correct, and its declaration of them absolutely binding.

After exhaustively examining the authorities cited by the Attorney-General to establish that proposition, and

[1] Ad. and Ell. ix. pp. 107, 108. [2] Ad. and Ell. ix. p. 108

to prove that questions of Parliamentary privilege are in no case examinable at law, he arrives clearly at the conclusion that *they establish no such proposition.* On the contrary, he finds that his great predecessor, Holt, having, on three several occasions, found himself compelled to deal with questions of Parliamentary privilege, on all of them not only examined the claim of privilege, but gave judgment against it.[1]

He, of course, founded himself chiefly on the great case of Ashby *v.* White, in which Holt, against the opinion of other judges of this Court, decided, and the House of Lords, confirming Holt's judgment, held, that even in questions of Parliamentary elections—a matter, if any, peculiary within the jurisdiction of the House of Commons—that Courts of Law were not bound by the opinion of the Commons House on matters of election, whereon that House claimed the sole right of judging, and had actually given judgment; but that the law must take its course, as if no such judgment had been given by the House of Commons, and no such privilege claimed.

Reverting, then, once again, from precedent to principle, Lord Denman, in concluding his argument as to this part of the case, says: "*In truth, no practical difference can be drawn between the right to sanction all things under the name of privilege, and the right to sanction all things whatever by merely ordering them to be done.*

"In both cases the law must be superseded by one Assembly, and however dignified and respectable that body—in whatever degree superior to all temptations of abusing their power—still, the power claimed is arbitrary and irresponsible, in itself the most monstrous and intolerable of all abuses."

On the second point, therefore, the opinion of Lord Denman was equally as clear as on the first, and his decision was that the House could not give themselves jurisdiction by merely adjudging that they possess it.

III. The Chief Justice then proceeded to examine the third and minor question, viz. whether the particular privilege claimed in this case—the privilege of publication—existed in law.

[1] See Lord Denman's judgment in Ad. and Ell. p. 134.

The proofs that it must so exist, he said, had been based on three grounds—Necessity, Practice, Universal Acquiescence.

As to *necessity*, he observed, that the supposed necessity was "absolutely non-proven, and had dwindled down, in the hands of the Attorney-General to merely a very dubious kind of expediency."

As to its *expediency*, Lord Denman remarked—and the remark is important, as will be seen hereafter, with reference to the act of the Legislature that closed the controversy—"It can hardly be necessary to guard myself against being supposed to discuss the *expediency* of keeping the law in its present state, or introducing any, and what alterations. It is no doubt suspectible of improvement, *but the improvement must be a legislative act;* it can not be effected under the name of privilege."[1]

As to *practice* and *long acquiescence*, he denied that any proof had been given, or could be found of any practice to authorize the printing and publication by the House of papers injurious to the character of a fellow-subject.

Even were it otherwise, he observed, "The practice of a ruling power in the State, coupled with public acquiescence, is but a feeble proof of its legality. I know not how long the *practice* of raising ship-money had prevailed before the *right* was denied by Hampden. *General Warrants* had been issued and enforced for centuries before they were quashed in action by Wilkes and his associates, who, by bringing them to the test of law, procured their condemnation and abandonment."

Towards the conclusion of his judgment Lord Denman thus referred to the remarks that had fallen from him at Nisi Prius, when the case was first tried before him in 1837:

"I can not lament that I gave utterance, at the proper occasion, to sentiments of which I deeply felt the importance, as well as the truth; nor can I doubt that a full consideration of the whole subject will lead to beneficial results. One thing alone I regret—a warmth of expression in asserting what law and justice appeared to me to require, which may have rendered it more difficult

[1] Ad. and Ell. ix. p. 153.

for the late House of Commons to recede from any claim which it had advanced.[1]

"Upon the whole matter (said Lord Denman in conclusion) I am of opinion that the defense pleaded is no defense in law, and that our judgment must be for the plaintiffs on this demurrer."

This celebrated judgment, notwithstanding its length—a length not greater than was absolutely necessary for the purpose of adequate judicial exposition—will be found, in the last analysis, to be mainly founded on a single broad principle, supported by a single illustrious precedent.

The *principle* is that no one branch of the Legislature, *acting separately and alone*, can, by any so-called privilege, alter, suspend, or supersede the established laws of the land, so as to prevent the subject from resorting to any remedy or enforcing any right which those laws have provided for or conferred on them.

The *precedent* is the famous judgment in *Ashby* v. *White*—the crowning glory of Lord Holt—whom Lord Denman always revered as the greatest among his predecessors in all the long and distinguished roll of the Chief Justices of England.

Among the many contributions which Denman, with unwearied zeal and diligence, made to the elucidation of this great question, few were more important than his publication, in 1837, of the judgment in *Ashby* v. *White*, and of the cognate case of *John Paty and others*, from a manuscript prepared under the eye of Lord Holt himself, and which was much fuller and more accurate than the text heretofore printed in the contemporary "Law Reports." This publication, which appeared without Lord Denman's name,[2] shortly after the House of Commons had passed the resolutions of May, 1837, was preceded by an able and argumentative introduction, from which the following passage may be extracted:

"The genuine and full report of his (Lord Holt's) judgment is believed to be now first published, and is highly

[1] Ad. and Ell. ix. p. 156.

[2] "The Judgments delivered by the Lord Chief Justice Holt in the Case of *Ashby* v. *White*, and in the Case of *John Paty and others*." Printed from original manuscripts, with an Introduction: Saunders and Benning, 1837. The citation in the text is from p. vii. of the Introduction.

deserving of attention. The Lords' Report on this subject (6 Parl. Hist. 420) is a noble document, but it is thought that Holt's revised statements of his own views ought by no means to be lost. Besides the learning and reasoning, who can fail to admire his plain and solemn statement of the sense of judicial duty; his far-sighted appreciation of the consequence of the disputed privilege on the whole frame of government in England; and the manly spirit which indicates the right of all Englishmen to assert their claims, and that of their advocates to maintain them, and that of the sworn judges of the land to decide upon them?"

The spirit here described as that which animated the great constitutional Chief Justice of an older time, is precisely that which animated his great successor; and England has equal reason to be proud of both.

Judgment on the *second* action having been thus given for the plaintiff on the demurrer, his damages were assessed at £100, a result which by no means satisfied Stockdale, who, during the parliamentary recess of 1839, having bought a third copy of the report, brought a *third* action against Messrs. Hansard.

To the *third* action the defendants (in obedience to the order of the House) put in no defense whatever. Judgment accordingly went by default, and on a writ of inquiry in the Sheriff's Court, damages were assessed at £600, which amount, together with an additional £40 for costs, &c., was levied by the Sheriffs (Messrs. Evans and Wheelton)[1] on December 16, 1839.

On the first day of the next Hilary Term (January 11, 1840) Stockdale obtained a rule returnable on the 17th, ordering the Sheriff to pay over to him the £640 which they had thus levied.

On the day before that fixed for the return of this rule—Jan. 16, 1840—Parliament met, and vigorous measures were at once taken by the House of Commons to assert its dignity.

On the very day of its meeting, the House, on the

[1] Messrs. Wheelton and Evans, the Sheriffs of London, in law constituted together the Sheriff of Middlesex, which throughout these proceedings, was their proper *legal* style, but they are generally in the text spoken of as the Sheriffs, in the plural.

motion of Lord John Russell, after an animated debate, resolved, by a majority of 119, that Stockdale and his attorney, Thomas Burton Howard, be called to the bar; by a majority of 89 they came to the same resolution in the case of the Sheriffs.

On January 17 Stockdale was committed to Newgate, Howard (having expressed regret for his fault) escaping with a severe reprimand.

On the 20th the Sheriffs were ordered to refund to Messrs. Hansard the moneys which they had levied, and which they admitted to be still in their possession and control.

The Sheriffs, believing they were bound to do so by their duty to the Court of Queen's Bench, whose sworn officers they were, having declined to comply with this order, it was resolved, on the 21st, by a majority of 101, that they should be committed to the custody of the Sergeant-at-Arms, and committed accordingly they were.

The imprisonment of these two gentlemen—"innocent victims," as Sir Erskine May well calls them, "of conflicting jurisdiction"—excited a considerable amount of public commiseration.

On January 24 the Sheriffs sued out their writ of Habeas Corpus, to which the Sergeant-at-Arms was directed to make a *general* return, that he held the bodies of the Sheriffs by virtue of a warrant, under the hand and seal of the Speaker, for a *contempt* and breach of the privileges of the House.

The Attorney-General, Sir John Campbell, in recommending the House to adopt this course, had informed them, and with entire accuracy, that the House had power to commit for *contempt*, and that when it appeared generally, on the face of the return to the writ, that it had so committed, the Court to which the writ was returned would have no power whatever to question the ground of the committal, or go into any inquiry as to its propriety or legality.

The legal principle thus stated by the Attorney-General was too firmly established to admit of any serious discussion; and, accordingly, when, on Jan. 25, the Sheriffs were brought up in custody of the Sergeant-at-

Arms, the Court of Queen's Bench, having overruled certain technical objections to the form of the warrant and the return, had no alternative but to direct, as it did, that the prisoners must return to the custody whence they came.[1]

Lord Denman, having stated it as clear law that the Court of Queen's Bench could not examine into the validity of the commitment, but must presume that what *any* Court, much more what either House of Parliament, acting on great legal authority, takes upon it to pronounce a contempt, is so, added, with grave sarcasm, "Indeed, it would be unseemly to suspect that a body acting under such sanctions as a House of Parliament, would, in making its warrant, suppress facts which, if discussed, might entitle the person committed to his liberty."[2]

The Judges of the Court of Queen's Bench, though thus precluded by the mode in which the Attorney-General had framed his warrant, from effectively interposing for the liberation of the Sheriffs, thought it right to take the opportunity of openly declaring their adhesion to the celebrated judgment pronounced by the Court, nearly eight months before. Lord Denman did so in the following bold and manly terms:

"I think it necessary to declare that the judgment delivered by this Court last Trinity term in the case of *Stockdale* v. *Hansard* appears to me in all respects correct. The Court there decided that there was no Power in this country above being questioned by Law. The House of Commons there attempted to place its privilege on the footing of an unquestionable and unlimited power. I endeavored to establish that the claim advanced in that case tended to despotic power, which could not be recognized or exist in this country, and that the privilege of publication as there asserted had no legal foundation.

"To *all* of these positions, I, on further consideration, adhere: *all* of them I believe in my conscience to be true.

"And if this were not so, it is strange that the case should not have been brought before the other ten

[1] See "Case of the Sheriff of Middlesex," reported in Ad. and Ell. xi. p 273.

[2] Ad. and Ell. xi. p. 292.

Judges by writ of error. The House would have suffered no loss of dignity by submitting to them [the Court of Error] the question it had already laid before us. In the last resort a further appeal might have been made to the House of Lords.

"In deciding the former case we looked to the law as our only safe guide, discarding all considerations of supposed expediency; and, under the same guidance, we have examined the question now before us. In the present case I am obliged to say that I find no authority under which we can discharge these gentlemen from their imprisonment."

The following passage from the "Annual Register" of the year 1840, relating to this application for the release of the Sheriffs, shows the nature of the public feeling which the proceedings of the House of Commons had already begun to excite.

"On the next day, January 25, Sir William Gossett (the Sergeant-at-Arms) appeared in the Court of Queen's Bench with the two Sheriffs in his custody, who were dressed in their robes of office. Their situation excited a lively interest, and the Court and its passages were crowded to excess. While proceeding from the apartment where they had been confined to the Court, they were loudly cheered by the crowd of persons assembled, who seemed to feel the utmost sympathy for their disagreeable position. This was about four o'clock in the afternoon; and at the time when Sir William Gossett with his prisoners reached the Court the Bench was empty; the whole of the fifteen Judges having been engaged during the day in hearing the point argued which had been reserved at the trial of Frost. Williams, and Jones, for high treason at Monmouth. In a short time, however, Lord Denman, Mr. Justice Littledale, Mr. Justice Williams, and Mr. Justice Coleridge, took their seats, and Sir William Gossett immediately handed in his return.

Counsel having been called upon, it was ably contended by Mr. Richards, Mr. Watson, and Mr. Kennedy, on behalf of the Sheriffs, that they were entitled to their discharge—that the Court would take cognizance of the particular breach of privilege of which it was alleged they were guilty; and, as it had previously decided against that privilege, it would release those who had merely obeyed, in the execution of their duty, its own orders. The Court, however, thought otherwise. The Judges gave their opinions *seriatim*, and held that the return to the *habeas corpus* was good and sufficient—that they could not *presume* anything, but must take it that the Sheriffs had, in some way or other, committed a contempt and breach of the privileges of the House of Commons, and that, therefore, they could only remand them to the custody of the Sergeant-at-Arms. It was now half-past eight, and Sir William Gossett retired from the Court with the Sheriffs in his custody.

The feeling shown on this occasion against the imprisonment of the Sheriffs was very strong, and the members of the Bar appeared to be almost unanimous in condemning the course adopted by the House of Commons.

The imprisoment of the Sheriffs was of some duration, and enforced with considerable rigor. A motion for their discharge, made on February 3, was rejected by a majority of 71. On February 12, indeed, on a medical certificate that his life would be endangered by further confinement, Mr. Sheriff Wheelton was discharged; but on February 14, and again on March 3, a similar application was refused in the case of Mr. Sheriff Evans, the House not being satisfied that the state of that gentleman's health rendered his discharge necessary; nor was he released from confinement, and then only provisionally, till March 5, after the introduction of the "Printed Papers Bill."

Meanwhile the irrepressible Stockdale, though fast in Newgate, continued to exercise his malign activity. On January 25 he had caused his attorney, Thomas Burton Howard, to commence a *fourth* action against the Messrs. Hansard—a fresh act of contempt, for which the attorney was sent to keep company in Newgate with his employer.

On February 17 a *fifth* action was commenced at the instance of Stockdale, by the attorney's son, which resulted in the committal the next day of Thomas Howard the younger, and of a miserable copying-clerk in his employment, one Thomas Pearce.

When matters had reached this point, it was universally felt that the dignity and character of the House were being seriously compromised. The public feeling was strongly excited; placards appeared in the streets of London expressive of the popular indignation; and the Press, almost without exception, loudly denounced the proceedings of the House as unconstitutional and oppressive. On February 18, when the order was made for the committal of Thomas Howard the younger, and his clerk, Pearce, Mr. Leader, the member for Westminster, "declared, that though he had hitherto voted with Lord John on all these questions of privilege, yet, he must say that public opinion was not with them on this occasion. He would assert that one could not meet with any person outside the House, except the hangers-on of the Government, who did not say that the House was acting tyrannically, and that it would be beaten at last."

It was evidently high time that the supreme authority of the Legislature (*i. e.*, of Queen, Lords and Commons) should interfere to put an end to a state of things so discreditable and vexatious. Accordingly, Lord John Russell, on March 5, obtained leave to bring in a Bill, generally known as "the Printed Papers Bill," the object of which was to terminate the unfortunate collision of authorities which had occurred, by providing, that in future all proceedings against persons for publication of papers printed by order of Parliament should be *stayed on delivery of a certificate and affidavit that such publication was by order of either House.*

The motion of Lord John Russell for leave to bring in this bill was carried by a majority of 149 (203 to 54), numbers sufficiently indicating how glad the House was to escape by any fair compromise from a position which had evidently became untenable.

The zealots of privilege, indeed, were not satisfied; but led by the Solicitor-General, Sir Thomas Wilde—more mindful on this occasion of his zeal for the House than of his allegiance to the Government—contended that by invoking the assistance of the whole Legislature, the House in effect waived the assertion of its own privilege as a separate branch of the Legislature.

"The Solicitor-General earnestly cautioned the House against doing anything that might appear to admit in any degree the validity of the judgment of the Court of Queen's Bench. By passing (he said) a legislative measure to stop future proceedings in a summary manner, the inference would be that the House admitted it could not set up its own order as an effectual plea in bar, but that some thing further was necessary. It would also be said that *they would not have left the judgment of the Court of Queen's Bench unimpugned, as they had done. had they not felt that they could not successfully have dissented from it. His objection to the bill was that when they did not venture to assert separately and independently their own privileges—when they had not expressed the slightest dissent from the legal authority of the judgment pronounced by the Court of Queen's Bench—they in effect affirmed that judgment for all practical purposes.*"

The reasonings of the Solicitor-General on this point seem unanswerable; and it must be taken that the House, by invoking the authority of the whole Legislature to give validity to the plea they had vainly set up in the action, and by not appealing against the judgment of the Court of Queen's Bench, had, in effect, admitted the correctness of that judgment and affirmed the great principle on which it was founded, viz., that no single branch of the Legislature can, by any assertion of its alleged privileges, alter, suspend, or supersede any known law of the land, or bar the resort of any Englishman to any remedy, or his exercise and enjoyment of any right, by that law established.

The "Printed Papers Bill" was in fact a compromise, leaving the authority of the judgment of the Queen's Bench, as an assertion of constitutional principle, not only unshaken, but to some extent confirmed.

The Bill having passed the Commons on March 20, was read a second time in the House of Lords on April 6. On that occasion Lord Denman delivered the speech from which extracts have already been made, and the whole of which will be found printed in the Appendix;[1] a speech of a very high order of excellence, calm, moderate, and dignified; giving a lucid history of the whole

[1] Appendix IV.

controversy from its first inception; firmly maintaining the ground taken by the Court of Queen's Bench; but not opposing in principle the Bill before the House as a means of legislatively putting an end to a collision of authorities which had been rather forced upon him than sought by him, and the existence of which no one had more regretted than himself. Notwithstanding some opposition by the Duke of Wellington, who protested against the passing of any measure the effect of which would be to make the House of Commons "the only authorized libelers in the country," the Bill finally passed the Lords—with some additions and amendments, principally suggested by Lord Denman himself—to which the Commons agreed, and on April 14 it received the Royal assent, and took its place in the Statute-book as the 3 and 4 Vic. c. 9, with the title of "An Act to give Summary Protection to Persons employed in the Publication of Parliamentary Papers."[1]

Thus ended this memorable controversy. Mr. Sheriff Evans, who had been released provisionally on March 5 (the day the Bill was brought into the House of Commons), was finally and absolutely discharged on April 14, the day it received the Royal assent; and on the same day Thomas Howard the younger, and his clerk, were let out of Newgate; where, however, Stockdale and Thomas Burton Howard were further detained till May 15.

The firmness, temperance, and dignity displayed by Lord Denman throughout the whole of this protracted and harassing controversy, were deservedly the theme of universal praise, and his name became endeared to the people of England as that of a bold and unshaken

[1] The principal provision of the Act is the first section, providing that proceedings, criminal or civil, against persons for publication of papers printed by order of Parliament, shall be stayed upon delivery of a certificate and affidavit to the effect that such publication is by order of either House of Parliament.

A concluding clause (the fourth) was added to soothe the susceptibilities of the Lower House, viz. "That nothing herein contained shall be deemed, or taken, or held, or construed, directly or indirectly, by implication or otherwi e, to affect the privileges of Parliament in any manner whatever." This elaborate verbiage could not prevent people from drawing their own inferences, nor conceal, by a cloud of words, the substantial defeat of the House.

supporter of their ancient liberties and immemorial rights.

He has preserved among his papers a letter by an unknown hand, which, by the indorsement, "*to be taken care of*," had evidently gratified him, and which, as a fair expression of the popular sentiment of the time, may be inserted here.

"*To the Lord Chief Justice Denman.*

"When the spirit of political intrigue, which pre-eminently distinguishes the present era, shall have passed away, and agitation have subsided throughout the land, the dispassionate judgments of another generation will gratefully appreciate the judicial virtues and the magnanimity of the Lord Chief Justice Denman.

"It is not fitting in me, my lord, an humble member of the English Bar, to offer to your Lordship the spontaneous tribute of admiration which is participated by a large portion of the profession; yet the homage of the citizen is not, on that account, the less due to the benefactor of his country, when he predicts of your Lordship that so long as Westminster Hall shall endure, so long as the British Constitution shall exist, so surely shall that which your Lordship has done for the people of England, in the case of Stockdale *v.* Hansard, stand recorded, a glorious memento, in the brightest page of our national annals. "CIVILIS.

"June 19, 1837."

It was not only the popular sentiment, however, which, revering in Lord Denman the fearless and upright magistrate, ranged itself in favor of the line taken by the Court of Queen's Bench; but the learned opinion also of Westminster Hall was entirely in favor of the correctness, in point of law, of the judgment in *Stockdale* v. *Hansard.*

This appears from a discussion which arose in the House of Lords, on March 28, 1843, regarding a speech then recently delivered by Sir Thomas Wilde in the House of Commons, and which, as incorrectly reported, attributed to Lord Denman an expression of opinion in the course of the judgment in *Stockdale* v. *Hansard*, which in point of fact he had never uttered. This led to a declaration on the part of Lord Denman of his being prepared to abide by every word of that judgment as correctly given in the authorized legal reports; to a re-affirmation of the principles laid down in the judgment, which, never having been appealed against, must be taken as correct in law; and to a vindication of the judges who had taken part in it from the disparagement [recently put forth by Lord Campbell in his "Lives of the Chief Justices"] of being "mere lawyers."[1]

This called up Lord Campbell, who declared it to be his firm opinion—1st, that the judgment of the Court of Queen's Bench was entirely erroneous, and had been at once condemned by Westminster Hall: 2ndly, "that the Printed Papers Publication Act amounted to a *Parliamentary reversal* of the judgment, inasmuch as the preamble of that Act distinctly recognized it to be essentially necessary to the due discharge of the functions of the two Houses that they should have the power of publishing whatever part of their proceedings they might deem requisite for the information of the public."

On both points Lord Campbell received an emphatic and decisive refutation.

As to the *opinion of Westminster Hall*, Lord Abinger (Sir James Scarlett)—certainly no partial witness in Denman's favor—said, "As far as I could learn the opinion of Westminster Hall on the subject (and Scarlett, in 1839, when the judgment was delivered, was the first man in the profession), I must say that the *general* feeling there coincided with what I believe to have been the *universal* feeling elsewhere" (viz., in favor of the judgment). Lord Abinger reminded Lord Campbell that "at the time the judgment was pronounced, he [Lord Campbell] was not in a position to ascertain truly what the real opinions of the bar were. He then held a high and influential situation under the Government [as Attorney-General], and was surrounded by persons who were not likely to differ from him in opinion."[2]

As to the alleged *Parliamentary reversal* of the judgment, by the passing of the Act of 3 & 4 Vic. c. 9,

[1] Hansard, Parl. Deb., third series, vol. lxvi. p. 1100 et seq.
[2] Hansard, Parl. Deb., third series, vol. lxvi. p. 1113.

Lord Denman (who, in giving judgment in Stockdale *v.* Hansard, had, as already pointed out, distinctly disclaimed expressing any opinion on the *expediency* or otherwise of altering the law as it then stood, although intimating that it was susceptible of improvement) supplied the following short and conclusive answer:—

"As a Judge, I denied that that privilege of publication existed *before*, to the injury of individuals; as a Legislator I concurred in its being permitted *for the future*. As a Judge I could only lay down the law as I found it; as a Member of Parliament I agreed to a change in the law for the public advantage."

As to the point of "*Parliamentary reversal*," the Duke of Wellington also, who had, not without difficulty, consented to the passing of the Act on Printed Papers, spoke as follows:—

"The noble and learned lord [Lord Campbell] says that Act was a contradiction of the judgment of the Court of Queen's Bench, and is wholly inconsistent with it. I wish just to state what passed in this House when that act was under your lordship's consideration—namely, that it was the noble and learned lord, the Chief Justice of the Queen's Bench, who himself supported the measure and prevailed on your lordships to adopt it. Answering only for myself, at least, I can say that *I was persuaded to vote for that measure entirely in consequence of the speech of the noble and learned lord, the Chief Justice*, who, I take it, would not have urged the Bill on the adoption of the House if it were so entirely inconsistent, as the noble and learned lord [Lord Campbell] has represented it to be, with the judgment of the Court of Queen's Bench."

Very few, if any, letters are to be found among Lord Denman's papers bearing directly upon the great controversy raised by Stockdale *v.* Hansard.

The two following, however, which have an indirect relation to it, may conveniently be inserted here.

In 1838 the venerable Lord Commissioner Adam had written Denman a letter (not preserved) in praise of his constitutional exertions, and inclosing some papers in reference to what he himself had done in 1793, when he had brought before Parliament the illegal sentence of the

Scotch Court of Judiciary in the case of Muir, and had been defeated by 171 to 31. The sentence in Muir's case was flagrant and monstrously illegal; he had been convicted of sedition (*for associating to obtain a Reform in Parliament!*) and sentenced to fourteen years' transportation, *such punishment for such offense being totally unknown to the law!!* Lord Commissioner Adam had sent these papers to Denman as showing how, in periods of political excitement, the sense of justice can be overcome in the House of Commons by the spirit of party.

Denman's reply was as follows:

"Middleton: August 27, 1838.

"My dear Lord,—One of the first occupations of my leisure has been the perusal of the valuable documents which you have been so good as to transmit to me. I beg you to accept my thanks, and to believe that few persons could be more gratified by any proof of your regard or more interested in the contents of the papers.

"It has ever been my opinion that the resistance made by Mr. Fox and his friends to the inroads of arbitrary power preserved the free Constitution of this country from the most imminent danger, and that not one of their efforts is entitled to more praise and gratitude than your able vindication of the law against the judicial outrage committed on the persons of Mr. Muir and his fellow-sufferers. It seems now astonishing that the torrent of power and party spirit could sweep away the safeguards of justice when so clearly pointed out; *but you fixed the landmark while the storm was raging, and it still remains, now that the waters have subsided, for the protective guidance of posterity.*

"The result must be delightful to your feelings. There can be no higher reward for a public man than to witness the triumph of those just principles which he had dared to assert under every discouragement. That you, my dear lord, may yet have the satisfaction of seeing a long series of these bloodless victories in the cause of freedom and humanity, is my earnest hope.

"Your lordship's obliged and faithful servant.

"DENMAN."

The other letter was written to the Duke of Wellington, just before the Privilege controversy was terminated by the passing of the Printed Papers Act. The Duke had taken throughout a strong interest in the discussion, and had fully supported the views enounced by Lord Denman. Denman had sent the Duke a copy of his own republication of Lord Holt's judgment in the case of Ashby *v.* White, and of John Paty and others; and the Duke had lent Denman the pamphlet referred to in the following letter. The tone of respectful homage which pervades Denman's communication is the sincere expression of his real sentiments for the great Captain to whom, personally, he always felt he had been under deep obligation, for procuring him the first great and indispensable step in his professional advancement—the rank of King's Counsel.

"Warwick: March 29, 1840.

"My dear Lord Duke,—I have the honor to return, with many thanks, the volume which you were so kind as to lend me. The account of what occurred in Parliament and the Queen's Bench with reference to the Five Men of Aylesbury, is very well drawn up: yet, if your Grace could find time to read the judgment in Paty's case, as reported in the little publication I sent, I think you will find the principles and reasonings both more eloquently stated and more fully developed.

"The value stamped by your Grace's approbation on the narrative of the Battle of Blenheim in the same volume has induced me to devote some short intervals of leisure to the perusal of it.

"Both these passages in our history appears to me extremely interesting, as well from the nature of the transactions as from their resemblance to events in our own times.

"The author's style rises with his subject. The Duke of Marlborough is brought upon the scene with great spirit: 'a person whom courage, experience, vigilance, and conduct recommended for a captain-general, and whom wisdom, penetration, temper, and affability fitted for a plenipotentiary.'

"Few will read this passage without finding a parallel which is only not exact, because still higher qualities ought to be added to complete the likeness.

"On the other hand, the successor of Lord Holt can enter into no competition with him, except, perhaps, on the score of good intentions.

"I am conscious of some presumption in placing myself, on any terms, in company with such illustrious names: but the observation has forced itself upon me.

"In common with all Englishmen, I claim an interest in your Grace's reputation, and I am proud to remember that you have some interest in mine, as being, to a certain extent, responsible for my promotion to an office that I never could have attained without the rank previously procured for me by your kindness and generosity.

"Permit me, my Lord, to express my hope that the Bill relating to Printed Papers may lead to the satisfactory adjustment of painful differences, though it will probably require modification and curtailment.

"I have the honor to be
"Your Grace's obliged and faithful servant,
"DENMAN."

In addition to the many publications and documents already referred to in the present chapter, a paper may be mentioned which Lord Denman himself communicated on this great question to *The Quarterly Review.*[1] It is not, however, necessary to do more than thus refer to it, for, though able and interesting, it adds nothing to the elucidation the subject had elsewhere received from his more authoritative deliverances—his judgments in the Court of Queen's Bench and his speeches in the Upper House of Parliament; while, from the easy accessibility of the volume in which it is contained, it has not been thought necessary to reprint it in the Appendix.

[1] Vol. lxv., No. for March 1840, Article ix.

CHAPTER XXVII.

SOCIAL AND FAMILY LIFE—FIRST SLAVE-TRADE SPEECH IN HOUSE OF LORDS.

1837 TO 1841. ÆT. 58 TO 62.

WITH a view of presenting a continuous account of the proceedings and discussions connected with and arising out of the great case of Stockdale *v.* Hansard, the course of the narrative has been suspended, and the order of time departed from.

The first trial of Stockdale *v.* Hansard took place, it will be recollected, in February, 1837; and the preparation, later in the spring of that year, of his pamphlet commenting on the resolution of the Commons Committee, coupled with the deep and extended researches into the Law of Privilege, to which, as his papers prove, he about this period devoted himself, sufficiently occupied the greater portion of the time which the Chief Justice could spare from his judicial functions.

On June 20, 1837, William IV. died, and Her present Majesty succeeded to the Throne.

In the session that preceded the consequent dissolution of Parliament, Denman had the high satisfaction of at length carrying through the House of Lords two bills, one finally abolishing death punishment in *all* cases of *forgery*, and the other putting an end to it in a great variety of other cases, where, though in fact capital punishment was hardly ever, if ever inflicted, the power of awarding it was, to the disgrace of the law, still suffered to remain.[1]

In the late autumn session which followed the dissolu-

[1] These two Bills received the Royal assent, one on July 11, the other on July 17, 1837. See Hansard, Parl. Deb., third series, vol. xxxviii. pp. 1773–1859–1907–8; the Act abolishing Death Punishment for Forgery is 1 Vic. c. 84.

tion—on December 3, 1837,—the Chief Justice lent cordial and efficient support to the Bill for the Abolition of Arrest on Mesne Process, the second reading of which was on that day moved by Lord Cottenham.[1]

Among the few letters of this year which have been preserved, is the following, written on August 4, for the amusement of his daughters, and giving an account of a dinner-party at Buckingham Palace, the first, apparently, which the Chief Justice had attended since the young Queen's accession.[2]

"Now for a description of the Queen's dinner. The dinner was at a quarter-past seven, at Buckingham Palace, and I was there within ten minutes after that time.[3] The Palace has been much maligned, and is really much handsomer than I expected. The hall and staircase are magnificent. A splendid room hung with green silk first receives you, then a round room with a vaulted roof, where several were assembled, and among the rest Tricoupi. In about five minutes folding doors to the right were thrown open, and the Queen came tripping in, with the Duchess of Kent and all her ladies. A *general* bow and some particular addresses, very short, and interrupted by 'God save the Queen,' softly and charmingly played by the Coldstream band. It was kindly received, for it meant dinner. She was led in by some foreign nobleman, and so in order. I am sorry I can not say who was led in by me. We passed through a large room—remarkably rich with gilding and yellow furniture, but deformed with numerous pillars of mock marble, of a deep raspberry-cream color, with which the gilded capitals harmonized very ill—into the dining-room. Candles were lighted, but we had sufficient daylight to show the fine trees in the garden, and might have been, as the Cockneys say, a hundred miles from London. I was seating myself at one end of the table, when Colonel Cavendish told me that place belonged to him as equerry, and so I was divorced from my anony-

[1] Hansard, Parl. Deb., third series, vol. xxxix. pp. 592–625. This Bill received the Royal assent on August 16, 1838, and is 1 & 2 Vic. c. 110.

[2] The letter was addressed to his third daughter, Fanny, now the Hon. Lady Baynes.

[3] Lord Denham had come up from Croydon, where he was presiding on the Home Circuit.

mous partner. This threw me next to Miss Spring Rice and mother, and another maid of honor whom I did not know, and to the same side of the table with Her Majesty, so that I could see but little of her.

"The party was, I think, twenty-six in number. The conversation was confined to small knots, but was lively and incessant, though carried on in subdued tones. It was very different from the kingly table I remember, where the Royal Host used to drink to the general health of the whole table, and singly with most of his company, and more than once. Shortly after dinner, while Miss Spring Rice was harrowing my feelings with the story of Norma, there was a little stir, and Colonel Cavendish called me by name out of my reverie. All stood and drank the Queen's health; half an hour then passed in conversation, and after a second ladyless half hour, we returned through the gorgeous apartment to the vaulted gathering-room, the folding-doors of which opened into a sober drawing-room, and others into the gallery of Flemish pictures—a most noble collection. The band was placed at the end of this gallery, and it played at dinner, and at intervals throughout the evening, very softly and sweetly.

"In the drawing-room whist was played at one table. Her Majesty was seated on a sofa between the Marchioness of Abercorn and Madame Tricoupi. Her Majesty desired chairs to be placed, and that all of us should sit down, so the conversation went on till about eleven, when the same national air again struck up, and the party broke up.

"Now I come to the important part of my description; but, though the general mourning is over, it was still court mourning. The Queen wore all black, with a train, her hair as usual, with thin rings of curls hardly larger than a shilling on the cheeks—that is one just below each ear: a little flowing black gauze was fastened in the hair behind; but I don't know what became of it, I rather suspect it was fastened somewhere about half-way down her back. The Queen is exactly the height of Madame Tricoupi, but looks much shorter when sitting. No human countenance was ever more expressive of happiness and good-nature; she had something to say to everybody, and asked me about your mother and about the circuit; not the smallest constraint with anyone; on retiring she shook hands with several of the ladies, and seemed to talk very confidentially with some. I heard her ask with much interest, 'Is it a nice child?' Her Majesty is not yet provided with a horse, so if you hear of anything very perfect for spirit and docility, you may as well make a purchase of it on speculation: she is determined to have a large horse, '*none of your cobs.*'"

On October 20, 1837, he writes from Middleton to Mrs. Baillie:

"The extraordinary beauty of this morning has tempted me to a short walk before commencing my daily occupation of writing letters. The glass is at 58° in the shade. I sincerely wish you could enjoy our quiet, dewy scene, which promises a whole day equally fine; but we will hope for similar weather next year. My former reading had thrown me on 'Mackintosh's Life,'[1] which I have read for the second time with increasing pleasure." In a subsequent letter he tells his sister: "I am deep in Madame de Sevigné's letters, which I never read before, and find equal to all their panegyrics."[2]

The following letter to Coleridge was written while Denman was presiding at the London sittings after Michaelmas Term of this year, immediately on receipt of an engraved likeness of his brother Judge, accompanied by a note, in which Coleridge begs his acceptance of it "in token of the great pleasure I have in serving in the same Court with and under you, and of my sense of your uniform kindness to me."

"December 15, 1837.

"Dear Coleridge,—Under any circumstances I must place a high value on an excellent likeness of you; but as a present from you, and *accompanied by such a letter*, it is inestimable.

"I was going to write to you about Awdry's letter,[3]

[1] First published in 1835.

[2] Denman had no doubt been induced to set himself to the perusal of the Sevigné letters by the enthusiastic eulogies of Mackintosh, who, in his "Memoirs," shows himself almost as much in love with the "charming woman" as Horace Walpole in his "Letters."

[3] Sir John Awdry, born 1795; Judge and Chief Justice of the Supreme

and express the hope that in his wide separation from us, he may represent and anticipate the judgment of posterity. To my posterity, at least, your portrait and letter shall descend.

"I don't know that I ever exchanged a word with your correspondent (Awdry), and of course am delighted with the manner in which he speaks of me. I am the less surprised at it because I fancy there is discoverable in his letter a strong sympathy between his habits of thinking and mine. Wordsworth's stanza, which he resents, made me so sore, five-and-thirty years ago, that I followed out his attack on professions by a parody running through all walks of life.[1]

"His (Awdry's) refutation of the sarcasm by referring to Cresswell's[2] looks, has something whimsical in it, from a personal anecdote of what occurred on a trial before Bolland at Carlisle, when I went the Northern Circuit with him in 1833. Lord Lonsdale prosecuted for libel, in consequence of a violent invective against himself in respect to the St. Bee's charity. Wordsworth, as Commissioner of Stamps, attended in court to prove the publisher's affidavit, and sat to the end of the trial. In his presence, Cresswell, for the defendant, read an eloquent passage from Wordsworth's pamphlet on the Convention of Cintra, stating as the most disgusting proof of moral degradation in any people, that its nobles abuse the charitable funds intrusted to their management. And this very pamphlet was understood to have been bought up by Lord Lonsdale to smooth the way to Wordsworth's appointment to that very office he now holds.

"At this moment Creswell and Thesiger are engaged before me, fighting a case on a mercantile contract, very well on both sides. I hope this prose to you has not

Court of Bombay from 1830 to 1842; first class in Classics at Oxford in 1816, and Fellow of Oriel.

[1] The stanza is no doubt that occurring in Wordsworth's poem, "A Poet's Epitaph"—

> "A lawyer art thou?—draw not nigh;
> Go, carry to some fitter place
> The keenness of that practiced eye,
> The hardness of that sallow face."

[2] The late Mr. Justice Cresswell, before his promotion to the Bench, was leader of the Northern Circuit.

diverted my attention from Thesiger's argument, which now draws to a close.

"I can not conclude my acknowledgments without assuring you how sensible I am of the value of your co-operation as a judge, and of that personal friendship which I most sincerely return.

"Ever, my dear Coleridge,
"Yours,
"DENMAN."

In the early part of the year 1838, Denman was made very happy by the union of his second daughter, Elizabeth, with his old friend and schoolfellow, Francis Hodgson, who had for some years been Vicar of Bakewell, the little Derbyshire town where Denman's grandfather had lived and where his father was born. The near neighborhood of Bakewell to Stony Middleton had led, since 1830, to a frequent intercourse between the Vicar and the Denman family. Hodgson, whose first wife had died some years before his second marriage with Miss Denman,[1] had, since 1836, become Archdeacon of Derbyshire and Vicar of Edensor, close to Chatsworth (in addition to Bakewell). In 1840, as will be afterwards seen, he was elected Provost of Eton, an appointment worth from two to three thousand a year, on obtaining which he resigned his former preferments.

In addition to very considerable classical and literary attainments,[2] Francis Hodgson was a most charming person in society, and an admirable talker. He was well received in the highest circles, and an especial favorite with the then Duke of Devonshire (the sixth duke), so long and so well known as a leader in the world of fashion.

In the spring of 1838 Hodgson was staying in London at Devonshire House, when he received from his old

[1] Hodgson's first wife (*née* Tayleur) was a graceful and accomplished person. This was the lady whom Moore saw when he visited Bakewell, in 1828, to learn all that Hodgson could tell him about his earlier intimacy with Byron—a visit of which he has given a pleasant account in his Diary under the dates of the 25th, 26th, 27th, and 28th of January, 1828.

[2] In addition to his excellent translation of Juvenal, Hodgson published, from time to time, a good deal of verse, of which a poem called "The Leaves of Laurel" was probably the best known. His early intimacy with Byron has elsewhere been alluded to; he was also much liked and appreciated by Moore.

friend a letter written on March 21, from Exeter, on the Western Circuit, where the Chief Justice was then presiding. It was evidently written, as the following extract shows, after having received from Hodgson an intimation of the state of his affections.

"You can not easily conceive the incessant occupation brought upon me by the present assizes; my only time for writing is in Court, where I am afraid, during the long, long speeches, of losing something that ought to affect the decision. I seize a few moments, therefore, from needful repose, to say how much I am pleased with the interest my dear daughter has excited in you, and with the prospect of that closer intimacy which our new relation must produce. I can not doubt that a union formed so entirely on perfect regard and esteem on both sides will be happy, and one of the greatest enjoyments of my life will be to witness and promote your comfort. I am literally almost dropping out of my chair, and must resume work at an early hour to-morrow. Good night, and many happy years to you."

In the course of a letter written on March 26, to his daughter Elizabeth, from Launceston, on the same circuit, he thus refers to the marriage, which, by that time, it seems, had been already arranged.

"The more I think of your prospects the better I like them. Nothing can promise so fairly to exalt the character and advance the happiness of a wife as such a temper and conversation, such manners, talents, and principles."

On May 24, 1838, while presiding at the sittings either at Westminster or Guildhall,[1] he wrote the following lively and entertaining letter to the newly-married couple, who were just completing their honeymoon at Hardwicke Hall, one of the Duke of Devonshire's rural palaces in Derbyshire.

"My dear Children,[2]—You must, I fear, have thought me an unnatural parent; but you, my dear Elizabeth, are well acquainted with the complete absorption of my

[1] Most probably at Guildhall, on the first day of the London sittings in Trinity Term, which had begun on May 22.

[2] This paternal style of address to a son-in-law nearly his own age was of course intended to raise a laugh.

whole being in sittings and visitings, so that nothing gives me the opportunity of putting pen to paper except a long consultation in the jury-box (which now happens), or a very long speech about nothing. I have been truly happy to hear of your enjoyment at Hardwicke, and delight in thinking that you will find Middleton not uncomfortable, and I trust, in high beauty. We have been very gay; on Monday, Lord Clarendon[1] gave a particularly pleasant party—Lords Grey and Holland, and several others. Lord Grey not in absolute good humor with his old friends; a little sore on many points; inclined to admire Sir Robert Peel's speech at Merchant Tailors' Hall;[2] not pleased with Brougham's last political article in the *Edinburgh*. The general asperities not softened by his being seated next to Lady Clarendon, who required him to carve all the dishes, especially a roast pig![3] Lord Holland, more amiable, good-humored, and entertaining than I ever saw even him before—quite aware of Lord Grey's infirmity, but only amused by it. Both deep in Wilberforce's biography, and agreed that it raised him in their estimation. Holland said in addition (but with some nervousness as to how it would be received) that the work also raised Pitt in his opinion. This was controverted, but not ungracefully. Grey condemned the 'Athenian Captive.'[4] He would not speak of it. Grey said he could not read 'Pickwick.' Holland spoke of it with discriminating discernment, but mentioned Boz's other book, 'Oliver Twist,' almost with tears. When Grey offered to help him to pig, he declined it hastily, and gave me the most comical look, as though he should have come between the lion and his wrath. Rogers mentioned that Fox used to be very angry with those who questioned Wilberforce's sincerity about slavery. When, however, some one said to Fox, 'Suppose Wilberforce had to choose between continuing slavery and turning Pitt out of power.' 'Ah,' said Fox, 'that would have been a

[1] The third Lord Clarendon, grandfather of the present Earl.
[2] On May 11.
[3] An infliction enough to have soured most tempers. The dinner a la Russe had not then been invented.
[4] Talfourd's play, then recently brought out.

hard choice for him. I am afraid he would have given the preference to Barabbas.'

"We had yesterday a very agreeable pretentionless dinner at home. Miss Pierce,[1] Mr. and Mrs. Merrivale, Charles Wright, &c. We were also gladdened by a letter from Cadiz, written by the commander-in-chief there.[2]

"Our fair ones at this moment are all doing honor to the [Queen's] birthday. I am showing respect for my Sovereign by administering justice to her subjects. But they are a queer set. We have a horse cause, with many interesting traits of low life, à la Pickwick and Nickleby. A widow, in crape, of an hostler, who died last December in a hospital; she said, 'We did not live very well together, but thank God we died very good friends.' It seems that she set out to go to see him, and on the way got so tipsy that she fell and cut her head, and became a patient in the same hospital for a fortnight, during which he died."[3]

It should have been, perhaps, mentioned, in connection with the Western Spring Assizes of 1838, that this was the first occasion on which Denman, as one of Her Majesty's Judges, was entertained by the Duke of Wellington at Strathfieldsaye—a visit which was afterwards frequently repeated. On this occasion, as usual, a large party of county magnates were invited to meet the Judges, amongst whom the present Lord Denman (who accompanied his father) recollects Lord Eversley, Assheton Smith, the famous master of hounds (an old Eton schoolfellow of Denman's), Mr. Darby Griffiths, Mr. Pigott (brother of the present Baron of the Exchequer), and many others. Denman's sister (Lady Croft) came over to see her brother from Strathfield Mortimer; and the Duke, having no ladies, gave her a private room to see him in. At breakfast the Duke and all his non-legal guests appeared in red coats for the

[1] Of Bedale, in the North Riding.

[2] Captain Joseph Denman, at the moment, I suppose, first officer of the West African squadron, then in Cadiz harbor.

[3] "Ah, dear," says Mrs. Gamp, "when Gamp was summonsed to his long home, and I saw him a-laying in Guy's Hospital, with a penny piece over each eye, and his wooden leg under his left arm, I thought I should have fainted away—but I bore up." Had Dickens ever heard Lord Denman's story of the hostler's widow? Likely enough.

meet, which was to take place that morning in the neighborhood; and it is a circumstance that seems to have made an impression on the present Lord Denman's memory, that the Duke had a "tag," or hook-and-eye apparatus, attached to the collar of his "pink," which enabled him to close it round the throat like a great coat.

In the session of 1838, Denman first brought before the House of Lords a subject which much interested him, and on which he had previously, by letter, consulted all the members of the Bench—*the substitution of affirmations for oaths* in all cases where witnesses entertained conscientious scruples against being sworn. The answers of the Judges were unfavorable; but the Chief Justice persevered, and, on June 15, 1838, moved, in the Lords, that the report on the "Oaths Validity Bill" be received.

This Bill, as Lord Denman explained to the House, contained two clauses, having for their object: the first, to enable all witnesses to be sworn according to the *form* binding on their consciences; the second, to enable all those who believed that no *oath* ought to be taken, to make *affirmation* instead.

The first clause, he stated, was merely a declaration of the Common Law of England, the principle of which was, that the *conscience of the individual* was the only law to be resorted to in swearing him in. Such affirmation of the Common Law had been rendered necessary by a recent decision of the Irish Judges, to the effect that the evidence of the well-known Dr. Cooke, of Belfast, who had been sworn, not in the usual mode, but with uplifted hands, according to the practice of the Presbyterians, had been wrongly admitted by the Judge who tried the case: the consequence of which decision had been that the prisoner, who had been convicted on the sole evidence of Dr. Cooke, had, though his guilt was most clear, been unavoidably discharged from custody.

The second clause of the Bill enabled witnesses who thought an oath wrong to take an affirmation instead. On this clause, Denman observed:

"Now, if the principle of allowing a witness to be sworn according to that *form* which was binding on his conscience were good, it followed that the second clause was equally fit and necessary to be introduced as part of the enactments of the country; for, if it were not fit to impose on a witness an oath in a different *form* from that in which he conscientiously believed, *it followed as a corollary that if a witness believed that no oath at all should be taken, his affirmation should be received instead.*"

Notwithstanding this entirely irrefragable argument, the Lords, influenced a good deal by Lord Abinger, who on this occasion represented the opposition of the great body of the Common-Law Judges, shrunk from taking the wise and moderate step in Law Reform to which the Chief Justice pointed the way; and he, seeing the sense of the House to be against him, was content with carrying the first clause only,[1] reserving the second to be embodied in a separate Bill, which, when subsequently brought before the House (on July 14), and pressed to a division, was rejected by a majority of 16, half the whole number that voted; the contents being 16, and the non-contents 32.[2]

There will be occasion hereafter to relate the subsequent Parliamentary exertions of the Chief Justice on the subject of substituting affirmations for oaths, and to state what the law of England, on the matter, at present is.

It was in this year, too, that the Chief Justice was mainly instrumental in promoting and carrying into effect that great and beneficial reform in the administration of Justice, by which the Common-Law Courts were enabled to sit in Banc, beyond the narrow limits of the four legal Terms, and to hear arguments and deliver judgments in Vacation.

Lord Denman used to calculate that in the twelve years that elapsed between 1838 and 1850 (the year of his retirement), no less than two additional years of sittings, were, by this measure, given to the public. This circumstance so gratified him, that he desired it to be recorded on his tomb—a desire carried out by his eldest son, who has caused the fact to be inscribed on the

[1] Hansard, Parl. Deb., third series, vol. xliii. pp. 756-767.

[2] Hansard, Parl. Deb., third series, vol. xliv. p. 319 et seq.

stone that covers his remains in Stoke Albany churchyard.

The Long Vacation of 1838 was spent as usual at Stony Middleton, in planting, thinning, and improving, entertaining friends, making visits and excursions, and keeping pace with the current literature of the day.

On September 27, writing from Middleton to his friend Coleridge, whose tastes and pursuits were very similar to his own, he says:

"My life has been much like yours. My literary taste, such as it is, I find quite as strong as ever, and perhaps rather more eager; but I have no fellow-student, so I can not venture on the ancient classics. One of yours, or very likely yourself, can perhaps tell me from what play I took a motto that has been a favorite with me nearly half a century—

Μὴ ζώην μετ' ἀμουσίας
'Αεὶ δ' ἐν κιθάραισιν εἴην.

In the same strain he writes to his sister, Mrs. Baillie:

"We have had a holiday rather too agreeable to me, as a life of literary quiet, to be just the thing for young ladies; but you know how good and considerate mine are. I flatter myself that both[1] are much improved in health, and my lady is a great deal stronger than she used to be. Last week I took George[2] to Cambridge, and settled him under Mr. Whewell[3] to my entire satisfaction, and with the earnest hope that he may distinguish himself. I may probably inclose his late master's testimonial."

The hope thus expressed was brilliantly realized. The name of the Honorable George Denman was first in the first class of the Classic Tripos for 1842, and the next year he became Fellow of Trinity—honors which caused inexpressible delight to his father, who had watched with sanguine, yet anxious fondness, every step in his son's University career.

The testimonial referred to in the letter to Mrs.

[1] His third and fourth daughters, Fanny and Margaret, now Lady Baynes and Mrs. Cropper.

[2] His fourth son, now the Hon. Mr. Justice Denman.

[3] The famous Master of Trinity.

Baillie was from the Rev. J. H. Macaulay, the master of Repton School, where George Denman had been educated.[1]

In the course of the same letter, Denman indulges in a little literary gossip about Brougham's then recently published "Characters," &c., which is interesting from the evidence it affords of Denman's deeply rooted and unchanged veneration for Fox.

"Brougham's 'Characters' are very lively, and his views in general, I think, just; but I have complained to him of his disparaging Fox. We are in high controversy about it, and, if I had time, I think I could not refrain from printing. I hope Lord Holland or some one else will. A review of those times convinces me of Fox's good qualities more than ever; yet Brougham hardly raises him above the level of Pitt, whose whole life, from the cradle to the grave, was nothing but the love of office."[2]

He then refers, as follows, to Macaulay's well-known article on Sir W. Temple:

"Macaulay ought to have vindicated Temple against his foolish biographer, of whom Bessie [Mrs. Hodgson] and I said last year that he found a white marble statue, and took delight in spoiling it by scrawling with a black lead pencil, first his own name, and then all manner of nonsense. It is as reasonable to quarrel with Temple for not being Russell or Sidney, as for not being Marlborough or Somers. It is not the heroic line; but an honorable, amiable, and consistent man, whose life was devoted to the honest service of the public and to literature, should have been left in possession of all the respect the world was paying him.

In the earlier part of 1839, the Chief Justice, as already

[1] The following is an extract from the testimonial:—"It is with great regret that I take leave of George, though with complete satisfaction as far as his state of preparation for Cambridge is concerned. If he continues throughout to exert himself with the same activity and perseverance which has marked the last year or two, nothing can prevent his highly distinguishing himself. With regard to the last two months, I can truly say I have never known an equal period of time more industriously or more profitably employed."

[2] A gross injustice to Pitt, of which Fox's idolators were too often guilty. The statesman who was killed by Austerlitz had something else in him than love of office—he had love for country and glory.

mentioned, was anxiously and laboriously engaged on the great question of Privilege, and he does not appear to have spoken in the House of Lords till July 18, when he supported the second reading of the bill (called "The Custody of Infants' Bill") for giving the wife right of access to her children in cases of separation. In the course of his speech he said:

"Some alteration, and that of a sweeping nature, was absolutely necessary to the due administration of justice, and for the prevention of the frightful injuries to society which the existing system gave birth to. The existing law was cruel to the wife, debasing to the husband, dangerous and probably ruinous to the health and morals of the children, who could not have any such sure guarantee against corruption under the tutelage of a profligate father as the occasional care of a mother."

The Chief Justice instanced the case of the King *v.* Greenhill, which had been decided in 1836, before himself and the rest of the Judges of the Court of King's Bench. "He believed," he said, "that there was not one judge on the Bench who had not felt ashamed of the state of the law, and that it was such as to render it odious in the eyes of the country. The effect in the case he had mentioned would have been, unless Mrs. Greenhill had fled from this country with her children, to have enabled the father to take his children from his young and blameless wife, and place them in charge of the woman with whom he then cohabited.[1]

The just and powerful observations of the Chief Justice, co-operating with the brilliant eloquence of Talfourd in the Commons, were mainly instrumental in bringing about such partial and incomplete change for the better, as has since been realized in this peculiarly difficult and delicate department of the law.

In the Summer Assizes of 1839, Denman presided on the Home Circuit, accompanied by the Chief Justice of the Common Pleas, Sir Nicholas C. Tindal, for whom he always entertained the highest respect and esteem, and who, on this occasion, paid him the unusual and

[1] Hansard, Parl. Deb., third series, vol. xlix. p. 491 et seq. This was the measure in the promotion of which, Talfourd so brilliantly distinguished himself in the House of Commons.

flattering compliment of going with him on circuit as second judge.[1]

It was while on this circuit that Denman received a pleasing reminiscence of the virtues of his excellent father, in the announcement of a legacy of £10,000, left among his unmarried daughters, under the will of the venerable Sir Francis Drake (a lineal descendant of the famous old sea hero), who, when a young captain in command of the "Edgar," had been most anxiously nursed and skillfully tended in a dangerous illness by Dr. Denman, then the ship's surgeon, whom he ever afterwards regarded as a brother. In his extreme old age, Sir Francis had bequeathed to the granddaughters of his old friend and benefactor this substantial token of his gratitude and affection.

Lord Denman hurried off from circuit to be present in the House of Lords on August 15, when, on the second reading of the Government "Bill for the Better Suppression of the Slave Trade," he made a most able and masterly speech, which greatly contributed to the success of the ministry, who had recently been outvoted in the Lords on the cognate measure known as the "Slave Trade (Portugal) Bill." This was the earliest of Denman's great exertions in the House of Lords on the question of the West African Slave Trade—a question which from this time forward was destined to make claims on his heart and brain, that had much to do with gradually undermining his constitution, and which, from its effect on his nervous system, prepared the way for the inroads of that disease which ultimately prostrated him.

On the present occasion, one of his great objects was to allay the alarms assiduously propagated by the Duke of Wellington and Lord Lyndhurst, and to satisfy the House that the fears of war with France, as likely to arise out of the execution of the more stringent methods of suppression sanctioned by the Bill, were, in truth, baseless and chimerical. His principal and entirely correct point was this, that no act of Parliament can give

[1] It hardly ever happens that two Chief Justices, or a Chief Justice and Chief Baron, go the same circuit.

the Crown powers of search, detention, and seizure which it does not possess by treaty.

"My lords, in respect of the possible seizure of *other* vessels, [*i. e.*, not Spanish or Portuguese], I am really sorry to say one word on the subject after what has fallen from my noble and learned friend [Brougham]. I feel ashamed to repeat that no act of Parliament can give the Crown power to seize vessels which it is precluded from seizing by treaties. The words 'any vessel' mean only any vessel which the Crown is now permitted to seize by treaties into which it has entered, and does not include any vessel which, under the treaties, it could not capture."

On the general question he said:

"Your lordships ought not to allow any opportunity to pass which will enable you to make the suppression of the Slave Trade not merely a name but a fact. When once it has been established that the slave trade is illegal, the restraints which treaties have put upon its abolition ought to be looked at with a jealous eye. That is the principle by which your lordships ought to be guided."

Adverting to the indemnity proposed to be given by the Bill to the officers engaged in the suppression of the trade, Lord Denman expressed himself as follows:

"I say the necessity is imposed on your lordships of providing that judges should henceforth be relieved from the necessity of stating that a man engaged in the capture of his fellow creatures for sale is engaged in a legal traffic, and, at the same time, of telling a jury that the man who, in obedience to your lordships' orders, has stopped him in his inhuman traffic, is guilty of a punishable offense. I say your lordships are called upon to do something for the protection of your own agents, acting under your own enactments. There must be the right of visitation and search, and, if a mistake is made, the officer making the mistake must be liable, or the State in his place. If it were not so, it would be impossible to take any steps for the suppression of the slave trade. By this bill the Government take upon themselves the responsibility of the whole matter, and call upon the House to do nothing but indemnify the officers of Her Majesty in the discharge of the duty imposed on them; and to allow the Admiralty Court to adjudicate on seizures made under the treaties."[1]

Denman's powerful and masterly appeal, urged with all the sincerity of deep conviction, and with a ripe maturity of legal knowledge, produced a great effect on the House; and the ministry, who had been anticipating defeat, were agreeably surprised to find themselves on the division in a majority of 11. Contents 39, against non-contents 28.

The Duke of Wellington, followed by thirteen peers, including Lord Lyndhurst, entered a protest against the second reading, which the Duke and seven peers repeated on August 19, when the bill was read a third time and passed. It received the royal assent on August 24, and on the 27th, Parliament was prorogued.

The two following communications, both under the same cover, which Denman wrote to his wife, one on August 15, just before making his speech, and the other on the 16th, after it had been delivered with success, are not without interest; the first was written in the library of the House of Lords, the second at the Old Bailey, where he was presiding as one of the judges on the rota of the Central Criminal Court.

"Thursday, August 15, 1839.

"My dearest Love,—I have stolen out of the House of Lords into the library, to tell you with my own hand that I am alive and well, though in a state of the utmost anxiety about the Slave Trade Bill. We are threatened with an opposition to it, the great Duke appearing disposed to persist in the error he committed a fortnight ago.[1] If it comes to a division, I must make a speech, and that is an operation by no means enviable here."

"Central Criminal Court (vulgarly, Old Bailey),
"Friday, August 16.

"I continue my narrative. The Duke persisted in his opposition; the debate went on with much heat on both sides, and a decided majority to all

[1] Denman's speech is reported in Hansard, Parl. Deb., third series, vol. l, pp. 330–334.

[2] On the "Slave Trade (Portugal) Bill," see Hansard, Parl. Deb., third series, vol. xlix. p. 1058 et seq.

appearance in his support. So as I could do no harm by making a speech, I tried to do some good, and I believe that I had some effect on the decision. The Bishop of London [Blomfield] had previously declared in his favor, and five other peers who usually vote with the Duke came over to the support of our measure. You will be pleased to hear that one of them was Lord Sondes. In the result we counted thirty-nine, our opponents only twenty-eight. You may conceive the captain's [now Admiral Denman's] delight, and he has good right to feel it, for his efforts have mainly contributed to annihilate this monstrous wickedness called the Slave Trade. Brougham made an excellent speech on the right side. Lyndhurst, though he followed his leader [the Duke of Wellington], had the grace to be silent."

What follows is a curious and vivid sketch from the life, of the predatory habits of London children of the criminal class:

"Two little girls are at this moment standing at the bar, ten and eleven years of age. Their foreheads hardly come in sight. They are charged with picking a lady's pocket in a jeweler's shop on Saturday night at eleven. Almost immediately after she had been robbed, the lady had the younger taken up, playing in the streets. She had already thrown away the purse, and changed a crown piece and two half-crowns, having purchased a doll and some trinkets. She said the elder girl had 'tapped' the lady's pocket, and that she then proceeded to pick it. As to the purse, she said she always threw away the purses!"

In September, 1839, Denman wrote from his favorite Middleton to his son, George, who was then reading in the vacation with a tutor:

"I am delighted to hear of your steady proceeding in your studies—all the more so, because you have got out of my depth There is no feeling more deeply rooted in human nature, than that ascribed to Hector,

"*Καί ποτέ τις εἴπῃσι, πατρὸς δ᾽ ὅγε πολλὸν ἀμείνων.*[1]

"A thousand times have I had cause to regret that I

[1] "Some one may, perchance, say in the aftertime, Why, the son is even a better man than the father;" from Hector's speech to Andromache.—*Iliad*, vi. 479.

stopped short in the career you are now pursuing: *Pergite, juvenes!*"

The year 1840 was that in which Denman saw the end of the Privilege controversy in the House of Lords. His principal effort was the remarkable and masterly speech, already sufficiently referred to in the last chapter, by which, on April 6, 1840, he prefaced his vote on the second reading of the Printed Papers Bill.

He had previously, on February 17, 1840, laid on the table of the House of Lords a bill which not long afterwards became law, the object of which was to provide that in all *actions of libel or slander* in which damages under 40*s.* were awarded, such damages should not carry costs beyond the amount of the verdict—a measure of obvious utility, inasmuch as actions for small libels were of constant occurrence, which were only introduced for the sake of the costs.[1]

Later in the session, on June 1, 1840, Lord Denman, on the second reading of the bill for the better *administration of justice in Chancery*, stated to the House that he had come, though with great reluctance, to a full conviction that it *was* necessary to increase the judicial strength of the Court of Chancery, and that the sooner that remedy was applied the better.[2]

In the spring of 1840, Denman was greatly interested in the election for the Provostship of Eton, which, after many complications, at length terminated in favor of his old friend and son-in-law, Archdeacon Hodgson.

The nature of the complications referred to are explained in the following letter to the Archdeacon, written two days after Denman's great speech in the Lords on the Printed Papers Bill.

"April 8, 1840.

"My dear Hodgson,—I am now about to tell you all I know about this extraordinary involvement of facts. William Herbert *was* the man, but was found ineligible, as on neither foundation at any time. You were *then* the man, and the state of things I described to you on Monday night arose. Lord Melbourne afterwards, indeed, said, 'Of course Hodgson is a B. D.—that *ad*

[1] Hansard, Parl. Deb., third series, vol. lii. p. 316.
[2] Hansard, Parl. Deb., third series, vol. liii. p. 1020.

minus the statutes require.' I was fully persuaded of the affirmative, principally from my full confidence in Drury's spirit of business, though Merivale thought he must have heard of your going to graduate. The Fellows, however, have now returned an answer to the Secretary of State, that you being unqualified as not B. D., they have proceeded to elect one qualified. I believe, and have no doubt, that this is Lonsdale [it was so]. In their answer, the Fellows stated their willingness to do what was required, but for this obstacle.

"Now, I much doubt whether Lonsdale will accept the appointment, which would be incompatible with some of his present preferment—the Golden Prebend, King's College and Lincoln's Inn—though he has a very good living tenable with the Provostship. If he resigns, a mandate must go down, of course, with your name again. I never saw the Duke [of Devonshire] look black till last night in the House, when, in answer to my first approach, he said, 'I don't understand it.' He is gone to Paris."

The Queen, who thought highly of Hodgson, and had set her mind on his appointment, was vexed with the Fellows for having rejected "her Provost" as she called him. A second special mandate was issued; Lonsdale, though desirous of the appointment, on an intimation of the royal feeling in the matter, declined to accept it;[1] Hodgson qualified at Cambridge as a B. D., and the legal difficulty being thus got over, he was at length duly elected Provost.[2]

Before the matter was quite decided Denman had written as follows to his daughter, Mrs. Hodgson, who, in the letter to which he replies, would appear to have said something about money difficulties, and also to have complained of the declaration made by some influential personage (possibly Lord Melbourne himself) of his determination not to take any active step in her husband's behalf.

[1] Lonsdale, not very long afterwards, became Bishop of Litchfield—a promotion undoubtedly due to his high character and professional claims, but with which his self-denial in the matter of the Provostship may possibly also have had some little connection.

[2] The value of the Provostship was then from £2,000 to £3,000 a year. Hodgson, on his election, resigned his other preferment.

"Your letter was very welcome to me, and delighted me with the statement of your happiness. With regard to what you mention towards the close of your letter, I fairly acknowledge that I am by no means surprised, having a strong impression that if there is any one person in England less addicted to economy than your own family it is your lord and master.

"One comfort is, that, on the principle of two negatives, your baby bids fair to be as prudent a young lady as Miss Coutts herself.

"You must, however, renounce the opinion that little can be done by care and experience. In truth, everything can be done with it—certainly nothing can be done without it. The largest income is insufficient without good regulation of the expenditure, and a very moderate one will do wonders for comfort and respectability if united with the necessary qualities. I do not refer our defects to nature, except in Fontenelle's sense, 'If custom is the second nature, tell me what is the first?' I take infinite pains to correct myself, in spite of the bumps behind the ear, and hope to succeed by the time I am actually leaving the world.

"On the other subject, I own I feel a surprise at so decided a declaration of non-interference. It is a strong proof of the multitude of besiegers of the dispensers of patronage. I have some reason to know this in my own case. You have probably heard me express some unwillingness as a judge to make such applications, and I can not tell how far this folly of the House of Commons[1] may affect whatever influence I possess. But you may fully rely, in this case, on my passing over no chance of obtaining what you desire and are so justly entitled to."

In the summer of 1840, with a view to comparatively light work and the enjoyment of fine scenery, Denman chose the North Wales Circuit, on which he was accompanied, as Marshal, by his youngest son, Lewis, then a youth of nineteen, now the Hon. and Rev. Lewis Denman, Rector of Willian, in Hertfordshire, who has kindly communicated an amusing incident that occurred

[1] In the Stockdale *v.* Hansard case. This was written while the discussions on the Printed Papers Bill were pending.

at the outset of the circuit, and which is here related in his own words:

"On July 25, 1840, I went with my father as Marshal, on the North Wales Circuit. The first place of holding the assizes was Newtown (now, with Welshpool, one of the two assize towns for Montgomeryshire), and I think this was the first occasion on which a[1] judge had ever been there. When about three miles from Newtown we were met by the Sheriff, Mr. Evans, with a coach and four good horses, and twenty mounted javelin men. My father had told me to order the post-boys to make the best of their way to the lodgings at Newtown, to get things ready for him, he himself going in the Sheriff's carriage, which he expected, as usual, would proceed at a walking pace. I ordered the post-boys to make the best of their way, and so they did; and, whether it was that there had been no experience of the general custom of a judge coming slowly into an assize town, or whether it was owing, as is quite possible, to the Welsh blood of the Sheriff's coachman being up, I can't say, but certain it is that the Sheriff's yellow coach and four, with my father and the Sheriff in it, came after me at a tremendous pace. Perhaps the coachman thought he ought to have taken the lead, but the post-boys did as I had told them, in accordance with my father's orders, and we held our own, doing the three or four miles at about the rate of twenty miles an hour. Nor was this all; the javelin men, of course, had to keep up with us, but, instead of keeping near the Sheriff, they went ahead of me, and made the running still stronger, now jostling one another into the ditches by the side of the road, now scrambling over heaps of stones, &c. The consequence was that my Lord got into Newton very much quicker than he expected; and he, having good nerves and not too much punctiliousness, was extremely glad of it."

From Ruthin, the assize town of Denbighshire, towards the close of the circuit, the Chief Justice wrote as follows to Lady Denman at Middleton:

"Here we are, my dearest love, having reached the

[1] Probably *the* Judge should be the reading, "*sed quære.*"

extreme point of our long travel, and from henceforth turning our horses' heads regularly though slowly towards home. We were much interested with Holyhead—which we left on Saturday afternoon, and at night slept at a most comfortable inn at Bangor. We proceeded soon after breakfast, and then traversed the finest country we have yet seen. It is a part I have never seen before, and I was most anxious to become acquainted with it. Never was curiosity better repaid. We stopped for one glorious object, a Rhaiadr, which means the fall of a river. The Ligwy runs far over a rocky bed, gradually sloping till it falls in one immense cascade of great height and descends yet lower, tumbling and foaming through great masses of stone. The steep banks are covered with fine wood—the sight, the dew, the spray on our faces, and the clear sunshine overhead, made the half-hour most truly delightful.

"It has almost put out of my head another object even more peculiar; this is the South-Stack Lighthouse, at the very extremity of the Isle of Anglesea, about three miles from Holyhead. We arrived at it over a barren moor covered with loose stones, and had the sea, which was almost at high water, on every side of us—the coast formed of a line of huge rocks. When we had reached what appeared the world's end, suddenly, on a much lower level, a long tongue of land ran out into the water, at whose extremity stands the lighthouse. Tom and I descended some hundreds of rude steps cut in the hill's precipitous sides, and, when near the bottom, found ourselves shut out by a locked door. Long and loud hallooing seemed thrown away, for not a creature was to be discovered. At length, as we were remounting our path in despair, a man came out of the dwelling house to the door—no small distance—and admitted us to a drawbridge suspended from rock to rock, a good height above the water which separates this little islet from Anglesea.

"We then visited the lighthouse, and were just so much farther out at sea. This little island is remarkable—about 400 yards long and 100 in breadth, perfectly barren, though it contains a few rabbits, and is haunted by large sea-gulls, whose transparent wings expanded against the sun make their flight beautiful, while their screams and their ways with one another were very amusing.

"We are here in a most dismal lodging, and threatened with heavy business—80 witnesses in one cause—with no other blessing than two haunches of venison and nobody to eat them."

From Stony Middleton, at the close of July, 1840, he writes to Merivale, then at Barton Place, telling him, in triumph, that he has been able to accomplish the journey from Portland Place in ten hours, and that his plantations have thriven so prosperously that instead of *Stony* Middleton his favorite retreat must thenceforth be called *Woody* Middleton, "formerly Petræ, now Felix." In the middle of August, he writes thence to his sister, Mrs. Baillie, who was then just entering on her 70th year, and was at the time staying at the Provost's Lodge at Eton, to be with Mrs. Hodgson during an approaching confinement:

"Being the only person in the family down stairs, I am obliged to take paper on which Lewis has been preparing his drawings.[1] I was very glad to hear from you on circuit, and delighted with what you say of Mrs. Brodie's[2] persevering activity and warmth of heart. Long may it continue. In fact, this class of old ladies has always commanded a great portion of my regard (as if I had foreseen that I was one day to be of their order), and, if possible, I shall love even you better, my dear sister, when you have decidedly entered the pale. It gives us great pleasure to hear that you have undertaken to preside over Bessy's nursery on the approaching occasion. I trust that engagement will rather tend to facilitate than to defeat your visit to this place. It is a considerable loss to me that you have not been here already, because, as it is, you can not be made to understand the advantage which the place has gained from a small acquisition of land. But the positive beauty which has thus been secured, is alone well worth being

[1] Denman's youngest son, now the Hon. and Rev. Lewis Denman: he had an extraordinary turn and a great talent for drawing coaches and four —the "Tantivies" and "Quicksilvers" of the days before railways.

[2] The widow of Rev. P. B. Brodie, Lord Denman's uncle, still living in 1840, in extreme old age.

acquainted with. The weather has been most favorable, and during the week I have been here we have had breakfast out of doors every morning. I had a most agreeable circuit, no over-work, and the finest weather for seeing the delightful scenery; in every quarter extreme hospitality and kindness. I took the opportunity of crossing the Mersey [from Chester to Liverpool] for the purpose of paying a visit to Richard's new relations;[1] nothing could be more satisfactory. He is now at Liverpool attending the assizes, and, as Emma hopes, to obtain his marriage license earlier than had been promised. George [now the Honorable Mr. Justice Denman] writes to Lewis [his younger brother] that he is reading 11 hours a day without at all suffering.[2] Theodosia [Mrs. Wright] is going on particularly well [after her confinement]; perhaps too well, for she had been up and in the garden within the fortnight, which you will not permit, I think, at the Provost's Lodge."

In October he writes as follows to Coleridge:

"I have to thank you for the most kind and friendly letters, which I could almost answer by copying them, as far as the account of our proceedings is concerned. No two people lead the same life in the country more completely than we do. Mine has been a very happy one, subject to no drawback but in respect of our friends, and that of no grave nature, as you may judge from the fact that none has touched me more than Patteson's disappointment in the field.[3] I hope he was not annoyed by William's question, which I sent him, whether he disposes of *points* that arise out of turnips with the same unvarying certainty as of inferior matters; but if the former faculty is really impaired by time, the latter has every chance of being (if possible) improved by it. I like Arnold's idea of considering the Eternal City [modern Rome] as a palimpsest, scrawled by monkery

[1] The Hon. Richard Denman, the third son of his father, was married on October 27, this year, to Emma, daughter of Hugh Jones, Esq., of Liverpool.

[2] He was staying up at Cambridge for the purpose of studying during the greater part of the Long Vacation.

[3] Mr. Justice Patteson had apparently connected the falling-off in his shooting with a general decay of his powers; his ill success as a sportsman was a standing joke with his brethren of the Bench.

over genius, like an MS. of Cicero's defaced by a treatise on foolish traditions. Mackintosh applies to it *opinionum commenta delet dies, naturæ judicia confirmat.* Something of this feeling has always made me think Athens, or even Venice, decaying in their real forms, more interesting for a visit than the Commonwealth buried under the fines of Emperors and Popes. Did Patteson tell you that Story has sent me, through Sumner, a complete approbation of our proceedings in *re Stockdale*—the more valuable because he is entirely opposed to a decision of ours of much less importance—*Decaux* v. *Salvador*.[2] I was not aware of his having sent us any work of his, but in answer to Sumner's question how he could best repay English hospitality, I said: 'Come again and bring Story.'

"We have invited and received visits more than usual —a fortnight in Yorkshire—running over the North Riding, going into Notts for a few days—then our Bishop came—and last week Tindall, with his sister and niece, enjoyed himself with our few amusements in a most delightful manner."

[2] A marine insurance case, in which the question was, whether there can be a "total loss" of part of a cargo, shipped in separate packages, under an insurance on so many packages; the Court of Queen's Bench held in the negative, the American Courts in the affirmative.

CHAPTER XXVIII.

LORD CARDIGAN'S CASE—CAPTAIN DENMAN AND THE BARRACOONS—GREAT YORK ASSIZE, SUMMER, 1842.

A. D. 1841, 1842. ÆT. 62, 63.

AT the commencement of 1841, a change took place in the Court of Queen's Bench by the retirement of Mr. Justice Littledale, then in the seventy-fourth year of his age, and the substitution in his place of Mr. Justice Wightman.

In one of Denman's letters to Coleridge, written in the Long Vacation of 1840, there is the following reference to Littledale's intended retirement:

"Tom [the present Lord Denman] was expressly told by Littledale that he should resign before next term [Michaelmas Term, 1840]. But in answer to a letter from me, which might very fairly have led to explanation, he says no such thing, but rather studiously, I think, avoids the topic. The nearest approach to it is: 'My health is tolerable, not quite perfect, and *with rather a tendency to be beginning to give way*, which, at my time of life, is not to be wondered at.'"

Many letters have been preserved which were written on this subject to Denman by this excellent and simple-minded judge, who, with few mental resources beyond the range of the profession, and with the keenest relish for the subtleties of legal argument, was naturally reluctant to quit the judgment seat which had so long been adorned by his learning and acuteness. At length, warned by increasing infirmities, he sent in his resignation at the end of Hilary Term (January 31), 1841. He did not long survive his retirement, dying at his house, in Bedford Square, on June 26, 1842, in the seventy-sixth year of his age.[1]

[1] See his life in Foss's "Lives of the Judges," vol. ix. p. 220.

His successor was Sir William Wightman, who, in modesty and learning, equaled the retiring judge, but who, as stated in an admirable memoir communicated to Foss's "Lives of the Judges" by, it is believed, Sir J. T. Coleridge, "brought with him a greater knowledge of mankind, and habits of more prompt decision." To the last day of his life (for he died in harness) Sir W. Wightman continued, for nearly three-and-twenty years, to discharge his duties as a judge with ever-increasing satisfaction to the profession and the public. He was carried off at York, in 1863, while attending the Northern Circuit, by an attack of apoplexy, in the eightieth year of his age. His great learning, sound reasoning faculty, and lucid style of expression (as especially shown in the preparation of written judgments) were of great service to Lord Denman, who had the highest appreciation of his estimable qualities and ready helpfulness. As stated by the writer of the memoir already referred to, "he served with three Chief Justices in succession (Denman, Campbell, Cockburn), and I believe there was not one of them who did not feel and gratefully acknowledge the value of his effective assistance, always zealously and never ostentatiously rendered."[1]

On February 16, 1841, Lord Denman (who, owing to the illness of the Chancellor, had been requested by Lord Melbourne to do so) presided as Lord High Steward at the trial in the House of Lords of the Earl of Cardigan, charged with having wounded, in a duel fought at Wimbledon, on September 12, 1840, a gentleman described in the indictment as Harvey Garnett Phipps Tuckett.

The Attorney-General, Sir John (afterwards Lord) Campbell, conducted the case for the Crown, and Sir William Follett was the leading counsel for Lord Cardigan.

The case for the Crown was so carelessly got up that there was an absolute failure to give strict proof, such as the English Criminal Law then required (and would,

[1] Foss's "Lives of the Judges," vol. ix. pp. 292–300. Sir W. Wightman was born A. D. 1784; University College, Oxford, and Michell Fellow of Queen's College, 1806; many years a special pleader; called to Bar, 1821; never took silk; Judge of Queen's Bench, 1841; died 1863.

probably, notwithstanding Lord Campbell's Act, still require) that the person named in the indictment was the same as the person whose bodily injuries were the subject of inquiry.

A certain number of witnesses had, on September 12, 1840, seen a gentleman fired at by Lord Cardigan, and afterwards lying wounded on the ground where the duel had just taken place, and some of these witnesses had subsequently seen the same gentleman lying wounded in lodgings at Hamilton Place, said to belong to a Captain Tuckett; but none of these witnesses could prove that the name of the wounded gentleman was, as laid in the indictment, Harvey Garnett Phipps Tuckett.

On the other hand, a Mr. Codd, an army agent, proved that he had been in the habit of paying half-pay to a captain of the 11th Light Dragoons, whose name he knew to be Harvey Garnett Phipps Tuckett; but Mr. Codd had never been taken, as he ought to have been, to Hamilton Place to identify the officer there lying wounded with the Harvey Garnett Phipps Tuckett to whom he had been in the habit of making payments: nor was the wounded officer himself produced, as he might and ought to have been, in the House of Lords, so as to have been then and there identified by both classes of witnesses.

Upon this state of facts, Lord Denman, as High Steward, was obliged to tell the Peers, as he did tell them, that there was an absolute want of strict proof to connect the individual at whom the shot was fired, and who was afterwards seen wounded in Hamilton Place, with the half-pay officer known to Mr. Codd as bearing the names of Harvey Garnett Phipps Tuckett, set forth in the indictment.

"There were," said his lordship, "two distinct lines of testimony, and they never met at the same point."

The Lord High Steward did not fail to point out that proper proof would have been easy. Their lordships' order might have been obtained for the appearance of Captain Tuckett at the bar, when the witnesses for the duel would have deposed to his having been the person wounded on the field; and Mr. Codd could then have identified him as the person whom he knew by the four names set forth in the indictment.

"It seems too much," said Lord Denman, "to require that your Lordships should volunteer the presumption of a fact, which, if true, might have been made clear and manifest by the shortest and simplest process."[1]

The Peers, acting on the view of the law laid down by the Lord High Steward, unanimously pronounced Lord Cardigan not guilty, and he was forthwith discharged.

There can not be the shadow of a doubt that Lord Denman was perfectly correct in his exposition of the law, but one thing must strike with wonder any one not brought up in habitual reverence for the highly artificial forms of English criminal procedure.

The attendance of Captain Tuckett, which would instantly have made the whole proof perfect and clear, might have been procured after a delay of some three or four hours. Why was not this delay accorded, and the missing link supplied by compelling, as the House had the power to compel, the attendance of the wounded officer?

The only answer that can be given to this very natural question, is that English criminal procedure does not so much seek the discovery of truth, pure and simple, as the discovery of truth according to certain artificial rules, one of which is, that the prosecution must come into Court with its case absolutely and entirely complete on the day of trial, failing which it shall, as a penalty, fail to bring the charge home to the prisoner, who must be convicted according to the strict rules of the legal game, or not convicted at all—and that, too, however clear his guilt may be—however manifest it may be that his escape arises solely from maladroitness on the part of the prosecution in neglecting to have ready at the appointed place and time, the required modicum of strict technical proof.

The good sense of the country was shocked at the solemn mockery of Lord Cardigan's acquittal; but men blamed the law for the result, and not Lord Denman,

[1] The above is taken from the Report of Lord Cardigan's case in Townsend's "Modern State Trials," vol. i. pp. 209-243.

who simply, as his duty was, declared the law to be what he found it.

Another case connected with a noble delinquent, the case of Lord Waldegrave, was, on March 29, 1841, brought by Lord Denman before the House of Lords, in order to clear himself from some extraordinary misrepresentations in connection with it which had appeared in the public press.

The short facts were these: Lord Waldegrave and Captain Duff Gordon had been indicted for a violent assault on a policeman.

The case was removed by certiorari into the Court of Queen's Bench, where it came on to be tried before Lord Denman.

Sir Frederick Pollock, who appeared for the defendants, withdrew their plea of not guilty, and pleaded guilty, at the same time expressing their most sincere regret at what had occurred, and their desire to make every possible apology and atonement.

Lord Denman said: "At least they are right now: let their former plea be withdrawn, and a plea of guilty be recorded. I hope the case is of such a nature as to admit of its being settled by private reparation." "And this," said Lord Denman, addressing the House of Lords, "is what has been tortured into an order that the prosecution should be bought off, and the offenders screened from justice."

The mere statement of the absurd calumny was sufficient for its refutation, especially in the case of Lord Denman, whose failing as a judge, if failing he had, was certainly not a leaning in favor of aristocratic delinquents.[1]

In March of this year (1841) news reached England of the dashing exploit of Denman's second son, Captain (now admiral) Joseph Denman, in taking and destroying a barracoon (or slave warehouse) of the West African slave traders, and liberating all the slaves stored in it.

On November 19, 1840, Captain Denman, then in command of the "Wanderer," proceeded to the Gallinas River, on the West Coast of Africa, and, having landed

[1] See this matter reported in Hansard, Parl. Deb., third series, vol. lvii. p. 651, et seq.

a sufficient force for the purpose, took military possession of a barracoon filled with chained negroes, and on November 23, having, in the meantime, made a short treaty with the native chief of the Gallinas, obtaining his permission for the destruction of the slave factory, and leaving to the chief the benefit of all the merchandise stored therein, he burnt the barracoon and carried away all the slaves, about 900 in number, to Sierra Leone, where, under the protection of England, they helped to form a colony of free negroes.

Denman was, with reason, very proud of his son's achievement, and extremely sanguine as to the effect which he trusted it would produce in discouraging the infernal traffic, an effect which it did produce in a very great degree, and would have produced in a much greater degree but for the subsequent chicanery of the lawyers, and the timorous over-caution of Lord Aberdeen when Foreign Minister in Peel's administration.

The Captain, in a letter dated "Christmas Day, 1840, off Sierra Leone," had communicated to his father, with sailor-like brevity, the facts above stated, adding some horrible details as to the way in which the wretched slaves were found stored in long rows in the barracoon, chained, some neck to neck, others leg to leg, and others arm to arm. A copy of this letter Denman, early in March, 1841, sent to his sons George and Lewis, then both at Cambridge, adding the following explanations, which set in a still clearer light the disinterested gallantry of Captain Denman's exploit:

"There is something very noble in Joe's conduct. The profits of the Anti-Slave Trade enterprises depend on the number of slaves *taken on board* the pirate cruisers; Government allowing £5 a head for every negro so taken. The British captain's interest, therefore, *is to allow the negroes to be shipped and then capture them.* But this proceeding is attended with infinite suffering to the slaves; and they are thrown overboard, if there is a chase, to lighten the vessel. By preventing the empty vessel from receiving the unfortunate negroes, all this misery and murder is saved; but then the prize is scarcely of any value. Again, these barracoons at Gallinas contains multitudes who could be shipped off at a moment's notice, and so make the prize valuable. But, by destroying the barracoons, the fund of slavery itself is destroyed, but the British cruisers get nothing by it.

"There can be no doubt that the heaviest blow that has ever been aimed at the nefarious traffic has been struck by your brother. There may possibly be some irregularity, but Lord John [Russell] has written me his congratulations on 'Joe's' spirited and successful conduct; and Lord Minto tells me that Lord Palmerston thinks the whole affair entirely justifiable."

It is highly to the credit of Lord Palmerston and Lord John Russell, then respectively Foreign and Colonial Ministers in the second administration of Lord Melbourne, that they lost no time in approving and ratifying this gallant act of the young officer.

The Foreign Office communication to the Admiralty was dated April 6, 1841, and ran as follows:

"I am to request you will state to the Lords Commissioners of the Admiralty, that Lord Palmerston is of opinion that the conduct of Captain Denman in his proceedings against the slave factories at the Gallinas ought to be approved; and I am to add that Lord Palmerston would recommend that similar operations should be executed against all the piratical slave establishments which may be met with on parts of the coast not occupied by any civilized power.

"The course pursued by Captain Denman seems best adapted for attaining the object in view; the commanding officers should endeavor to obtain formal permission from the native chiefs for the destruction of the slave factories within their territories, leaving to those chiefs all the merchandise that may be stored in them—the British officers contenting themselves with destroying the factories and carrying to Sierra Leone the slaves that may be found in them."

The communication from the Colonial Office (dated April 7, 1841) was to a similar effect, and contained besides a request on behalf of Lord John Russell to the then Secretary to the Admiralty, that he would "move the Lords Commissioners to express to Commander Denman the high sense which Her Majesty's Government entertain of his very spirited and able conduct at the Gallinas, and of its important results in the interests of humanity."

These letters, as will be seen hereafter, were destined to be of the greatest service to Captain Denman, when, having been sued for damages in a British Court of Justice by one of the slave traders who was a part owner of the demolished barracoon, and four British Judges having refused to hold that slave trading was piracy by the law of nations, he was driven to take refuge in the defense "that Government, by these letters of the then Foreign and Colonial Secretaries, had, in approving and ratifying his act, made it their own, and thereby rendered the Government (if any one), and not Captain Denman, responsible in damages to the slave-trading and slave-owning plaintiff."

When, on the fall of the Melbourne administration and the accession to power of Sir Robert Peel, Lord Aberdeen became Foreign Minister, a colder, tamer, and more timorous spirit prevailed in Downing Street, as will be seen by the following letter from Lord Aberdeen to the Lords Commissioners of the Admiralty, dated May 20, 1842, about a year later than the letters just cited of Lord Palmerston and Lord John Russell:

"I beg to call your attention to the subject of the instructions given to H. M.'s naval officers employed in suppressing the Slave Trade on the West Coast of Africa:

"Her Majesty's Advocate-General has reported that he can not take upon himself to advise that all the proceedings described as having taken place at Gallinas, &c., are strictly justifiable, or that the instructions to Her Majesty's naval officers as referred to in these papers are such as can with perfect legality be carried into execution.

"I would submit to the consideration of your lordships that Her Majesty's naval officers employed in suppressing the Slave Trade should be instructed to abstain from destroying slave factories and carrying off persons held in slavery, *unless the Power within whose territory or jurisdiction the factories or slaves be found should by treaty with Great Britain, or formal agreement and treaty with Her Majesty's naval officer*, have employed Her Majesty's naval forces to take those steps for the suppression of the Slave Trade."

Thus was the "native hue of resolution sicklied o'er by the pale cast" of law, the moral effect of Captain Denman's gallant exploit materially impaired, and the hopes and wicked activity of the slave traders revived. It will be seen, hereafter, how Lord Denman, in the House of Lords, denounced the policy and set forth the effects of this ill-judged and unfortunate letter.

The veteran friends of the African cause, meanwhile, Thomas Clarkson and Fowell Buxton, to whom Denman had communicated the good news of his son's achievement, were not slow to congratulate him on it."

The letter from Fowell Buxton runs thus:

"Brewery, Spitalfields; March 18, 1841.

"My dear Lord,—Owing to an accident, I did not till this moment receive the news of your son's most glorious exploit. I must allow myself the pleasure of offering my most hearty congratulations to your lordship, and of adding that if anything could increase my satisfaction at the (as I hope) fatal blow which has been struck at the Slave Trade on that part of the coast, it is that the honor of the achievement devolves on the son of one who was a faithful friend of the negro when the herd of politicians stood aloof from the cause.

"Believe me, my dear Lord,
"Your faithful servant,
"T. FOWELL BUXTON."

A little later the venerable Clarkson writes as follows:

"Playford Hall: March 29, 1841.

"My Lord,—I feel very grateful to you, not only for your letter of March 20, but for the newspaper which accompanied it, and also for the House of Commons papers on the same subject, received yesterday.

"I congratulate you on the well-planned success of your son, who has acquitted himself with so much credit to himself, and with such beneficial service to the great cause of humanity,

"I am sure that he has struck the greatest blow that

has ever been given to the Slave Trade on the West Coast of Africa, either within my memory or on record, and its influence will be felt in different places, in different parts of the world. I should not be surprised if it had a tendency completely to destroy the Slave Trade for a while in the neighboring countries to the Gallinas. The slave hunter will now have for some time no market to pay him for his plunder. The slave agents (Portuguese or Spanish) will be in fear for their respective factories, lest those also should be burnt or destroyed. But what is the best feature in the prospect is that it will do still more in Cuba, now the greatest slave mart in the world. After the loss of seven or eight ships, and of two beaten off, whose voyages must be greatly spoiled, and after the immense loss of goods in the slave factories in Africa, will not the people of Cuba be thunderstruck, will they not pause, and pause a good while, before they will venture to send articles of traffic to be kept in store for the purchase of future slaves?

"But, my Lord, I am too ill at this moment to dwell on these future prospects. Only let me advise you, when you write to your son, to put him on his guard relative to retaliation. I have known these bloodthirsty monsters—the white agents of the slave traders in Africa—for 57 years. They will stick at nothing for revenge, nor should I wonder if they were to stir up the native chiefs in the bordering territories to take part in their quarrel, to come down with overwhelming force on Gallinas itself, and make the king pay dear for the destruction of the factories.

"I am, my Lord, with great respect and esteem,

"Your sincere friend,

"THOMAS CLARKSON.

"P.S. I have this day entered into the 82nd year of my age, and alas! am not fit to help the sacred cause much longer. I hope when you have time you will read my last book, the last I shall ever be able to write, on account of age and infirmities."[1]

Denman, who always kept up a correspondence with

[1] The handwriting of this letter is small, neat, perfectly legible, without the slightest sign of age or debility. Clarkson lived five years after this, not dying till 1846, in his 87th year.

the United States, received, this spring, from the accomplished Charles Summer (who, in a recent visit to England had seen much of the Chief Justice), a letter containing some interesting references to the celebrated Judge Story.

"Boston, April 15, 1841.

"My dear Lord,—I owe you many thanks for your kind letter of September 29th, written from your country retreat. Judge Story was much gratified by the flattering terms in which you alluded to him. He loves England and her jurisprudence. Whether he will ever summon the resolution to leave his family and encounter a sea-voyage, shortened as it has been by steam, that he may see with his own eyes what interests him so much in your country, I can not tell. He is now 61, and his time is constantly occupied by his judicial duties and self-imposed labors as professor and author. He has just published a second edition of his 'Conflict of Laws,' with extensive additions, a copy of which he is desirous of forwarding by some proper channel for your acceptance.

"Mr. Stevenson, our minister in London, will be immediately recalled. It is not yet known who will be his successor. Judge Story has been spoken of, but it is not probable that he will be permitted to leave the Bench. I trust the rumors of war will cease. We are all for peace. I have great confidence in the discretion, good sense, and desire of peace which animate the rulers of both countries. A war between us would be fratricidal. Perhaps I may say that we are both able to do each other incalculable mischief. But we will not have a war. I cry out with Lord Falkland in the Civil War—'Peace! Peace!'

"I remember England with the strongest affection, and am, with the highest regard, dear Lord Denman,

"Most faithfully yours,

"CHARLES SUMNER."

In May, 1841, Denman was called upon to preside at the 400th anniversary festival of Eton College (founded by Henry VI., A. D. 1441).

Among the Etonians present on this occasion (little short of 300 in number) were his old friend and son-in-law, Hodgson, then Provost, his equally old friend, Launcelot Shadwell, then Vice-Chancellor of England, and his deeply esteemed brethren on the Bench, Patteson and Coleridge.

Denman, as might have been expected, made a first-rate chairman, and the whole affair went off brilliantly; but nothing, perhaps, in connection with it gave him more pleasure than the following letter, from that illustrious old Etonian, the venerable Marquis of Wellesley, then in his eighty-second year,[1] who, from age and infirmity, had been reluctantly compelled to decline the chair on the present occasion.

"My dear Lord,—If I could receive any consolation for the affliction which deprives me of the happiness of accepting the high honor offered to me on this occasion by my beloved and revered fellow-scholars of the College of Eton, it would be afforded by their happy choice of your Lordship to fill the place originally destined for me by their kindness and favor. That choice, indeed, is not more honorable to the object of it than to me, and to those who manifested so much judgment in making it. Your Lordship's great name well becomes the four hundredth anniversary of the foundation of that noble and illustrious institution, now in the full zenith of fame and glory, and which, through its whole course of splendor, displays no brighter spot than that character, shining in the exercise of the highest judicial functions, and recently displayed with additional luster in the exalted station of Lord High Steward. The chair of the Eton meeting has not yet been filled by equal rank and dignity. May Providence favor us with a result equally auspicious! and may this great assemblage of the produce of Eton, tend to strengthen, to cultivate, and to perpetuate the national benefits which this glorious empire has derived through successive ages, in every department of the State and of the country, from this parental source of wisdom, religion, and happiness! It would be vain at this day for me to make professions of my attachment to the interests and prosperity of Eton.

[1] The Marquis of Wellesley, born in 1760 (nine years before his still more famous brother, the Great Duke); died in 1842—ten years before him.

My whole fame, my whole character, whatever success has attended my life, whatever I am now, whatever I can hope to be hereafter, are all drawn from that (to me sacred and hallowed) spring. I trust that I have not been untrue to the lessons which I received from all my preceptors at that place, but more especially from Dr. Jonathan Davies and Dr. Norbury, both eminent scholars, but whose memory is more endeared to me by their constant and assiduous care to assist and encourage me in the true course of seeking ingenuous and honest fame by diligent and attentive study.

"To the memory of a more exalted personage I am bound, on this occasion, to pay an humble but most ardently grateful tribute of gratitude, veneration, and dutiful affection—to our deceased Sovereign, George the Third, the great and constant patron of Eton, whose patronage and favor animated and encouraged me and all Eton in our labors, and by his gracious presence and countenance, rendered all our exertions public, and the distinctions we severally gained almost national.

"I felt this truly royal act as a new spirit, urging me to all that was praiseworthy. I can not forbear from mentioning it. To this hour I feel all its animation; nor can I conclude with a wish and prayer nearer to my heart, nor one of which the fulfillment would be more beneficial to Eton and to the empire, than that all future Sovereigns may extend a similar protection to our beloved parent, and give a similar countenance to her prosperity and glory.

"Believe me always, my dear Lord, with true respect, esteem, gratitude, and affection, your faithful and obliged servant, "WELLESLEY.

"Kingston House: May 22, 1841."

In the summer of 1841, a case of some interest to the literary world came before the Chief Justice at Westminster—the prosecution of Moxon, the well-known publisher, for blasphemy, in having brought out the whole of Shelley's poems, including the "Queen Mab."

The case was brilliantly defended by Talfourd. Lord Denman told the jury that, as the law stood, they must find against the publisher if they came to the conclusion that he published with the intent alleged.

"How far it might, in general, be expedient to have recourse to prosecution for the purpose of suppressing such publications was," he said, "a question to be considered by those who had the right and the power of instituting such proceedings.

"For himself, he was of opinion that the best and most efficacious method of acting with respect to such publications, was to proceed by way of argument or reasoning: they would be more effectually suppressed or neutralized by confuting the sentiments themselves than by prosecuting the authors of them."[1]

The verdict of the jury was for the Crown, but Mr. Moxon was never called up for judgment.

It had long been clear to all accustomed to read the political signs of the times, that the second Melbourne administration was tottering to its fall. The dissolution which took place on June 23, 1841, served only to precipitate its ruin, and show the strength and extent of the Conservative reaction.

The new Parliament met on Thursday, August 19; the Queen's speech was delivered on the 24th, and on Saturday the 28th, after a four nights' debate on the Address, there was a majority in the Commons against the ministry of 91, the ayes being 269 and the noes 360.

On the next Monday, August 30, Lord Melbourne in the Lords, and Lord John Russell in the Commons, announced the resignation of the Cabinet, and Sir Robert Peel proceeded to form the memorable administration which, after a five years' tenure of power, was broken up in 1846, by the party schisms arising out of the abolition of the Corn Laws.

The succeeding year, 1842, was a busy one with Denman, both in the House and on circuit.

On the first occasion of his addressing the Lords (February 14, 1842), on the question raised by the case of the "Creole," as to the principles of international law regulating the practice on claims of extradition, Denman took the opportunity of paying a high and deserved compliment to the illustrious jurists of the United States. He said:

[1] From *The Times* report of the case.

"The opinions he had cited were not confined to the lawyers of Europe: the great lawyers of America—men distinguished by their profound erudition, whose decisions were so highly respected amongst us, and whose valuable works on great legal points are consulted in this country with the highest advantage—held the same doctrine."[1]

It was not long after this that Denman received the following gratifying letter from the greatest of the great lawyers of whom he had thus spoken with just appreciation, the venerable Chancellor Kent, who, together with the letter, transmitted to the English Chief Justice a copy of the fourth edition of his "Commentaries:"

"New York; March 30, 1842.

"My Lord,—I beg leave to present to your Lordship the fourth edition of my 'Commentaries on American Law,' as I perceive that your Lordship has done me the honor repeatedly to allude to the work.

"I have long wished for a fit occasion to express in some personal way my profound respect and veneration for the character of the Judges of the Courts at Westminster, and especially my sense of the distinguished ability with which your Lordship presides over the Court of Queen's Bench. This letter, I hope, will be deemed a pardonable intrusion. I never had the honor of a personal acquaintance, or of any correspondence whatever with any judicial character in England, yet my familiarity with the English law and the decisions of the English Courts for the last half century, makes me feel as if I was on this occasion in some degree addressing a companion.

"I am now far advanced in the seventy-ninth year of my age, and though I am, as I always have been, healthy and active, I am not without gentle admonitions of late of my very advanced life.

"As I retired from the New York Court of Chancery at the age of sixty, the 'Commentaries' are the fruit of my subsequent leisure, and, together with chamber business, have given me sufficient occupation ever since; and I may truly add, as a fact pleasant to be known, that the last eighteen years of my life have afforded me

[1] Hansard, Parl. Deb., third series, vol. lx. p. 322.

the most agreeable and the most profitable employment.

"With my best wishes for your Lordship's continued health and happiness, and with the highest respect and esteem,

"I have the honor to subscribe myself,

"Your Lordship's most obedient servant,

"JAMES KENT."

On March 8, 1842, the Chief Justice, carrying into act the ideas which eighteen years before he had embodied in his able article on the defects of our Law of Evidence, in the "Edinburgh Review," rose to move the second reading of his bill for amending the Law of Evidence *by preventing the exclusion of testimony on the ground of incompetency from interest or from previous conviction.*

It is hardly necessary to advert at any length to the arguments which Lord Denman, in his very able speech, addressed to the House. None now would attempt to gainsay them: the difficulty rather is to go back in thought to a state of legal opinion in which it would be necessary gravely to adduce such arguments to any deliberative assembly. Suffice it to say that the Chief Justice, by his clear and able address, succeeded in convincing even the House of Lords of that day of the truth of the great principles long since laid down by Bentham, viz., that all persons, whether interested or not, or whether previously convicted of crime or not, should be allowed to give their evidence, leaving it to the jury to estimate its value.

The bill embodying this great and rational improvement in the English Law of Evidence, passed the House of Lords on June 8, 1842, though it did not receive the Royal assent till August 22, 1843, when it became part and parcel of the law of the land, as the Act 6 and 7 Vic. c. 85.[1]

After presiding for the Spring Assizes of 1842 on the Home Circuit, Lord Denman spent a few days of the Easter Vacation at Stony Middleton, whence he wrote the following letter to his fourth daughter, Margaret, (now the honorable Mrs. Cropper), who, in the summer

[1] For Lord Denman's speech on the second reading, see Hansard, Parl. Deb., third series, vol. lxi. p. 208, et seq.

of the preceding year, had married, as her first husband, Mr. Henry William Macaulay, brother of the celebrated Thomas Babington (afterwards Lord) Macaulay.

"Middleton: April 5, 1842.

"My dearest Margaret,—Even if I had not vowed my first leisure to you, everything here brings you to my mind, especially during the last year, from our short visit twelve months ago to witness the first effect of the improvements, to the happy meeting at breakfast on the lawn, on a morning even more brilliant than this, when your happy letters announced the most important event of your life—the most important, and, of course, if happy, the happiest to yourself and all to whom you are dear. What a joyful thing to me to hear from yourself, and from all around you, that that union of hearts and minds, without which the most prosperous circumstances are of no value, secures your enjoyment of the greatest blessing of life in every lot that can befall you.

"You will think this romantic effusion the result of long premeditation on the promised letter, but it really flows from me spontaneously the moment I sit down to think of you and look on this beautiful scene. I hope you will both see it in its most favorable season this year, and to much more advantage than either of you have seen it yet. We left Cubley (Rev. R. Vevers' living, near Ashburn) yesterday under a lowering sky. The day was dismal from Ashburn to Bakewell, but when we approached our own district, the valley of Derwent was filled with broad sunshine, and our own trees and turf most splendid. The Captain [his son Joseph] is pleased with our improvements generally, and my Lady and the two girls [Ann and Caroline] in joyous spirits."

Denman, in May, 1842, succeeded in prevailing upon the great historian, Hallam, to take the chair at the Eton anniversary dinner for that year. He thus intimates to his son-in-law, Hodgson, the Provost, his notion that Hallam might consent if applied to:

"Westminster Hall: May 2, 1842.

"My dear Hodgson,—Meeting Hallam at the Royal Academy dinner, I thought him a desirable chairman, and spoke to him about it. He did not more than half decline, but rather appeared to be more than half willing to be pressed. If the College think him most desirable, application to him would, I think, gratify and fix him."

At the request of the Provost and Fellows, Denman wrote to Hallam on the subject, and received from the distinguished historian the following characteristic note of half-reluctant, half-gratified acceptance:

"24 Wilton Cresent: May 9, 1842.

"Dear Lord Denman,—The proposal contained in your note of yesterday, that I should take the chair at the next anniversary dinner of our schoolfellows, is one which I can not accept without reluctance.

"Nothing, indeed, but a sense that I ought not to decline too pertinaciously what is pressed upon by one whom I respect as I do you, would induce me to place myself in a position neither suited to my years,[1] nor, in the opinion perhaps of many, to my rank, or rather want of rank in society. I must also add that the domestic misfortunes which have repeatedly fallen on my head, have led to an increased unwillingness to stand forward in the bustling scenes of life, and, in particular, I have never attended the Eton meeting since the loss of my eldest son, nine years ago.[2] It has, indeed, happened that I have been compelled to take a more prominent part than I designed, and have had honors of this kind conferred on me which I have little expected or desired.

"I rely on your having good reason to believe that my taking the chair will not be unacceptable to the leading Etonians.

"I am, dear Lord Denman,
"Very truly yours,
"HENRY HALLAM."

On June 2, 1842, Lord Denman, renewing the attempt which he had made unsuccessfully in 1838, laid on the table of the House of Lords a bill "to provide for the

[1] Hallam was then only just turned of sixty, having been born in 1781, two years after Denman.

[2] Arthur Hallam, the inspirer of Tennyson's "In Memoriam," who died in 1833.

Affirmation of persons having conscientious objections to taking *Oaths*;[1] and on June 27, he moved the second reading of his bill, in an admirable speech, the only one, it is believed, of his Parliamentary discourses which he revised for the press, and caused to be published in a separate form.[2]

The bill encountered considerable opposition. Lord Abinger, as the mouthpiece of the Common-Law Judges, urged that if persons professing to have religious scruples had an opportunity of giving evidence without the sanction of an oath, there might be many who, on false pretense of such scruples, would evade being sworn. Many of their lordships expressed the opinion that the matter wanted further inquiry; and finally, on the suggestion of the Bishop of London that it would be better to refer the whole subject of judicial oaths and affirmations to a Select Committee, Lord Denman, though with considerable reluctance, consented to withdraw his bill.[3]

The whole of this excellent speech is reprinted in the Appendix,[4] and all readers who feel interested on the important subject to which it relates, are earnestly recommended to peruse it there. Its arguments are so close and connected, that it is difficult, if not impossible, to present any passage apart from its context without impairing its force and lessening its value. It is a perfect model of the style in which such questions should be dealt with before a high deliberative assembly—lucid, vigorous, dignified, and convincing.

Denman caused copies of this speech to be sent to several of his friends, and amongst others to Sydney Smith, from whom, before the year was out, he received the following characteristic acknowledgment:

"Combe Florey, Taunton: October 18, 1842.

"My dear Lord,—I have received your speech upon

[1] Hansard, Parl. Deb, third series, vol. lxiii. p. 1237.

[2] The report in Hansard is a reprint from the corrected speech. See Hansard, Parl. Deb., third series, vol. lxiv. pp. 617–627.

[3] Hansard, Parl. Deb., third series, vol. lxiv. p. 655. Lord Denman again introduced a bill for the same object, but slightly varied in form, in 1849. The provisions of *this* bill, its rejection, and the present state of the law on the subject, will fall to be considered hereafter.

[4] Appendix No. V.

'Affirmations,' and, though it is not said so on the white leaf, I believe you sent it me; or if not, leave me in the honorable delusion.

"Your great difficulty is akin to that of proving that two and two are equivalent to four. All that the Legislature ought to inquire, is, whether this scruple has now become so common as to cause the frequent interruption of justice. This admitted, the remedy ought to follow as a matter of course. We are to get the best evidence for discovering truth—not the best we can imagine, but the best we can procure—and if you can't get oaths you must put up with affirmations, as far better than no evidence at all; but one is ashamed to descant on such obvious truths.

"One obvious truth, however, I have always great pleasure in descanting upon, and that is, that I always see the Chief Justice leading the way in everything that is brave, liberal, and wise. I beg he will accept my best wishes and best regards. SYDNEY SMITH."[1]

A juster or more dexterous compliment was perhaps never paid.

In the Summer Assizes of 1842, Lord Denman, with Mr. Justice Maule, went the Northern Circuit, where the work, especially at York, was exceptionally severe. It was the time of one of the great Chartist risings in the North,[2] and the work of trying the Chartist rioters, in addition to a very considerable number of other prisoners, devolved on Lord Denman and his colleague, who was then suffering very severely from asthma.

This was probably the hardest judicial labor that even Lord Denman ever went through, and the encountering it was entirely his own voluntary act, for the Government had intended to try the Chartist prisoners under a Special Commission, as appears from the following letter of Sir James Graham, then Secretary of State for the Home Department.

"Whitehall: August 19, 1842.

"My dear Lord Denman,—Lord Wharncliffe writes me

[1] The above is printed from the original, in the handwriting of the immortal Sydney; a copy was made and given to Lady Holland for insertion in her charming memoir of her illustrious father.

[2] The one so well told in Mr. Disraeli's "Sybil," and Miss Brontë's "Shirley."

word that he had addressed a letter to you, in which he has requested that you will not discharge the grand jury, with the view of bringing to trial at the present assizes the prisoners newly committed to York Castle.

"It is not possible in the present state of affairs that we should be prepared to go to trial immediately. Our present duty is to suppress the insurrection; our future endeavor will be to convict the prisoners now in custody, when we shall have had time to sift the evidence and to collect the information we may receive. In these circumstances, I hope you will be disposed to leave the prisoners committed within the last few days for trial at a Special Commission, which the Crown will be disposed to issue, and that you will close the present assize at York in ordinary course, without reference to the present unhappy circumstances which have so suddenly arisen.

"I have little time to write to you, and I can not enter more fully into the subject, but Lord Wharncliffe's letter rendered this communication necessary.

"I am, my dear Lord,
"Yours very faithfully,
"J. G. GRAHAM."

Denman had a very strong conviction that nothing could so effectually tend to suppress the insurrectionary spirit of the North at that time, as the prompt and immediate trial of the insurgents. The enormously increased burden of work which would thus be thrown upon him, in addition to a large list of nearly a hundred causes which had come before him for trial in the ordinary course, had no weight with him when compared with this consideration. He accordingly wrote to the Home Office that in his opinion a Special Commission was unnecessary, and that he and his colleague were quite prepared to proceed at once to the trial of the Chartists. The grand jury, which had not been dismissed, was accordingly adjourned for a few days, until the evidence was prepared; and within one month from the outbreak, every rioter who had been apprehended was tried.[1]

Denman always looked back with pleasure and just

[1] The number of additional prisoners was about 200.

pride upon this passage in his judicial career, rightly considering that nothing could so powerfully have impressed the excited mind of the populace as this prompt and vigorous assertion of the power of the law. The effect, too, as he had correctly calculated, was more striking when it was seen that no extraordinary powers were put in force, but that the ordinary machinery of the law was amply sufficient to put down sedition and punish the offenders against the peace of the country. Doubtless much valuable property, and even many lives, were saved by this vigorous exertion, while the country was spared the serious expense always attending a Special Commission.

Several letters written by him to his wife and other members of his family while engaged at York in these arduous labors have been preserved, from which the following passages may be extracted:

On August 15, he writes to Lady Denman, soon after his arrival at York:

"The calendar is heavy, the cause list of great length. We are just launched on our great sea of work. *I am winding myself up to the state of patience and quiet which can alone guide me through it with the least possible annoyance.* The worst of it is that my brother judge [Maule] seems very suffering indeed."

The words italicized contain one of the great secrets of Lord Denman's rapid and successful dispatch of judicial business; vigilance, quietness, patience, and promptitude were judicial qualities he possessed in a degree rarely, if ever, surpassed.

At the close of the first week's work, he writes again:

"At length, my dearest love, there is a little leisure for me to tell you that this laborious week has passed away, not without some fatigue, but leaving me quite well, and Tom [present Lord Denman] very much improved. Indeed, he would no longer have any treatment of an invalid from me, if it did not provide the means of keeping him as prudent as he has been hitherto. For my part, though my days and two first evenings (for I felt myself unequal to more dissipation) were so crammed, yet I slept all night long every night, and have had an excellent appetite. I have just got to the top of the hill of business, having disposed of forty-eight causes out of ninety-two, but must not expect to descend at so rapid a rate, as the heavier matters remain to the last. Yesterday we dined, six miles out of York, at a new house in Elizabethan style, with a magnificent hall like Lord Middleton's at Wollaston. It is the property of a Mr. Prentice. The company was agreeable, and amongst other things, I heard a piece of wit directed against Sydney Smith, which I will tell you. He was quizzing a lady's fears about the cholera, and told her she would swell up till her whole frame was a large whitlow, and then burst. She was shocked and angry, and replied that it would be better to be a *whit low* than a *low wit*. I shall send you a flight of newspapers to-day. You can hardly have learnt yet that Maltby is the new Bishop of Durham, more retrenched [in income] than I have been, I fear."

On the 21st he writes to his daughter Fanny (Lady Baynes), then staying with the Hodgsons at Eton:

"The tumults appear to be put down; the local soldiery are disbanded. A seditious meeting advertised to be held to-day at Knavesmire (the race course) has been prohibited by the magistrates, and has not been held. York, which looked like a city expecting the approach of a besieging army, resumes its peaceful character.

"The Duke of Cambridge called here this morning, and afterwards attended the Minster, which presented a magnificent spectacle, containing within its narrowed dimensions not fewer than 5,000 people. The choir was so thronged that a passage to the altar was not easy for the ministers. The anthem was *half* the Old Hundreth Psalm. Why dimidiated? The Dean's[1] sermon, in its first sentence declared a controversy with the authors of 'Tracts for the Times,' 'penned with so much caution and obscurity that it is not easy to find anything objectionable in them.' He spoke afterwards of our 'Oxford Teachers,' concluding with four lines from a *moral* poet (Heber, perhaps), the last of which is—

'But only in thy deepest heart adore him.'

Tom and I are to have the honor of dining with His

[1] Sir William Cockburn, ninth Baronet, uncle of the present Chief Justice of the Queen's Bench, who succeeded him in 1858.

Royal Highness, my brother judge not being well enough, for one of the distresses of our position is that he suffers at times severely from asthma.

"The Provost will have perceived that some of my gossip is for him, but I must address him and dear Bessie [Mrs. Hodgson] a little more pointedly.

"I think he might have reported something of the Queen besides her going 'early to bed,' which is only commendable along with 'early to rise.' I hope Brighton may answer all its intended purposes, and should like to know this from time to time. If mamma has not time to write, I am sure that Betty [Mrs. Hodgson's little girl] has not come to these years without acquiring that accomplishment."

The next day, August 22, he writes to Lady Denman:

"The outrageous movement appears to be now effectually stopped, and I no longer fear any other ill consequences from it, except to the judges who may have the trouble to try the offenders. Whether we shall be those judges is rather doubtful, as Government wish to have a Special Commission, and certainly our hard work hitherto gives us a fair right to repose. At a sumptuous dinner given yesterday by one of the aldermen [Hudson, soon afterwards famous as the Railway King], Tom and I had the honor of being guests, Maule excusing himself on the score of health. The illustrious stranger [the Duke of Cambridge] was rather amusing, but more full of questions, more excited, and laughing louder than ever. He told Tom he had been writing answers to *addresses that he expects* from the towns he is about to visit. He comes to this part of the world on his way to celebrate Lord Seaham's son's coming of age. Prince George[1] has been busy in putting down the riots, and showing proper firmness and activity, while evincing (as his father also did) an amiable dislike of being employed as a soldier against his fellow-subjects.

"I must tell you that the Duke asked very kindly after the Provost, and said he was a great favorite at the Castle. He also inquired how much a year his office

[1] The present Duke of Cambridge and Commander-in-Chief.

produces, and put a similar question to Wortley[1] about his fees.

"This morning at breakfast the servants announced, as I thought, *Mr.* Charles Anderson, but, to my joy and surprise, it was your uncle, *Sir* Charles, looking extremely well, with the same affectionate and cheerful countenance as ever, his figure much stoutened. He is just come in from Bedale, gives the best reports of all there, and speaks of our Captain [Admiral Joseph Denman] with delight. They had no great sport on the moors, but all, especially Miss Pierce, enjoyed the expedition greatly. You perceive that I missed my visit to Milnes[2] at Pontefract, or rather I must tell you so now, for on Saturday I was obliged to remain in Court till after the train was off. I am growing sadly dull with prosing cases, and must spare any more prose of my own. To-morrow Lord Normanby[3] comes in for the races, and dines with us. I shall try and keep Sir Charles to meet him."

On the 24th, he writes:

"The troubles are certainly at an end for the present, and I trust for ever. The folly and the wickedness have luckily gone hand in hand, and the former has defeated the latter. Prisoners continue to be sent to York Castle. They are said to be decent-looking men, who were earning good wages and living in comparative comfort. It is devoutly to be hoped that some of the leaders who led them astray will be caught. Such must be severely punished.

"I think I told you Sir Charles [Anderson] was to dine with us yesterday. He met Lord Normanby and some very pleasant men, who took all the trouble of talking off his hands. He seemed very well entertained, and has been with us this morning to take leave. Maule and he have taken a great liking to each other. I had a pleasant letter from Joe [Admiral Denman] yesterday, and a good long one from Fanny [Lady Baynes] to-

[1] The late Hon. W. Stuart Wortley, then one of the leaders on the Northern Circuit.

[2] Father of the present Lord Houghton.

[3] The first Marquis of Normanby, so well known as a successful novelist and still more successful Viceroy of Ireland.

day. I hope you will find her much better, and make her much better still. Make her as well as she is good."

On the 27th, he writes:

"You will be rather sorry to hear that we have refused to hand over the prisoners to a Special Commission, which was asked for by the Government solicitor on the grounds which we thought wholly insufficient. The consequence is that, under the authority of our ordinary commission, we must proceed to try them, and thereby, of course, prolong our labors. What has occurred to me as a scheme which will make this inconvenience more tolerable, and fall in with some of our other objects, is this, that you should indulge me with your presence here about Tuesday or Wednesday, and proceed next day to Bedale, where I may be able to join you, and remain a few days at the end of the week. My own opinion is that the whole assizes will then be brought to an end. If you approve of my scheme, I should hope to return to Middleton with you in a very few days.

"You will see with great regret that Tindal has lost his eldest son. I had no idea of his being in danger, though he always appeared far from strong. I shall write to the Chief Justice by the next post."

The protracted assizes, notwithstanding the vigorous efforts and unwearied labors of the Chief Justice and his most able and self-sacrificing coadjutor, Mr. Justice Maule, lasted well into September.

The repose of Stony Middleton, amid his family and his favorite rural pursuits of planting, improving, and landscape-gardening, must have been doubly delightful to the Chief Justice after his long and harassing labors.

The wish to which he had frequently recurred in his letters to Mrs. Baillie, to have herself and her twin-sister, Lady Croft, at Stony Middleton, was gratified during this Long Vacation. He thus writes to Mrs. Baillie shortly before the visit took place:

"My Lady makes me very happy by telling me that you seem at length really disposed to come and look at our beautiful scenery. I need not tell you what pleasure it will give me. Indeed, the place wants something essential to my fully appreciating it till you and my sister have given it your sanction. The country goes on increasing in beauty till September. This year is the best season for the foliage I have ever witnessed. Will you report what I have said to my sister, and proceed to make arrangements with her in a business-like manner."

He writes thence, on October 18, 1842, to Hodgson, who, as Provost of Eton, had recently been attending the funeral of the celebrated Marquis of Wellesley:

"Your feelings as to the writing have been nearly the same as my own, but I have besides felt idleness to be in the nature of a conscientious duty, after so much work, and before so much more. Though you do not mention the funeral, I consider your letter as a complete answer to all the inquiries I was anxious to make. You have caught no cold, nor suffered more than from the occasion was unavoidable, after so many pleasing glimpses of the illustrious old Etonian. Your noble institution must derive benefit from his example—οἷος ἐκεῖνος—but it is unfortunate that so large a proportion of his great deeds was done in India, and will never be properly appreciated, even by well-informed men, at home.[1]

"Chatsworth has been altogether amiable and kind. Morpeth[2] came on Friday. I saw him on Saturday, looking well, thinner, bronzed, pleazed with his visit to America. It is charming to see how both parents [Lord (the sixth Earl) and Lady Carlisle, then staying at Chatsworth] are revived by his return.

"You probably know that Tom and Georgiana[3] are about to live apart from us. I trust and believe that they will settle very comfortably, and am convinced of the propriety of the change. We may hope to see you oftener in London, but I fairly own that your promise of coming to us here is much more agreeable to me, for here I could enjoy your society, and should delight in seeing Bessie and the children enjoying these beautiful

[1] How true! but, for the interests both of England and India, how much to be regretted.

[2] Long so known—afterwards the seventh Earl of Carlisle, for many years Viceroy of Ireland.

[3] The present Lord Denman and his first wife, who for some time had formed part of Lord Denman's family.

scenes. After the next Summer Circuit—*si validus, si sanus, si denique bene*—here will I come at an early period, and get my friends and offspring more about me. These falling leaves reconcile me to our return to town, but a longer enjoyment of sunshine and verdure would have been a richer treasure for the memory. The improvement here is universally admitted and is really striking.

CHAPTER XXIX.

LITERARY SOCIETY—REG. *v.* MILLIS—OPENING OF MAZZINI'S LETTERS AT THE POST-OFFICE.

A. D. 1843, 1844. ÆT. 64, 65.

DENMAN, after his elevation to the Chief Justiceship, had not only kept up but extended his social relations with men of letters. Among those of the older generation he had a close, cordial, and abiding intimacy with Samuel Rogers, whom, when in town, he rarely passed many days without seeing. He saw as much of Sydney Smith on his visits to London from Combe Florey as was compatible with the universal demand made by society on the time of the celebrated humorist, who used to describe himself on such occasions as submerged "in a Caspian Sea of Soup." Among the rising men of mark he saw most, probably, of Talfourd and Charles Dickens.

For the genial, generous nature, brilliant eloquence and distinguished literary faculty of Talfourd he had the highest and warmest appreciation; while, as to Dickens, it may be doubted whether in the three kingdoms any one could be found who reveled with greater delight in the boundless and amazing creativeness of the Great Humorist.

Among the stray notes that have cropped up from amid the chaos of the Denman papers is an urgent one dispatched by the Chief Justice from circuit to Lady Denman, earnestly enjoining her to lose no time in securing the best box that may still be available for the first night of Talfourds's "Ion" (1835). Mr. Foster's delightful memoirs of Dickens supply ample proof of the cordial relations existing between the celebrated writer and the celebrated Chief Justice. Denman, in May, 1844, was one of the chosen friends who, with Lord Normanby,

Sydney Smith, and others, attended the farewell dinner that preceded Dickens's departure for Italy.[1] In October of the same year, Dickens writes from Genoa, after reading the great O'Connell judgment, delivered in the preceding month: "Denman delights me; I am glad to think I have always liked him so well. I am sure when he makes a mistake it [alluding no doubt to the Privilege question] *is* a mistake; and that no one lives who has a grander and nobler scorn of every mean and dastard action. I would to heaven it were decorous to pay him some public tribute of respect."[2] When "Dombey and Son" was in course of publication, Mr. Forster notes how, at a dinner party at Talfourd's, the deep voice of Denman was heard exclaiming across the table, with that zeal of conviction which all who knew him can so well realize, "And isn't Bunsby good!"[3]

Nor was his intercourse with the men of letters of the newer generation confined to the two celebrities just mentioned; it extended also to several others, among whom may be mentioned Dr. Samuel Warren, the learned and ingenious author of "Now and Then" and "Ten Thousand a Year," who, from some stray notes scattered here and there among the Denman papers, appears to have enjoyed the pleasure of the Chief Justice's acquaintance, and the occasional honor of his correspondence.

Among several mere scraps from Sydney Smith, has been found the following characteristic note, written during the height of the London season of 1841, on occasion of Sydney's having asked Denman and his wife to join a dinner party to which he had also invited Lady Holland, then in the first year of her widowhood, and who, as is well-known, was not generally met or visited by the stricter part of the female world:

June 8, 1841.

"Dear Lord Denman,—Mrs. Sydney and I have made a blunder, which I am sure you will have the goodness to excuse, and the more especially as it proceeded from

[1] "Memoirs of Dickens," vol. ii. chap. iv. p. 85.
[2] Ibid. vol. ii. chap. v. p. 110.
[3] Ibid. vol. ii. chap. xvi. p. 337, in note.

our desire to secure Lady Denman's company in conjunction with yours.

"Lady Holland dines with us on the 17th. Does Lady Denman know Lady Holland, and, if not, will that deprive us of the pleasure of Lady Denman's company? Lady Holland sinned early in life,[1] with Methuselah and Enoch, but still she is out of the pale of the regular ladies, and the case ought to have been put. Pray tell me if this will make any difference. Your answer will be received by me in the strictest confidence.

"I remain, my dear Lord,

"Always with sincere respect and regard, yours,

"SYDNEY SMITH."

As Denman, to Sydney Smith's knowledge, had been at this time for more than twenty years on intimate terms with the Hollands, it seems at first sight a little singular that he should have thought any explanation as to Lady Holland's social position necessary; but he may well have been in ignorance whether Lady Denman had ever accompanied her husband to Holland House, or met its witty and distinguished mistress elsewhere, and he was therefore clearly quite right in "putting the case."

In the Parliamentary session of 1843, Denman's exertions were principally confined to questions more or less connected with the suppression of the Slave Trade, a subject that yearly, from this time forward, absorbed more and more of his time and energy.

On April 7, 1843, Brougham having, in an elaborately prepared speech, moved that the thanks of the House be given to Lord Ashburton for his services in concluding the Treaty of Washington, Denman, while concurring in the motion, took occasion, in consequence of something that had fallen from Lord Aberdeen in the course of the debate, to refer to his lordship's already cited letter of May 20, 1842, which he (Denman) construed as reflecting on his son, Captain Denman's, proceedings at the Gallinas.

[1] Lady Holland's marriage with her first husband, Sir Godfrey Webster, was dissolved in 1797 or 1798, immediately on which she married Lord Holland, with whom she had previously eloped. In 1841 she was a recent widow, Lord Holland having died in 1840.

In a speech, the report of which he himself seems to have corrected for Messrs. Hansard,[1] Lord Denman said:

"A letter has been written which I was not prepared to hear spoken of as it has been by the noble earl [Aberdeen].

"It seems to me, whether I look at it as a question of injustice to an individual, or as a matter of importance to the public service, that it is a question how far it was proper that such a letter should have been written.

"Some explanation is necessary. I avow for myself I think this great subject has never been regarded in its true light. Things ought to be called by their true names, and the Slave Trade never mentioned but to be stigmatized as the *worst of crimes*. If this be so, the important consequence is involved that *all mankind have a right to put it down. It is more than a Right—it is a Duty*. If we may arrest the arm of the murderer when raised in our presence; if we may release the kidnapped man from his kidnapper—we may surely combine to put down the traffic in human beings. Every civilized nation has agreed that this is a crime which ought to be extirpated off the face of the earth, and the only question now remaining is, by what means this is to be done!

"I will not enter into a distinction between the right of *Search*, and the right of *Visit*; I stand up for the *right of prevention*. I am not insensible of the importance of co-operation with other powers; but I maintain that every restriction imposed by treaty on that natural right [of Prevention of Crime] is a concession not lightly to be made.

"It is quite clear to me that no other means for the suppression of the Slave Trade can be so effectual as the employment of cruisers on the coast. But *seizure at sea* is too late; for, when once the cargo of human beings has been placed on board the vessel, half the mischief is done. She may escape to Cuba or Brazil, or even if not, the very chase is generally accompanied by

[1] See Hansard, Parl. Deb., third series, vol. lxviii., Appendix 1461. It does not greatly vary from the uncorrected report commencing at p. 673.

wholesale murder—the throwing overboard many of the victims, in order to lighten the vessel for escape. The great object, then, is to prevent the embarkation of the negroes from these barracoons on the coast, where they are regularly stored, like any other merchandise, for the purpose of immediate transportation. And if an officer, happening to command on such coast, should strike out a new line of prevention, and, acting on his own responsibility, but in strict accordance with the spirit of his instructions, should make *embarkation impossible* by releasing the slaves from these barracoons, who would deny that such a man entitled himself to the thanks of his country.

"This had been done by an officer, who received for what he had done the full approbation both of the late and of the present Board of Admiralty, and who had been shortly afterwards promoted. He had the happiness of giving freedom to more than 900 of his fellow-creatures, who were now settled at Sierra Leone; a deadly blow had been struck at the trade itself, and not a drop of blood had been shed.

"I say, with pride, that this conduct entitles the officer to whom I have alluded, to be regarded as a public benefactor. It was, therefore, with no small surprise that I read in the public journals the letter of the noble earl to the Lords of the Admiralty [letter of May 20, 1842]—a letter appearing to reflect on these proceedings; for it alluded by name to the Gallinas River, where they had been carried on, and suggested that new instructions should be given to the officers, as if their former conduct was open to censure. I must venture to think that any language susceptible of such construction is highly inexpedient for the public service."

Four days later (April 11, 1843), on Brougham's laying before the House a "bill for the more effectual suppression of slavery," Lord Aberdeen took occasion to explain that in his leter of May 20, 1842, he had intended no reference to the proceedings of Captain Denman. "Nothing," he said, "was further from his intention than to cast any such imputation. Even restricted," as he admitted his own views were, "as to what could legally be done by our cruisers on the coast of Africa, that gallant officer in anything he had done had not come within the exception he (Lord Aberdeen) had laid down; and he must add that there was no one who had more distinguished himself in this important service, nor for whom he entertained a higher respect than for the gallant officer."[1]

Lord Denman, after expressing his gratification at the statement of the noble earl, went on to observe:

"That he was not sure his opinions did not go further even than those of his noble and learned friends [Brougham and Campbell], for he had ventured to speak of a natural law of right and wrong, which declared a pirate an enemy of the human race, and the Slave Trade obnoxious to the principles of that law.

"Nothing, however, was further from his intention than to act indiscriminately upon the principles of that law, for he deemed it necessary to endeavor to obtain the assistance of other nations to make it effectual. But, he believed the government would do better in their negotiations by starting on the wider principle—viewing the Slave Trade in the light of a crime which all nations had a right to prevent, and then proceeding to discuss practically what measures would be most effectual for its suppression—than if they commenced by petitioning other nations to do them the favor to join in putting it down."[2]

In the Spring Assizes of 1843, Denman presided on the Home, and in the Summer Assizes on the Norfolk, Circuit. The following extract from a letter to Lady Denman, written from Bedford on the Norfolk Circuit in July, relates to a dinner given to the Judges at the Stowe by the second Duke of Buckingham, and bears witness to the profuse magnificence by which, amongst other means, that lavish and splendid nobleman contrived to squander a vast revenue and impoverish a princely property.[3]

"So splendid a dinner as the Duke of Buckingham

[1] This is all mighty well, but utterly irreconcilable with the spirit, if not with the terms, of the letter of May 20, 1842.

[2] Hansard, Parl. Deb., third series, vol. lxviii. p. 826, &c.

[3] The second duke died in 1861. This dinner was one item on a long train of extravagance, that led ultimately to the sale, under execution, of the furniture and collections at Stowe.

gave us yesterday I never saw, except at the christening of the Prince of Wales [at Windsor Castle, in January, 1842, at which Denman had been present]. An immense party of the magistrates and gentlemen, more than 100 in number; a most excellent dinner, plate on sideboards the whole length of each side of the long room. The host very hearty and good-natured. We went there again this morning and saw the pictures, some very fine. The Duke had returned to town."

In the summer months of 1843, Denman was very greatly occupied (as his papers show) in preparing his judgment, to be delivered in the House of Lords, in the important case of the *Queen* v. *Millis*, the material facts of which are thus concisely stated, with perfect accuracy, in the marginal note of the case, as published in the tenth volume of Messrs. Clark and Finelly's "Reports."[1]

A member of the Established Church in Ireland went with a Presbyterian woman to the house of a regularly placed Presbyterian minister of the parish, and there entered into a present contract of marriage with her, the minister performing a religious ceremony between them, according to the rites of the Presbyterian Church. The man having afterwards, but before the death of the woman, married another person in England, the question arose whether the first ceremony was a valid marriage, so as to support the charge of bigamy.

In the House of Lords, on appeal from the Irish judges, who had decided this point in the negative, the six law lords who delivered their opinions on the case equally divided: Brougham, Denman, and Campbell held that the first marriage was valid; Lyndhurst, Cottenham, and Abinger that it was not.

The general maxim applicable to such an exactly even balance of judicial opinion prevailed. The culprit was discharged, and the case was afterwards provided for by express legislation.

Denman's judgment (delivered on August 11, 1843),[2] in the preparation of which he had spared no pains, was very able.

[1] *Reg.* v. *Millis*, 10 Clark and Finelly, House of Lords Cases.
[2] Reported 10 Clark and Finelly, pp. 804–831.

His principal point was that the Irish judges had gone wrong *by reversing the order of proof.*

"The burden of proof," he said, "has been supposed to rest on those who assert that a marriage may be lawful without the intervention of a priest. Now, I most confidently maintain that *marriage, being a civil contract, flowing from the natural law, must be taken as lawful till some enactment which annuls it can be produced and proved by those who deny its lawfulness.*"

He concluded his learned and closely-reasoned judgment in these words:

"Upon the whole, I am most clearly of opinion that a contract *per verba de presente* was, before Lord Hardwicke's Act (of 1753) passed, by the English law, a good marriage—*ipsum matrimonium.*

"From the ground I have taken I can not descend to anything like compromise on the principle that *communis error facit jus*—on the supposition, that is, that there may indeed be error in the judicial opinion hitherto prevailing, but that it has been committed by so many persons of the highest authority that it ought now to be sanctioned by a legislative declaration.

"I think there is no error in that opinion—no proof whatever that the church would at any time have hesitated to enforce this contract, or to consider it a marriage for any purpose.

"It seems to me that if there had been such a *communis error* it is not the opinion of the great lawyers and judges who have been named, but the vulgar notion current in the world, confounding *the solemnization of a priest* with the marriage contract, to which it gave at once authenticity and respectability.

"The prevalence of that notion is explained by the practice; and it has laid hold of the public mind from that *propensity to take for granted* which we have so often seen leading to wrong conclusions.

"In spite of it, however, the judicial mind of England has now for ages held with equal tenacity the opposite faith; not reported in cases (for the prudent usages of men rendered these almost impossible), but from an enlightened consideration of the nature of the contract."[1]

[1] Clark and Finelly, pp. 829, 830.

In the Spring Assizes of the year 1844, Lord Denman (accompanied by Mr. Baron Alderson), again presided on the Home Circuit, which he preferred to any other, from the facility it afforded him of occasionally running up to town.

It was while sitting in the Civil Court at Maidstone, on March 12, 1844, that he wrote as follows to Mr. Justice Coleridge (then on the Oxford Circuit), commencing with a few lines of Maccaronic Latin, at the expense of the late Mr. Sergeant Dowling,[1] who, somewhat in the style of the immortal Sergeant Buzfuz, was leading for the plaintiff in a seduction case before a Kentish common jury.

"(*Dowling aperiente casùm seductionis multâ cum gravitate in procœmo, subito postea levissime gossipiente.*)[2] Your fate at Worcester awaits me here. Cause list 24—Special Juries 10—all the cases to be of enormous length—40, even 60, witnesses familiarly talked of—three cases at least to last two days. Alderson, with 102, not series cases on the criminal side, will probably render some assistance. He is very well and very agreeable.

"I am desired by Sir James Graham [then Minister for the Home Department in Sir R. Peel's administration] to ask for a return of all salaries, fees, and emoluments. I presume yours to be £5,000; but, if you answer me this question, you will tell me also something about yourself and your goings on.

"Dowling, looking and gesticulating like Othello,[3] now informs the jury that the seduced has already been awarded £100 in a previous action for breach of marriage promise, but that the heartless seducer has taken his property abroad, so her father fires this second shot after the delinquent.

"Brougham is excessively indignant, Alderson not much less so, at the sentence of death pronounced in

[1] Afterwards Judge of the County Court at York (Circuit No. 15); he died, 1868.

[2] "Dowling opening a case of seduction with vast solemnity at the outset, but suddenly dropping down in the poorest gossipping."

[3] The excellent and learned Sergeant was proverbially ill-favored—lank and swarthy, with a vast nose, and a mouth and lips more resembling those of "a man and a brother" than is usual in the Caucasian races.

Louisiana on the crime of aiding a slave to escape. The execution is to follow in April. Could any expression of sentiment by our judicial body avail anything? Interference *might* only exasperate, but Everett[1] thinks it may possibly be useful; there seems little reason to think it can do harm. Now farewell; remember me kindly to Parke."[2]

The Chief Justice, acting on the suggestion mentioned in the last paragraph of the above letter, hurried up from circuit, and six days afterwards, on March 18, rose up in his place in the House of Lords, to state the atrocious sentence, and in the name of the Judges of England to protest against its enormity. He said:

"He had been led to advert to the subject in that House from the deep respect entertained in this country for the manner in which justice was administered in America—the humanity and legal knowledge which guided its proceedings, and inspired the eminent men who presided in its courts. He called on all in authority there to pause a moment and consider whether such a sentence as death for aiding a slave to escape ought to be carried out."[3]

In the course of the Easter Term that followed, Denman sustained a severe loss in the death of the most intimate of all his old friends—the excellent and accomplished John Herman Merivale. Mr. Merivale died suddenly at his house in Bedford Square, on April 25, 1844, from an immediately fatal attack of apoplexy. He had been out walking with his daughters, and on his return retired to his own room, where, a few hours after, he was found quite dead. He was one of the most brilliant scholars of his time, particularly excelling in an almost unrivaled faculty of reproducing the gems of Greek and Latin poetry in English verse translations of singular fidelity and elegance. He was also a frequent contributor to the highest periodical literature of the day—a day in which Jeffery and Brougham and Macaulay, Scott and Southey and Milman, were among those who

[1] Then Minister for the United States at the Court of St. James.

[2] Afterwards Lord Wensleydale, then traveling the Oxford Circuit with Coleridge, as Senior Judge of Assize.

[3] Hansard, Parl. Deb., third series, vol. lxxii. p. 1156.

wrote for the "Edinburgh" and the "Quarterly." His high talents, his private virtues, and his endearing social qualities rendered him worthy of the friendship which for nearly half a century bound him so closely and intimately to his illustrious friend. Denman deeply deplored his loss, though, from the circumstance of his death occurring in town, where all their common friends were then residing, no written expression of his grief is to be found among his papers.[1]

During the Parliamentary session of 1844, Denman was not an unfrequent speaker. The following are among the subjects of professional or general interest upon which he addressed the House.

On April 1 he voted for the third reading of Lord Lyndhurst's Bill on Ecclesiastical Courts, though, from the conviction of Government that they could not carry the wider measure, the abolition of the *Diocesan* Courts was omitted from the bill. Lord Denman said as to this, that

"He could not help regarding it as a most melancholy and mortifying circumstance that Courts whose abolition had been recommended for fourteen years—Courts which were a public nuisance—Courts whose operations was most oppressive towards individuals, which had been condemned by all authorities of every description entitled to respect—should baffle the attempts of so powerful a Government to effect their abolition."[2]

On May 13, Brougham having, in a speech of great elaboration, moved the second reading of a Bill for the *Consolidation of the Criminal Law*, Denman supported the second reading, observing that

"Beyond all doubt the object to which, upon the subject of the criminal law, the attention of the legislature should now be directed was the simplification of our criminal code. He thought the modification of that law a fit subject to be undertaken by the legislature and the Government, and he entirely agreed that it was an ob-

[1] His widow long survived him, having died at a very advanced age in the course of last year. His eldest son, Mr. Herman Merivale, C. B., Permanent Under-Secretary of State for India, is well-known as the inheritor, not only of the brilliant scholarship, but of the estimable qualities of his father.

[2] Hansard, Parl. Deb., third series, vol. lxxiii. p. 1688.

ject of paramount importance that the criminal code of the country should be rendered as effective and, at the same time, as humane as possible.[1]

On June 21, Lord Lyndhurst having moved that Lord Cottenham's *Creditors and Debtors Bill* be referred to a select committee, Lord Denman made an earnest appeal against the proposal :

"He confessed the very principle of the abolition of imprisonment for debt was now placed in great jeopardy. If it was not the intention of his noble and learned friend (Lord Lyndhurst) to abolish imprisonment for debt, then he would press it upon the noble duke personally, and with the greatest energy, that he, as minister of this country, should lend all the weight of his high character and station to bring this matter to a real and decisive issue, in order that they might not go from month to month, and from year to year, playing with the feelings of a great body of people who were entitled to their lordships' commiseration, and also leaving in doubt what the actual law of the country on so important a subject was to be."[2]

In the summer of 1844, commenced the long and angry discussions that arose on the subject of the *opening of Mazzini's letters at the Post Office,* under warrant from Sir James Graham, the Secretary of State of the Home Department in Sir Robert Peel's administration.

Lord Radnor having brought on the subject in the House of Lords, on June 17, 1844, Denman spoke, as he felt, very strongly on the matter, as one of vast importance, not only to foreigners resident in this country, but also to our own people.

"Could anything [he asked] be more revolting to the feelings than that any man might have all his letters opened in consequence of some information having been given about him to the Secretary of State? or that the contents of letters he might never have received, might be made use of for the purpose of proceeding against him in a Court of Justice? The letters of a man might be opened, and he might not have the slightest intimation that he had been betrayed. How is such a state of

[1] Hansard, Parl. Deb., third series, vol. lxxiv. pp. 985-1005.

[2] Hansard, Parl. Deb., third series, vol. lxxv. p. 1204.

things to be tolerated in a free country? He must say, without the slightest hesitation, that it ought not to be borne with for a single hour."[1]

Lord Radnor having renewed his motion on June 25, Denman again spoke on the question. He said:

"It was imperative on Parliament to inquire into the mode in which this power was exercised, and to ascertain whether rules could not be laid down under which alone the power could ever usefully, beneficially, or consistently with honor, be exercised at all.

"He thought it very doubtful whether the Secretary of State, *acting alone and as an individual minister*, had this right; whether it was not confined to the Secretary of State acting in concert with all the ministers representing the Government. That such power might be so vested *in the whole* Government, from the necessity of the case, which might be so overpowering as to form a temporary excuse for the suspension and violation of all law, no one would deny. But that the power should be suffered to exist in a manner so oppressive, without the slightest opportunity of any reparation, or any responsibility, was what he did not think an English Parliament or the English people would any longer endure.

"He did not think this a question of expediency or inexpediency, but a question of right and wrong. He could no more believe it necessary to show that such a power ought not to be vested in the discretion of any individual than he should feel it necessary to argue that it was wrong to pick a pocket."[2]

In the summer of this same year, 1844, the Chief Justice presided on his favorite old circuit, the Midland, whence he sent Lady Denman a letter, begun at Leicester and ended at Coventry, under somewhat whimsical circumstances:

"What do you think, my dearest Love, gives me this opportunity of writing to you? S———'s having forgotten to pack up my hat, for want of which I can not get forward to Coventry, but sit in the back room behind the now empty court at Leceister, waiting till that valuable piece of property is brought. Well, then, I must

[1] Hansard, Parl. Deb., third series, vol. lxxv., pp. 975–986.

[2] Hansard, Parl. Deb., third series, vol. lxxv. pp. 1338–1340.

tell you I went over to Godderly yesterday; towards the afternoon the weather, which had been rainy in the morning, cleared up, the horses were got ready, and the Colonel took Tom and me a ride of some twelve miles over that most smiling country. It reminded me of the old times, when your father [Rev. R. Vevers, of Saxby] used to take me on horseback with him over the same district;—we were never a single moment without bright sunshine, and I never enjoyed a more agreeable ride."

Here the Leicester letter breaks off, and the narrative is continued the next day from Coventry:

"Then came the hat, since which we have proceeded to Coventry, opened the Commission, charged the Grand Jury, attended divine service, and returned to Court, where we are now sitting till the cases are ready for trial. The church is that which displays the beautiful spire, its size is immense, and it was quite full of people, a thing almost unknown on week days, and a proof, I fear, that work is very scarce here with the multitude.

"I have just received and accepted an invitation to dine with Lord Leigh on Saturday, but I trust the break-down of the business here, before that time, will enable me to excuse myself there, or, at all events, that Sunday will bring me to you."

Writing the next day from the same place, he tells his wife how he had found time, while at Leicester, to ride over to her late father's old living at Saxby, where he had visited the church, "to which," he writes, "I owe the greatest blessings of my life." It was there that they had been married nearly forty years before.

From Middleton, a few days after this, he writes to Mr. Justice Coleridge, who had just completed the North Wales Circuit:

"August 13, 1844.

"My dear Coleridge,—Your letter gave me the greatest pleasure: among other reasons because it supplied a want, no other Circuit having passed without a letter from a judicial brother. Since coming here on Sunday night I have heard from Williams, in all the luxury of ire at the O'Connell arrangement.[1] The numerous

[1] By which the judges were summoned to give their opinions in the House

points ought be fully discussed among us. Coltman[1] seemed to feel much doubt on the whole matter, but judges on circuit have other things to occupy them. Cottenham [then Lord Chancellor] was struck with the difficulties which seem to beset you—the counts and findings. Campbell thought the Swearing-before-Grand-Jury-Act almost, if not altogether, fatal. I have somehow conquered my objection on the former, and think I could get over the latter, though the words are surely hard and obstinate. *But the jury-panel is my stumbling-block and scandal.* Is the challenge to the array taken away entirely? If not, must it not be in force, wherever there is default in the Sheriff (or any of those officers who by recent acts are appointed to divide among them his ancient duties)—a default, I mean, of such a nature as to provide for the party a different array from what the law contemplates? and can this be more effectually done than by cutting a monstrous cantling out of it (the jury panel)? Such is the state of opinion to which I brought myself in the few days between the Guildhall sittings and Northampton [the commencement of the circuit]. That opportunity I took of rummaging the few cases cited by Lord Coke from the Year Books, the principal one of which I translated, and will send it to you if you would like to have it. Some expressions are remarkable: of the other points I think nothing.

"Your circuit is a succession of agreeable pictures. I must visit North Wales once more, for the sake of Llanberris—hitherto by some accident always left unvisited, and, from report, the best worth seeing of all. The Midland is always agreeable to me from "aulde lang syne," and Coltman is a most easy and pleasant companion. Civil causes few, but some of them rather heavy; criminal work not overpowering, but the time well filled. The proportion of entries in the different Courts [Queen's Bench, Common Pleas, and Exchequer] almost the same as you describe. Our country is beau-

of Lords on the legal points raised in the O'Connell case during the Long Vacation.

[1] Sir Thomas Coltman, born 1781; Fellow of Trinity College, Cambridge, 1805; King's Counsel, 1832; Judge of Common Pleas, 1837; died of cholera, 1849. Mr. Justice Coltman had this summer traveled the Midland Circuit with the Chief Justice.

tiful now; the Marshal and Georgiana [present Lord Denman and his first wife] leave us for Devonshire in a few days, and speak with much pleasure of seeing you during your abode there.[1]

"The loss of Erskine[2] is indeed grievous; my notion would rather be favorable to a change of climate and scene, but you are better acquainted with his condition."

In the course of the same letter he avows himself a stanch believer in the personal unity of Homer, and adds some gossip as to his general Long Vacation reading:

"I suppose 'Keeble's Prælectiones' are in Latin, which I can not relish, but I like his Homer-worship, and am fully convinced of the falsehood of Payne Knight's heresy that he was more than one. I should be glad to father the 'Battle of the Gods' on some journeyman, but all the rest is the consistent work of one great genius, a man of the most enlarged wisdom and the most exalted liberality—witness those extraordinary speeches of Hector and Sarpedon. He is excelled by none but Shakespeare. [Lord] Nugent left us yesterday, overflowing with Athens and Palestine, and I hope will make a readable book of travels. My principal study has been Burke's 'Correspondence,' which verifies Goldsmith's character of him wonderfully. His unpracticality and clumsiness in affairs form a curious contrast to his noble character and gifted mind. I think it a most instructive and improving work, 'Lord Malmesbury' [Life of] is also very good reading. The 'Quarterly Review' stimulated me to order (at our book club) that strange so-called biography of William Taylor, but there is no interest in it, except the ill-nature, and Lockhart managed to bring that all out in speaking of his deceased fellow-laborer. Arnold's life has not yet come round to me. Do you much admire his lectures on history? Guizot's lectures on European civilization have also been a study of mine—rather too vague, but acute and very sensible—they make me desirous of knowing his views

[1] At Mr. Justice Coleridge's country seat of Heath's Court, Ottery St. Mary, Devon.

[2] Right Hon. Thomas Erskine, son of the great advocate: born, 1788; King's Counsel, 1827; Judge of Common Pleas, 1839; retired from ill-health, November, 1844; died November, 1864.

on our Civil Wars. What he says in a letter to Brougham on the chances of war at present is nearly in these words: *Pour la guerre il faut que les fous soient devenus les maitres, ou que les sages soient devenus fous.* He proceeds to say that the clamorers for war do not really wish it, but only to remove him, and that if they excite war they certainly will get rid of him, for he will not carry it on."[1]

The celebrated O'Connell case, to which reference is made in the foregoing letter, will be reserved for consideration in the next chapter, the present one may be concluded with the following communication to his daughter, the Honorable Mrs. Hodgson, who, as wife of the Provost of Eton, had lately been partaking of the festivities with which the Queen and Prince Albert had been welcoming Louis Philippe at Windsor Castle in return for the hospitality which the Citizen King had shown them, in the summer of the preceding year, at the Chateau d'Eu.[2]

"Stony Middleton: October 20, 1844.

"My dearest Bessie,—We were quite delighted to see in the papers that you were present at that magnificent banquet at the Castle, and very thankful for your sketch of the proceedings. The visit to you at Eton is a still more interesting subject, and we admire the behavior of all your young ladies, and expect to find them models of courtesy. What a happiness that they and their dear parents are so well.

"Your question about my acquaintance with the French King (or L. P., as Tom styles him) is a poser. One of the peculiarities of Royal memories is a faculty of remembering things that never happened, and those who remember correctly must take care never to destroy their illusions. Possibly, indeed, His Majesty may remember what I forget. The mistake about Recorder and Common Sergeant is of small moment. He used the latter and correct title when Tom and Georgiana [present Lord Denman and his first wife] were presented

[1] This was at the time of the excitement caused by the affair of Pritchard, the British Consul at Otaheite, 1843.

[2] Louis Philippe, on this visit, reached Windsor Castle on October 7, and returned to France, accompanied by a most violent storm, on the 15th.

at Paris. Now, it is possible that during his exile[1] he may have made his appearance before me on some unlucky occasion—but most probably it would be under some fictitious name—at the Court formerly called the Old Bailey. Common people are not fond of reverting to such occurrences, but with kings it may be different.

"As to Captain Denman—he of the name who gave His Majesty a passage—he is no son of mine; if he were we must be counting our seventieth wedding-day at least, instead of our fortieth. He was an officer of some distinction, and commanded a ship in the squadron which took Napoleon to St. Helena. I remember his being afterwards in Burlington Street (Dr. Denman's). I think he is still alive.

"But we must thank you both for your kind congratulations on our festival, which passed off admirably. My Lady looks handsomer than she did in 1804: both of us are extremely well, and shall, to the end of our time, be your affectionate parents.

"I hope to look in at the Lodge some day before Christmas. We are getting all in order for you here next summer. I talk of paying Joe and his wife a short visit at the inn at Bolton Abbey."

The "festival" mentioned in the concluding sentences of the letter just cited was the fortieth anniversary of Lord and Lady Denman's wedding-day (October 18, 1844). The expression as to Lady Denman looking handsomer at sixty-five than she did at twenty-five,[2] must, of course, be set down, in a great measure, to the amiable delusion of a husband who had never ceased to be a lover; but the fact is that Lady Denman *did* preserve her good looks to a very advanced period of her life. The strength and romance of the attachment that still subsisted between Denman and his wife is not ill expressed in the following simple lines that had passed between them, in this very year (1844), on occasion of his birthday (February 21).

[1] As Denman was not Common Sergeant till 1822, and the exile of Louis Philippe had terminated eight years before, in 1814, this seems not a possible solution.

[2] Lady Denman was born in November 21, 1799, in the same year as her husband, but about nine months later.

The wife writes:

"Noble, generous, brave, and kind,
Graceful in person as in mind,
With manners elegant, and wit refined,
Most justly is he loved by all mankind.
With knowledge deep, and memory strong,
No worldly motives lead him wrong,
If thus abroad his virtues shine,
Oh think how blest a lot is mine."

The husband replies:

"Though well I know that Love is blind,
Oft fancying what no eye can see,
A wife's dear praises may remind
The husband what he ought to be."

Those have not lived in vain, who, after forty years of wedlock, cherish for each other such feelings as these.

CHAPTER XXX.

THE JUDGMENT IN O'CONNELL'S CASE.

A. D. 1844. ÆT. 65.

THE celebrated judgment in O'Connell's case tended in a high degree to confirm the public estimate of Lord Denman as one fearlessly determined, with a single eye to truth and justice, and a total disregard to possible ulterior consequences, to carry out to the uttermost the views he had deliberately formed as to the real rights of every case brought before him for decision.

The noble and lofty strain of dignified judicial eloquence which pervaded the judgment produced its full effect on all who read it, while those who were fortunate enough to hear it will never forget the impressive tones and inimitable manner of the speaker.

A very brief sketch of the previous history of the O'Connell case, of the points presented for decision in the House of Lords, and of Lord Denman's opinion upon them, is all that will be here attempted.

In the year 1843, the great agitator entered upon his campaign of "Monster Meetings" for the repeal of the Union. Beginning with an assemblage of 30,000 at Trim, on March 14, the numbers at these gatherings had increased, by August 15, to 250,000 at Tara, and on October 8, a still vaster multitude was expected to assemble at Clontarf.

The Government at length resolved to act with vigor. On October 7, they issued a proclamation prohibiting the Clontarf meeting for the next day; on the 14th, O'Connell (with others) was arrested on a charge of conspiracy and sedition; on February 12, 1844, after a protracted trial, he was convicted; and on May 24, after long arguments before the Irish Court of Queen's Bench, he was sentenced to a year's imprisonment and a fine of £2,000.

A writ of error having been moved for, two principal objections against the validity of this sentence were argued before the House of Lords.

The first objection was this: that sixty names of qualified special jurors had been improperly omitted from the list sent by the Recorder to the Sheriff for the purpose of making up the jurors' book and special jurors' list, and that the array selected for the trial of O'Connell was made up from the list so mutilated.

This objection had been taken at the trial, and the array challenged (i. e. objected to) on this ground. It had also been argued on demurrer to the challenge of the array before the Judges of the Queen's Bench in Ireland, sitting in Banc, and by them, with only one dissenting voice, overruled.

The second objection, though not completely technical, was more so than the first. It arose thus: The indictment was of monstrous length, and contained several counts (or separate charges). Some of these counts were held to be void in law. Yet the verdict and judgment were general; that is, given generally upon the whole of the indictment, not separately on each separate count of the indictment. The objection was that such general judgment was bad, and could not be taken to apply to the good counts only. This objection had not been taken before the Irish Judges.

The first objection was obviously the more substantial, for it was founded on this—that the accused party was not tried by such a jury as by law he had a right to be tried by.

The Judges of England, as is usual in cases of great difficulty, were summoned to give the House of Lords the benefit of their opinion on both points.

With the single exception of Mr. Justice Coleridge, who, though too ill to attend the House, had intimated in writing to Lord Denman that he inclined to think the mutilation of the jury-list a good ground of challenge to the array, all the Judges of England were unanimously against the first objection.

With regard to the second objection, six of the English

Judges thought it invalid, against two (Parke and Coltman) who were of the contrary opinion.

The weight of judicial authority, therefore, preponderated immensely against both the objections.

In the House of Lords, where judgment was pronounced on September 4, the majority was the other way: Lords Lyndhurst and Brougham were against the validity of the objections; Lords Cottenham, Campbell, and Denman in favor of it. The majority prevailed, the sentence was quashed, and O'Connell released from custody.

No one in the profession of the law now doubts that on both points the judgment of the majority of the Law Lords was right, and there is, perhaps, no judgment on record which has had a more wholesome effect in curing the looseness of the previous practice of Criminal Courts, both in England and Ireland.

It required some moral courage to pronounce a decision in direct contravention to so vast a preponderance (in fact, as regards the first objection, to so close an approach to absolute unanimity) of opinion on the part of the Judges of England. But, Denman, clear in the correctness of his own opinion, and animated by a high sense of duty, was superior to any feelings of moral timorousness on an occasion like this. Admitting that the Lords were bound to respect in the highest degree, and consider with the utmost care, the opinion of the judges, he added: "But, my Lords, you have a duty of your own to perform. *Your* consciences are to be satisfied, *your* minds are to be made up; your privilege affords you the assistance of the most learned men living, but your duty forbids you to delegate your office to them."

In order fully to appreciate the vigor and closeness of his arguments, the masterly judgment of Lord Denman must be studied in its entirety; an extract here and there will, however, serve to indicate generally the line of its reasoning, and to show the loftiness and earnestness of its tone.

The key-note is struck in the very opening sentences, which conclude with the memorable phrase which has ever since become one of the household words of the English language:

"My Lords, in considering the important questions involved in the case now before your lordships, it appears to me convenient to advert, in the first place, to that which has been last argued by my noble and learned friend who has just sat down [Lord Brougham]—I mean the objection to the judgment given in the Court below, allowing the demurrer to the challenge to the array.

"I am induced to begin with this subject, not only because it is preliminary in the course of the proceedings, but because it is important, to a degree that does not admit of exaggeration, to the administration of justice throughout the United Kingdom; for, if it is possible that such a practice as that which has taken place in the present instance should be allowed to pass without remedy (and no other remedy than that of the challenge to the array has been suggested), *trial by jury itself, instead of being a security to persons who are accused, will be a* MOCKERY, *a* DELUSION, *and a* SNARE."

The narrow ground upon which the Judges had held that the challenge to the array (admittedly the only remedy) was not open to the defendant was this: that challenge to the array, as the precedents proved, could only be allowed in cases where there had been default by the *Sheriff*, whereas, in the case under argument, there had been no default in the *Sheriff;* the mutilation of the list had not been the act of the *Sheriff*, but of the Recorder or other functionary who had delivered the list, already mutilated, into the Sheriff's hands.

Against this view, which made the remedy of the aggrieved party depend not upon the question whether he had or had not been tried by a lawfully constituted jury, but upon the question, wholly foreign to him, whether the Sheriff had or had not been a wrong-doer, Denman thus protested:

"The traversers (defendants) have challenged the array on account of the fraudulent omission of sixty names from the list of jurors of the County of the City of Dublin. The Attorney-General demurs to that challenge, admitting thereby that that fact has taken place.[1] It

[1] It is a familiar doctrine in law that he who demurs, i. e. objects to the legal sufficiency of any claim or defense, admits the truth of all the facts stated therein. The *wrongful omission of the sixty names* was, therefore,

appears to me that that challenge ought to have been allowed. I think that the principle of Challenge to the Array is not confined to the narrow issue whether the Sheriff has done wrong, *but involves that larger question whether the party has had the security of trial by a lawful jury of his county*."

With great force and cogency of argument, the Chief Justice, on bases not to be shaken, established this point, that *the true principle of the Challenge to the Array is the party's security that a jury shall be fairly taken*; and that if not fairly taken, he has a right to say he has not been lawfully tried, and on that ground to demand the reversal of any adverse verdict that such a jury may have given against him.

With regard to the argument of the practical inconvenience that might arise from visiting with consequences so serious the culpable carelessness of the ministerial functionary of the Court, be he Sheriff, or other officer upon whom by Act of Parliament has been cast a portion of the Sheriff's duty, Lord Denman's mode of dealing with it is conclusive: "I humbly ask," he says, "what balance is there between the two sets of inconvenient consequences? Is it not right to hold the public officer to the strict and faithful discharge of his easy duty? Can anything be more wrong than that he should enjoy full license to tamper with these sacred documents [the jury lists] according to his pleasure?"

But perhaps no part of the judgment is more conclusive and convincing than that which points out that if the Challenge to the Array be excluded a great and admitted wrong would be left absolutely without remedy or redress:

"Now, my Lords, what follows appears to me to be of the very highest importance. That there may be the greatest wrong and injury committed by the omission of names from the list is universally acknowledged. And the Chief Justice[1] says, 'that there must be some mode of relief for an injury occasioned by such non-observance

admitted in this case by the demurrer to the challenge, because such fact was stated as the ground of challenge.

[1] Tindal, who had delivered the opinion of the Judges on the first objection.

of the directions of an Act of Parliament is undeniable.' So all the judges in Ireland still more emphatically assert. So says my noble and learned friend on the woolsack [Lord Lyndhurst]. So says my noble and learned friend who has just addressed your lordships [Lord Brougham]. What, then, is the mode of relief?

"My noble and learned friend on the woolsack did certainly raise my expectations to a very high pitch upon the subject. In one part of his argument he said, 'The party is not without a remedy; the party can set himself right. There may have been a great error, a great injury, a great mistake, but there is a correction of that mistake; there is a redress for that error; there is a prevention of future injustice by such a trial as the law never contemplates, and would not have endured.' Then I wanted to hear from that high authority what is that remedy? what is that redress? and what is that mode of preventing one of the Queen's subjects accused from being tried by such a jury as the law never provided for him? 'Oh,' says my noble and learned friend, 'you must excuse me there. I shall put off telling you what the remedy is to some future occasion'—as if any occasion could more pressingly require that statement.

"When my Lord Chief Justices and the other learned Judges of England, and the learned Judges of Ireland, and my Lord Chancellor, can inform us of no remedy whatever against this, which is admitted to be possibly the greatest wrong, and productive of the greatest confusion and interference with the security of the law which it is possible for man to contemplate, I will venture to go a step further, and to declare affirmatively that (supposing the challenge to the array to be excluded) the law provides no remedy; and I will not believe that the law can have placed its subjects in such a situation. Unless I see the old and well-known constitutional practice of challenge to the array—founded primarily on the principle of the array being itself incorrect and injurious to the party, although involving also the question of criminality in the Sheriff as an officer of the Court—unless I see that ancient process repealed by a direct Act of Parliament—I will not believe that that remedy is not still reserved to the subject. *The absence of all other remedy in a case of such immense importance is to me demonstrative proof that that old remedy still exists, that the objection has been well taken, that the challenge ought to have been allowed—and that the trial has erroneously proceeded.* If this be otherwise, if the old redress is abrogated and no new one provided, that improved law, which was intended to place the constitution of juries beyond all abuse and all suspicion, would have the effect of securing success to the worst manœuvres, and of unsettling the public confidence in the most important function of justice."

Not less powerful, though from the more technical nature of the reasons less generally interesting, was his argument on the other objection, namely, that a General Judgment on an indictment containing many counts, some of which were admitted to be bad, could not be supported.

That the objection, indeed, was not wholly of a technical character he very clearly pointed out. "So far from being merely technical," he said, "it may involve the greatest injustice, because you may inflict the heaviest punishment for the lightest offense, or, indeed, for that which may turn out to be no subject of punishment at all." In another part of his judgment he puts the same point still more tersely. "To pass sentence for three offenses, where a party is well convicted of only two, can not be right."

In this part of his argument, Lord Denman animadverted with becoming severity on an abuse which was then prevalent in English Criminal Law procedure, and which, though since much abated by legislative enactment, has not yet wholly been got rid of—the cumbrous length and formality of criminal indictments, especially those for conspiracy and kindred offenses.

"I must take the liberty," he said, "of throwing out the observation that in my opinion, there can not be a much greater grievance or oppression than these endless, voluminous, and unintelligible indictments. An indictment which fills fifty-seven close folio pages,[1] is an abuse to be put down, not a practice to be encouraged."

The judgment of Lord Denman and the majority of

[1] As did the indictment in O'Connell's case.

the House of Lords on this second objection, has since been universally followed in the administration of the Criminal Law. It is, indeed, obvious, when once pointed out, that, as every count states a distinct offense, the verdict ought also to state upon what particular counts the jury find a prisoner guilty, and the judgment ought to follow the verdict. The decision in O'Connell's case has entirely put an end to the loose practice which had so long prevailed, of giving a general verdict and judgment on an indictment comprising several distinct charges.[1]

Lord Denman's admirable judgment, though, of course, the result of long and anxious research and reflection, was mainly oral, and, in its language, extemporaneous. This circumstance, undoubtedly, added very much to its effect in delivery, and enabled those references to be made to the arguments of previous speakers which so much enhance the spirit and animation of a spoken discourse, but are, of course, impossible in a written composition.

A writer in the *Morning Post*, not favorable to the conclusion arrived at by the majority of the Law Lords, had expressed himself, in reference to Lord Denman's judgment, to the following effect:

"The dignified impressiveness of his Lordship's manner, and the graceful earnestness of his elocution, are such, that they not only engage the attention, but almost win the assent of any feeling auditory, even before the subject-matter is fully compassed by the understanding."

The *Morning Chronicle* of the following day, commenting on this passage, observed:

"Whoever had the good fortune to be present on the occasion, will certainly never forget the effect produced

[1] The advocate who had the great merit of raising and arguing with rare ability this new and important point was Mr. (now the Right Hon. Sir Barnes) Peacock, formerly legal member of the Supreme Council in India, and Chief Justice of Calcutta, now one of the Judges of the Court of Appeal. A strong proof how long bad law may prevail if not questioned, is to be found in Lord Denman's frank avowal: "I felt, as my learned brothers did, great surprise when I heard the most able and ingenious argument that was addressed to the House on this point, and I confess I had never felt any doubt on the subject till that argument was submitted to my mind. But I must add that I never had occasion to give judicial consideration to the matter."

by the qualities which our contemporary describes. But we confidently believe, that, however much that audience was overpowered by the noble delivery of noble sentiments, gushing forth with hearth-warm sincerity in the defense of liberty, and finding utterance in a voice of incomparable beauty, still, the force of his Lordship's arguments upon the reason of his hearers, must have been equal to that of his personal qualities on their sesnibility; and that, after the subject-matter had been 'fully compassed by the understanding,' the calm decision of their intellects must have confirmed all the prepossessions that had previously been produced on the feelings."

The action of the speaker was not less impressive than his delivery: his son George (now the Honorable Mr. Justice Denman), who was present, was particularly struck by the mode in which he expressed his sense of the manner in which the law had been violated by the mutilation of the jury list: "This, my Lords," he said, holding a long slip of paper in his hand, "is the jury panel to which the defendants had a right by law, and this," he added, tearing off a third and holding up the residue, "this is all that, *in fact*, the defendants had allowed them." [1]

The effect of the judgment on the profession and the public was great and instantaneous, and Denman received from all competent quarters the warmest assurances of adhesion to the opinions he had pronounced, and of admiration for the fearlessness and ability with which he had expressed them.

The general opinion of the more enlightened part of the public was thus well expressed by the *Morning Chronicle*, then the leading organ of the Opposition :

"This masterly judgment will transmit the name of Lord Denman with the highest luster to the remotest posterity, as long as the people of this country shall continue, and we hope that to the end of all time they will continue, to be distinguished for their irrepressible attachment to the principles of civil liberty, and their

[1] Mr. Justice Denman adds a curious circumstance. Walking down with his father from the House after the delivery of the judgment, and praising, among other things, the celebrated words, "a mockery, a delusion, and a snare." "Ah," said Lord Denman, "I am sorry I used those words; they were not judicial."

determination to secure at all hazards the immaculate administration of justice."

Of the many letters which Denman at this time received on the subject of his judgment, few gratified him more than one written to him by Shadwell—the comrade of his school and college days, and the intimate of his maturer years, the excellent and warm-hearted man of whose long and close connection with his father, his son George has written: "Intimate at Eton, at Cambridge, and at Lincoln's Inn, they may be said to have gone through life arm-in-arm together."

The Vice-Chancellor, who was then enjoying his Long Vacation in the country, wrote as follows:

"Studley Park: September 7, 1844.

"My dear Denman,—Yesterday the papers arrived at the place where I happened to be by the sea-side, in Durham. I immediately sat down to read the speeches in the House of Lords, which appeared to be given verbatim, and, except a few errors in the names of cases, &c., accurately.

"The speeches of yourself and the Chancellor [Lyndhurst] appeared to me to be remarkably characteristic, and I was so much pleased with the display of the natural firmness and nobility of mind exhibited in your speech, that I could talk of nothing else and think of nothing else. I allude especially to what you said as to the challenge of the array. Everything seemed so fair and so just, so consistent with the Saxon notions exemplified in our early history, that I could not help feeling in how distinguished a position you were placed by the sentiments that you uttered, and which I know you have cherished from the time when we first met together as friends. I was so full of this feeling of admiration that I could not help sending you a line to tell you so. I think it is a matter of great importance that the question on the writ of error has been decided in a manner that proves the fairness with which law is administered in this great and glorious country, with such a Chief Justice at its head. "Believe me, dear Denman,

"Ever yours, very sincerely,

"LAUNCELOT SHADWELL.

His friend, Empson, Jeffrey's son-in-law, at that time Principal of Haileybury College, and Editor of the "Edinburgh Review," writes as follows, looking at the matter from a somewhat different and more political point of view:

"A few words only, my dear Denman, to tell you with what delight Jeffrey and myself read your judgment yesterday. It is quite a relief to me, a burden and a blot off my mind, that this Irish trial is got rid of—judicially expunged—and the public satisfied. What I feel at it is very much heightened by the part you have taken in it; especially in all you say about the jury system. Looking at the subject in another point of view, one may fairly hope that the moral and political effect of this judgment will tell more decidedly against the alleged facts, reasonings, and feelings, by which the Repeal steam has been got up, than anything else that has been or that could have been done."

With the probable political consequences of his judgment, Denman had, of course, nothing to do, when delivering his opinion, as one of the Law Lords, on the writ of error. But it was the general, and probably not ill-founded belief of reasonable men at the time, that the release of O'Connell was a fortunate circumstance for Sir Robert Peel's Government. The vigor which had been shown, had, for the time, completely disconcerted the Repealers,[1] while the executive were spared the necessity of carrying out sentences which would have exasperated Ireland from one end to the other, stirring up to a fierce fever heat the ever-ready hatred which is the sad, and it would almost seem the unappeasable, Nemesis for long centuries of misgovernment and wrong.

Denman seems himself to have been of opinion that the political effect of the reversal of the sentence would probably be beneficial, at least for a time. Writing from Middleton, on September 29, to his brother-in-law, the Rev. R. Vevers, he says:

[1] The sentence destroyed O'Connell's prestige, and prayed upon his health and spirits. He never recovered the shock, and died a broken man less than three years afterwards, on his way to Rome, at Genoa, on May 15, 1847, æt. seventy-two.

"I rejoice in your agreement with me, in thinking that the decision of the 6th instant may have a good effect in Ireland. Of course we, who had to consider points of law only, could have nothing to do with consequences, but it is delightful to think that these are also likely to be beneficial. My speech is about to be published separately, and it *must* have the effect of reforming the scandalous abuses that have prevailed in the selection of juries in Ireland. I must tell you that Coleridge (who agreed with me about the array) writes me word that he is much inclined to think the Lords right on the *counts* also, and that Erskine's leaning is the same way. Thus, the majority of the English Judges is materially diminished, and the argument is really too clear for doubt. Paragraphs are now and then sent me showing how greatly O'Connell's animosity is tamed by the reversal." [1]

A few days before, on September 20, Denman had written to Mr. Justice Coleridge a letter, the following passages from which are of some interest in reference to what took place both before and at the time of the delivery of Judgment on September 4:

"Tindal's inconsiderate statement of your opinion [as coinciding with that of the rest of the Judges on the first objection] left me no alternative but to read your letter, which at once qualified the unanimity on the array. The week before our appointed day of meeting, Brougham wrote to me on the subject of his Insolvency Bill (he is called 'The Liberator')[2] and my answer told him of my doubts on the array. He said he had felt no

[1] The immediate effect of the judgment in Ireland may be gathered from the following paragraphs from the *Dublin Evening Post*: "It would be an idle attempt—we acknowledge it—to express adequately the veneration we feel for the three Whig Lords who saved England and the Empire from the infamy of confirming the judgment of the Irish Judges, and it is needless to add that we are utterly incapable of finding words to express our admiration for the Lord Chief Justice of England. While he lives—and long, long may he enjoy his honors, and his dignity, and his fame! long may England glory in her first Judge, as Ireland shall long remember him with gratitude and exultation—as long as Denman lives no such gross injustice will be allowed to go unstigmatized or unpunished. The example will be enduring as the Constitution."

[2] From his bill proposing to abolish imprisonmont for debt. It is hardly necessary to say that "the Liberator" was then the Irish name for O'Connell.

doubt, but would reconsider it. On the Monday night we had some talk on it: the following day I gave him my collection to read. He returned them at night, saying he had read them with much fruit, but without conviction. In the meantime, Parke [Mr. Baron Parke, afterwards Lord Wensleydale] had stated his doubts on the second point [as to the counts]. On this point my mind had undergone exactly the same fluctuations that you describe. I saw no answer to his arguments, and am convinced there is none. But I prayed for a consultation of the five Law Lords on the Wednesday morning, not without some idea that my doubts [on the counts] might be removed, nor without some hopes that Lyndhurst might be convinced [on the first point, as to the array], and that on this point, after another day's consideration, Brougham might give way. This was not thought expedient. Nothing could be better in language and manner than Lyndhurst's speech, but his clearness only served to light up the hollow vacuity of his case. I *spoke* with due preparation and great care. Brougham *read* his judgment. It fell to me, as next in seniority, to follow him. I had prepared a *written* judgment on the array, much fuller and better than what I delivered but, having written nothing on the second point [the counts], I thought it best to *speak* all. Cottenham and Campbell had both written. I am perfectly confident of the assent of the *εἶς μὲν ἐπιστάμενος* who can read and think, and will lead the *τρὶς μυρίοι*, and I shall still call the *ἀναριθμοι, οὐδεὶς* knowing that they have had but one principle of judging, namely—'Dan is in prison, and it is much the best place for him.' Tom diverts me by a quotation from Woolner: 'He was misled by that crotchet, Trial by Jury.'"

On the *second* objection, the two Judges who gave their opinion in favor of it, against the six who opposed it, were Parke and Coltman. There were people found base enough to insinuate that Parke, in giving his judgment on this point, had been influenced by resentment against the Government, for having, in the preceding April, appointed the then Attorney-General, Sir Frederick Pollock, instead of himself, to be Chief Baron of the Exchequer on Lord Abinger's death. It is to this base and ridiculously groundless imputation that reference is made in the following passage from the letter now under citation:

"The leaning of your opinion and Erskine's [in favor of the second objection] is to me a very pleasing circumstance, nor can I doubt that if more time and pains had been taken, other Judges might have come round. The interests of justice and the cause of truth are infinitely indebted to Parke, who kept not only his political feelings, but his personal fear of imputations, which were sure to be cast, and which were cast. 'If he had but been made Chief Baron.' His weight of authority required much less courage in me in coming to the right decision [on the second point] than if Coltman had stood alone, though I hope that even then I should have seen the right and acted on it."[1]

A still fuller account of many of the circumstances attending this celebrated judgment, and particularly of the rapidity with which Denman had in the end to make up his mind on the question of the counts, is contained in the following letter to his son-in-law, H. W. Macaulay, the brother of Lord Macaulay, and first husband of Denman's fourth daughter, Margaret, a gentleman for whose character and talents his father-in-law had a high esteem, and who was then residing with his wife and children at Buena Vista, Cape de Verde Islands:

"Middleton: September 9, 1844.

"My dear Henry,—I thought my proximity to head-quarters would make it worth your while to hear from me on the O'Connell case, and I proceed to the performance of my promise by telling you that after fagging hard at the legal points in it, I set off by rail on September 1, reached home late in the evening, and saw no one but George [now Mr. Justice Denman], till both he and I went to the House of Lords on the 2nd.

"Tindal pronounced the unanimous opinion of the Judges on nine of the eleven questions submitted. The

[1] In reference to this base imputation, Denman, in his letter of September 29, to his brother-in-law, had said, "Pray if your county paper contains any extracts from *Herald* or *Standard*, imputing Parke's opinion to his disappointment in not being made Chief Baron, take the trouble of either sending me the paper or copying the paragraph."

third and the eleventh, on which a difference existed, were resolvable into one [the question of the counts].

"But I had conceived an inveterate opinion that the jury was unlawfully composed. Coleridge, with whom I had had some correspondence, warmly agreed with me on this point.

"On the other point [that of the counts], Parke and Coltman dissented from the general opinion of the judges. To this point I had given comparatively little attention, and was bound to examine it with care.

"George and I dined at Brougham's on Monday. On Tuesday he took us to his brother-in-law's (Eden) at Wimbledon, where we dined and slept. Two pleasanter evenings I never passed, but Brougham and I could not agree on the controversy.

"On Wednesday morning (the 4th), all resorted again to the Lords, and the papers will inform you what passed there. They, however, do not know that I had hardly made up my mind on the third and eleventh questions [the counts], and expected that all the Law Lords would have a meeting and talk the matter over before we gave our judgment. At the last moment I was told that this could not be, and had to consider the arguments of the Chancellor [Lyndhurst] and Brougham before I delivered or had even finally formed my own opinion.

"I must say that on both the points the law came out at last as clear to my mind as the sun which is just now emerging from the clouds.

"1. The jury by which the parties were tried was not that to which they were legally entitled, and so the whole proceeding fell to the ground.

"2. Some counts of the indictment were bad in law, but the Court in Dublin awarded the punishment on those, as well as the rest, from the impossibility of dividing or apportioning it, or of discovering how much of it belonged to one set of counts, how much to the other; and so it follows that the whole must fall.

"Cottenham and Campbell took the same view. Thus the Law Lords were 3 to 2. The Lay Lords wished to vote, but Lord Wharncliffe[1] persuaded them to with-

[1] At the instance of the Duke of Wellington.

draw, not without much difficulty. The prisoners, therefore, walk out of the penitentiary.

"What will be the consequence? That most naturally to be expected is a feeling, for a time at least, of reconcilement to England. The Liberator is weakened, I think, by losing this grievance. Had the result been different, it seems to me that the weakness of the legal arguments would have convinced nine-tenths of Ireland and three-fourths of England, that the judgment was a political one; and, if the Lay Lords had succeeded in overthrowing the majority of those called learned, to whom all the judicial business in the last resort is confided, surely rebellion would have blazed out, with no bad apology, in Ireland. No doubt, the Duke sent Wharncliffe to prevent so great a scandal, but the Ministry had committed the incredible fault of circulating treasury notes to require the attendance of their regular majority, who were, not unreasonably, unwilling to abstain from voting.

"My speech has had great success. It gave an unexpected turn to the proceeding. Its reasoning was simple, the matter important, and connected with some of the most popular principles. What infinite mischief if public opinion had been all on one side, but the Peers had decided the other way by the casting vote of the Chief Justice!"

CHAPTER XXXI.

DEATH OF MRS. BAILLIE—SLAVE TRADE—THE "FELICIDADE" CASE—SUGAR DUTIES BILL.

A. D. 1845–1846. ÆT. 66 TO 67.

IN the Parliamentary session of 1845, the discussions on the subject of opening letters at the Post-office, under warrant from a Secretary of State, was renewed in the House of Lords on May 30, on the occasion of Lord Radnor's moving the second reading of a bill which he had introduced for limiting and regulating the practice.

On this occasion Lord Denman spoke at some length, and with great force and eloquence, in favor of the second reading.[1]

He stated the question thus:

"Their Lordships had to consider the grave question whether it was really to be permitted that in England all letters should be subjected to the authority of the Ministers of the Crown—whether the private correspondence of every man in the country should be placed wholly at the discretion of the Secretary of State.

"The power," he contended, "was utterly useless. Neither of the Committees could state an instance in which it had ever done the smallest service to the State.

"In fact, it might be dangerous, for as soon as the practice was known, nothing would be more easy than for seditiously disposed persons to entrap the Government, by false intelligence, carefully and expressly prepared—as, for instance, if the state of the country were such that troops were really wanted, say in the north, to

[1] His speech is reported in Hansard, Parl. Deb., third series, vol. lxxx. pp. 1051-1065.

write such letters as, being opened at the Post-office, might cause the troops to be sent away to the east, west, or south.

"The, Committees, no doubt, have stated that the Secretaries of State would be reluctant to see the power abolished; but who," he asks, "does not like power, whether he expects office, or is at present in office, or has once possessed office?

"This country ought not to be made the police-office of any foreign State whatever.

"Is it possible to imagine a more inconvenient situation than for a Government to be told by some foreign State: 'You have a certain Mazzini living among you. He is a dangerous man. Take care how you deal with him, and don't fail to open his letters, to prevent him from carrying on his revolutionary practices.'

"If England does this for one foreign State, she must do it for all; if we grant this favor to Austria, Naples, or the Pope, how are we to refuse it to the Emperor of Russia, in regard, for instance, to the numerous Poles who have taken refuge in this country?

"He could not agree in the expression of regret that we had not an Alien Act. He thanked God we had not an Alien Act. He remembered the seige that had been laid to that iniquitous Act in the other House of Parliament. Year after year had that siege been carried on, and he did not believe that Sir Robert Peel had yet forgotten the cheers with which he was greeted when he came forward, in 1826, and declared that the Alien Act was gone. He trusted it was gone forever; but this opening of letters was a substitute for it—much less effectual, it is true, but still more dangerous in its results. 1844 was the first year that we had seen the opening of foreign letters for the benefit of foreign States, *bonâ fide* done for that purpose, and for avoiding embarrassment in our relations with those States.

"The practice was new, and, as he thought, dangerous and utterly unknown to the people of England. They were not aware of its existence till it came before Parliament last year. It is true that this power had for a long series of years been actually contained in Acts of Parliament; but to Parliament itself its existence was in fact utterly unknown. It had its origin under Cromwell [respecting the suspicious terrors of whose later days, Lord Denman read the well-known passage from Hume, and then continued—]

"If he wanted a contrast between two individuals, he should find it between Oliver Cromwell and that illustrious man whose victories in war were crowned by his influence in civil affairs—whose victories had all been journeys on the road to peace, and whose moderation and virtues were the pride, the boast, and the bulwark of this country. He wished the Noble Duke would take that contrast into his consideration; would see that the individuals were not more contrasted than the times in which they lived; and that if this hateful power originated in the fears of a gloomy and hypocritical tyrant, there never was a man more proper or more suited to repeal it—to relieve the Government from the odium and the people of England from the oppression and insult of it—than was the Noble Duke himself in the times in which we lived."

Notwithstanding this appeal, the House of Lords, satisfied that for reasons of State the power ought to exist in some shape, and not at all satisfied that it could be adequately defined and modified by the express terms of an Act of Parliament, rejected Lord Radnor's bill by the overwhelming majority of forty-six, in a house of sixty four, the contents being only nine, and the non-contents fifty-five.

Lord Denman drew up and entered on the Journals of the House two protests against the rejection of the bill, one signed by himself and Lord Radnor, the other by himself, Lord Radnor, Lord Campbell, and Lord Kinnaird.

Apart from a short speech which he made on July 3, on moving the second reading of a bill giving judges discretionary power to mitigate punishments affixed to offenses by statute,[1] Lord Denman does not seem to have taken any further active part in debate during the remainder of the session of 1845.

In 1845, Denman sustained a loss which he felt very deeply in the death of his beloved sister and life-long

[1] Hansard, Parl. Deb., third series, vol. lxxxi. 1431.

correspondent, Mrs. Baillie. She died at Hampstead, at the house of her sisters-in-law, Agnes and Joanna Baillie, on August 5, of this year, while the Chief Justice was still detained in the Oxford Circuit.

On July 30, he had written to his wife from Hereford:

"I fear the hopes of recovery at Hampstead are less flattering. George [now Mr. Justice Denman] received an unfavorable report yesterday from Henrietta, and I am afraid we must make up our minds to the worst. There is great consolation in my dear sister's state of mind, and the affectionate care of her children. I have begun a letter to her, finding myself in the unexpected enjoyment of leisure in this quiet city, where there is only one cause for trial. It is the last place on the circuit but two, and there is no appearance of much work ahead of us."

He hurried up to town directly the circuit was over, but arrived too late to be present at his sister's last moments. Writing to Lady Denman immediately on his arrival, on August 7, he says:

"I have just been up to Hampstead, where I have seen the beloved remains, very little altered, quite composed, and much resembling my dear mother. All were greatly distressed, but are now a little recovering from fatigue as well as extreme sorrow, and, I trust, not suffering in health. Among all the endearing remembrances that consoled her last days, I have the happiness of finding that your constant affection and the attention of all our dear children held a high and just place. The old ladies [Agnes and Joanna Baillie] bear up with wonderful composure, but are full of tender feeling. I told them to make this house [38 Portland Place] their home whenever it may suit them to come to London, and promised that we would all exert ourselves to the utmost to make them feel at home."

Mrs. Baillie, who was in her seventy-fifth year when she died, was a most excellent, superior, and highly cultivated person. She had materially assisted in the development and improvement of her beloved brother's mind during his childhood, boyhood, and youth; and, from his Eton school-days to her death, was, for more than half a century, his constant correspondent. With affectionate diligence she copied out all his occasional writings, in prose and verse, drew up a charming sketch of his life, down to his elevation to the Peerage (often quoted from in the present Memoir), welcomed with pride and pleasure every fresh step forward in his brilliant and honorable career, and carefully treasured up every public token of the esteem and reverence with which his countrymen regarded him.'

From the ordinary struggle of mere party politics, Denman, ever since he became Chief Justice of England, had, unlike some of his predecessors, very properly abstained. On questions, however, affecting the social well-being of the community and the general interests of humanity, such as the Reform of the Law and the suppression of the Slave Trade, he had, throughout, taken, and to the last hour of his attendance continued to take, an active part in the House of Lords. In the important question of the Bank Act of 1844, and still more in the Corn Law discussions of 1845 and 1846, though not actively engaging in debate, he took a very deep interest. On "Cash, Corn, and Catholics," his views had always been those of a steady Liberal, and a sound free-trader, and when Sir Robert Peel felt that he could no longer resist the overwhelming case made out by Cobden and Bright for the repeal of the Corn Laws, Denman's sympathies were entirely on the side of the minister who had the courage to act on the opinions which he had been too slow to adopt, but which, when adopted, he spared no sacrifice to enforce. Denman disapproved of Lord John Russell's celebrated letter of November 22, 1845, in favor of a total repeal, as a party move, and was not displeased, when, on Sir Robert Peel's resignation, his lordship failed to form a Cabinet. His views on the short political crisis that terminated, as is well known, before the close of the year 1845, in Sir Robert Peel's resumption of power, may be seen by the following passages from two letters written to his son Joseph (then Captain, now Admiral), the first on December 13, and the second on Christmas Day, 1845. In the first he writes:

[1] The present representative of Dr. Baillie's family is his son, W. H. Baillie, Esq., of Dunsbourne House, near Cirencester.

"To-day's *Chronicle* contradicts the report of an interview between Lord John and Sir Robert, and states difficulty, if not reluctance, in forming a new ministry. It looks as if Lord John's *shell*, which dispersed the Cabinet, had been thrown back to him, and was still blazing so as to threaten burning of fingers, and prevent a new arrangement."

In the letter of the 25th, written after Peel had been reinstated in power, he says:

"Recent political events have in my opinion, inflicted a decisive blow on the Whig party, perhaps on all party. My view is that Lord John had no right to address that letter to his constituents unless he was prepared both with men and measures to enter on a new Government. Lord Grey was the obstacle: he proposed Cobden for office, but did not press him. In the last moment he objected to Palmerston as Foreign Minister, and hence came the explosion. I can not help thinking that Lord John ought (having published his letter) to have proceeded, notwithstanding Lord Grey's refusal to join. I can not agree in any outcry against Peel, whom I think as free to change his mind as Lord John."

Some short time before these events had taken place, the Chief Justice had been a good deal annoyed by the decision of the Court of Criminal Appeal in the case ot the *Felicidade*.

The case arose out of the trial and conviction, on a chargc of murder, before Mr. Baron Platt, at the Exeter Summer Assizes for 1845, of one Serva, a Spaniard, and six other foreigners, under the following circumstances.

On February 26, 1845, the *Felicidade*, a Brazilian schooner, bound on a voyage from the Brazils to Africa, *for the purpose of bringing back a cargo of slaves, and fitted up for the reception of such cargo*, while hovering about sixteen miles off the African coast, and before she had embarked any slaves on board, was taken by the armed boats of Her Majesty's ship *Wasp*, the boats being under the command of Lieutenant Stupart.

The *Felicidade* was then placed under the command of Lieutenant Stupart, with sixteen British seamen, and the Lieutenant was then directed to and did give chase in the *Felicidade* to the *Echo*, another Brazilian vessel.

having 434 slaves on board, and commanded by the chief prisoner, Serva.

After this capture, Lieutenant Stupart placed Mr. Palmer, a midshipman, and nine British seamen on board the *Felicidade*, to which he also transferred Serva, the late master of the *Echo*, and thirteen others of the *Echo's* crew.

Lieutenant Stupart, with the other seven British seamen, himself remained on board the *Echo*.

Within an hour after they had been thus placed on board the *Felicidade*, Serva and the rest of the *Echo* crew rose upon Mr. Palmer and his nine seamen, and, after a short but desperate struggle, succeeded in slaughtering them all, with circumstances of atrocious barbarity.

Mr. Baron Platt, on trying the case, was of opinion, after hearing arguments on the point, that the *Felicidade*, at the time when Serva and his crew rose upon and slew Mr. Palmer and his men, was a British ship, and that, therefore, if the jury should on the evidence pronounce the prisoners guilty, their crime would be not manslaughter but murder. The jury having on the evidence, which was perfectly clear, returned a verdict of guilty, the presiding judge, struck with the horrible and cold-blooded atrocity of the crime, sentenced all the seven prisoners to death by hanging, reserving, however, the legal point argued before him for the decision of the Court of Criminal Appeal, and respiting the execution of his sentence till after such decision should have been pronounced.

The Court of Criminal Appeal was composed of thirteen judges (only two—Cresswell and Coleridge—being absent). They heard two arguments, one on November 20, 1845, by Common lawyers, another on December 3, by Civilians.

On December 11, an overwhelming majority of the judges present at the argument—eleven to two—were of opinion that the conviction was wrong, on the ground of want of jurisdiction, and the prisoners were accordingly discharged.

The two dissentient judges were Lord Denman and Mr. Baron Platt, before whom the case was tried.

Lord Denman's opinion was expressed in the following terms:

"I thought the conviction right. It appeared to me that the possession of the Brazilian vessel by the British officers was a lawful possession, under a seizure by them of the said ship while employed by Brazilian subjects in the Slave Trade, and I thought that the vessel so in possession of British officers, under a general authority from the Crown, was a British vessel for the purpose of founding the jurisdiction of the Court of Admiralty, and, of course, since the late Act, of the Court of Oyer and Terminer sitting at Exeter to try crimes committed on board such vessel.[1]

It is not easy to discover the precise grounds on which the majority of the Court thought that jurisdiction did not exist or was not shown to exist, for, according to the bad custom of the Criminal Court of Appeal, their judgment was pronounced without a statement of the reasons on which it proceeded. From considering, however, the course of the argument as reported, and the occasional remarks let fall by the Judge, it would seem that a circumstance which had great weight with them was this: the *Felicidade*, when taken, though equipped and fitted out for slave-trading, *had no slaves on board*, nor was it shown that she had had any on board in the course of the voyage. Now, though the instructions on board the *Wasp* were, "that vessels are to be detained if there be reasonable ground for suspecting that they are engaged in the Slave Trade," yet, by a former Treaty between England and Portugal, incorporated into the Treaty then in force between England and Brazil, it was distinctly stipulated that "no British cruisers shall detain *any slave-ship, not having slaves actually on board.*" As this was precisely the case of the *Felicidade* when taken, the Court probably proceeded on the ground that her capture and detention was illegal, that she therefore never became a British ship, and consequently the offense was one which a British Court had no jurisdiction to try.

Denman went on the broader ground that these

[1] The case is reported in Denison's "Crown Cases reserved," vol. i. pp. 104–156.

prisoners, being Brazilian subjects, caught in carrying on the Slave Trade, by British officers intrusted with the suppression of that trade, were pirates by the Treaty between England and Brazil, in 1826, and the 7 and 8 Geo. IV. c. 74, and, consequently, that their slave ship, the *Felicidade*, was lawfully detained and captured, and so became a British ship for the purpose of founding criminal jurisdiction.

The decision of the majority of the Court on the *Felicidade* case was very grievous to Denman. In a paper which he shortly after drew up and submitted to the Home Secretary, upon the origin, constitution, and procedure of the Court of Criminal Appeal, with a view to the much-needed reform of that tribunal,[1] he thus alludes to the probable consequences of that decision, and to the unsatisfactory mode in which it was arrived at:

"The result appears to destroy all reasonable hope of suppressing the Slave Trade, and to hold out to it the promise of entire indemnity; to place the lives of British officers engaged in that service, at the mercy of the slave trader; to turn the pirate into an injured man, and expose the officer of justice to the penalties and dangers of piracy. And all this is effected through the medium of an opinion formed under the circumstances which I have described, without any statement of the reasons on which it proceeded, and without the expectation of having to assign those reasons in the face of the profession and the public."

Writing to his son, Captain Denman, on December 12, 1845, the day after the judgment, he says:

"The case was, in fact, decided on the ground of jurisdiction, the *Felicidade* being holden not a king's ship, so as to form a part of the British territory. I thought her in the lawful custody of one of H. M.'s officers, and therefore a British ship. It seems to me the poorest of quibbles, and the most mischievous of doctrines to deny this. But it is wonderful and disheartening to observe the reluctance to recede from the old iniquity."

[1] This valuable paper, which will be found very interesting by Law Reformers, is printed *in extenso* in the Appendix, as Appendix VI.

In the letter already cited, of December 25, he says, in further reference to the same subject:

"When the Government was supposed to be going out, Sir James Graham sent to the Chancellor [Lyndhurst] various suggestions for the improvement of the law. One respected the tribunal of the fifteen judges, the unsatisfactory character of which he illustrated by the late pirate's [*Felicidade*] case. At the same time, frightened, like Aberdeen, at the probable result of that decision, he sent Lushington to Parke's house, to consider how the matter should be put so as to do the least possible mischief. They brought me a letter written to Sir James Graham by Alderson, reporting, not very accurately, what passed among the Judges. This movement authorized and required me to write fully to Sir James Graham, my reasons for dissenting from the judgment of the Court of Criminal Appeal; and he, the next day [December 23], the very day of his returning to be reinstated in office at Windsor, sent me an acknowledgment of entire satisfaction and great joy, hoping that the mischief may be corrected. I requested him to show what I had written to Lord Aberdeen, and have myself sent a copy to the Chancellor. They will, of course, be cautious in condemning what has been done by a large judicial majority, but in the Lords I doubt not that Brougham will agree with me, and most probably Campbell, and even the Chancellor to a certain extent, adopting Lord Stowell's prudence, but greatly qualifying his general legal doctrine of piracy. On the whole I have great hope that the rash and ill-considered decision will be stript of all authority, and that my principal proposition will take its place among the undeniable and elementary truths of the law."

The case, however, was never brought before the Lords, and so the hopes above expressed by Denman as to its being stript of all authority there, were not in that respect fulfilled.

The paper to which, in the letter just cited, the Chief Justice refers as having been sent to Sir James Graham, and as containing his reasons for dissenting from the judgment of the Court of Criminal Appeal, is, as Sir James styles it in his letter of acknowledgement, dated

December 23, 1845, "a very masterly exposition of opinion." It mainly proceeds on the principle—a principle frequently, as has been seen, enounced by Denman in his speeches and his writings—viz. that the duty imposed on all civilized communities by the law of nature and of nations of dealing with the Slave Trade as a crime, and with slave-traders as pirates, is paramount to the special clauses of treaties introduced in derogation of it, even supposing that in the case under consideration—a supposition which he doubts—the clause in the old treaty with Portugal, incorporated into that with Brazil, limiting the right of capture to slave ships *having actually slaves on board at the time*, had not expired before the seizure and detention of the *Felicidade* took place. Whether this principle would ever have been asserted by the Law Lords in the Upper House had the case of the *Felicidade* been carried there, is a point which must be regarded as at least doubtful. By the judges of the superior Courts of Westminster Hall, who followed in this respect the lead of Lord Stowell, the principle had been always steadily and uniformly rejected.

In the earlier part of the session of 1846, Denman does not appear to have taken part in any questions of general public importance as a speaker in the House of Lords.

In the interval between the sittings after Easter and the commencement of Trinity Term, 1846, he had stolen down for a brief holiday at Stony Middleton, whence he writes as follows to Coleridge, who had been suffering in health, and throwing out, it appears, some hints as to retirement:

"May 21, 1846.

"My dear Coleridge,—Your letter scarcely precedes the conclusion of my short and happy retirement here, which has effected not only great reforms in the grounds, but also a good deal of judicial work, quietly got through, and rather as a resource from idleness than as an exertion. No week of my life has ever been better employed.

"Patteson wrote to me respecting your health, which has been suffering, it seems, from temporary causes.

The worst of that detestable influenza is the long depression it produces. I am glad you are sensible of the necessity of lying up for a time, and I should strongly recommend you to forego all thought of coming into active work before the Long Vacation. We are all, thank God, able and willing, and we may very probably send you some of our essays [written judgments] for correction at leisure. I am not sure that an opinion so obtained, without any of the fever of Court, may not often be more valuable. You use some expressions of a very ominous and painful character, but your spirits had recovered before you wrote. In case of a similar feeling again taking possession of you, and prompting you suddenly to do what all mankind and yourself would afterwards lament, I should like to exact a promise (indeed, I shall consider this suggestion, unanswered, as an engagement on your part) not to take any such step without a previous communication with each of your brethren of the Queen's Bench, or without a certain time (say one month, in time of work, and three in time of vacation) taken to deliberate. The want of wealth is no object of regret if we place our families well in the world, and by prudent and liberal outlay put our sons in a condition to help themselves and others."

Denman watched, with keen interest, through the spring and summer of 1846, the great struggle of Corn Law abolition, a struggle which, as is well known, led to the triumph of the ministerial measure, soon to be followed by the resignation (on June 29, 1846) of the minister himself. Writing to his son Joseph, on other matters, on June 23, he says, "Peel weathers the storm, I think, in the Commons and in the country, but the aspect of the Lords last night was threatening. We [the Whig party] cut a fine figure."

Writing again on June 30, the day after Peel's resignation, he says:

"The Whig dynasty will, I presume, be now restored, and the old government machine be reconstructed on the ruin and disgrace of the minister who has passed *both* of their measures—Corn and Coercion. It does seem to me the most shocking departure from honor and justice that politics have ever witnessed."

It was about the same time that his third daughter, Frances, the "dearest Fanny" and "dear little Queen" of his earlier correspondence, became, greatly to his satisfaction, the wife of a gallant brother officer of Captain Denman's—Captain (afterwards Admiral Sir Robert Lambert) Baynes, K.C.B.[1] The bride and bridegroom went to spend their honeymoon at Stony Middleton, of whose improvement the former had long been the most active superintendent.

In the Summer Assizes of this year, Denman again went the North Wales Circuit, whence, from under the shadow of Cader Idris, he writes to Lady Denman:

"Dolgelly: July 18, 1846.

"My dearest Love,—We go on in the same quiet, comfortable manner. Sir Robert Vaughan (the Sheriff) and his lady have been all kindness. We dined there on Thursday, and Georgiana,[2] passed all yesterday with Lady Vaughan, at their charming place among the mountains, two miles off; and last evening we drank tea there, after completing the whole work of the Assizes. We go to Carnarvon this afternoon, taking as many beautiful objects as possible on our way. Tell Joe [Captain Denman] I have been reading in the 'Quarterly' and 'Edinburgh' the interesting account of Mr. Brooke's[3] proceedings in Borneo, and have mentioned them to Brougham, to be contrasted with those doings in Africa, which some persons wish us to encourage for the sake of a halfpenny a pound in the price of sugar.

"I have not desired him (Brougham) to bring up the subject of my salary, but have only written to tell him that his memory is quite incorrect—in truth, if fault there be, he is the sole offender. I don't think anything will come of this stir. Lady Vaughan's mother played Welsh airs so well that we were reminded of you, but the music was not necessary as a reminder for your ever faithful and affectionate husband."

The reference in the last sentence but one of the

[1] He died, 1869.

[2] First wife of the present Lord Denman, who, as Marshal and Associate, officially accompanied the Chief Justice on circuit, and on this, as on some other occasions, took his wife round with him.

[3] Afterwards Sir James Brooke, Rajah of Sarawak.

above letter, as to salary, relates to the debate which took place in the House of Lords, on June 14, 1846, on the subject of the salaries of the Chief Justices, and the result of which has been shortly given in a former chapter, when stating the acceptance, by Lord Denman, of a reduced salary, at the time of his elevation to the Chief Justiceship of the King's Bench.

He refers to the same subject in a letter written a few days later, to Coleridge (on July 25, from Holyhead), the substance of which, as far as regards this matter, has been given in the chapter just mentioned, but other parts of which are of sufficient interest to justify a more extended citation here. After setting forth, in the terms elsewhere stated, the exact circumstances regarding his acceptance of the lower salary, he adds:

"This is all that passed; no haggling or bargaining, but merely a suggestion of my own, accepted by the Government, and acted on first by myself, and then by them. Brougham says my executors will have a claim to the whole amount for the last six years of my life at least;[1] and if it is determined to give £10,000 after my time, I certainly should think myself hardly used if the same amount were not secured to me for the remainder of my term.[2] Pray tell me your opinion and Patteson's, to be considered if the occasion should arise, which I do not much think it will, for other waves come rushing in and sweep this subject out of every mind. Brougham, beginning his communication with my salary, carries it on solely on the great question on which a Liberal Government seek the support of popular opinion—the right to become an accomplice in *that congeries of crimes—miscalled the Slave Trade*—the right to encourage and extend, without limit, the kidnapping of free Africans in their own country, to be consigned, in torture, to slavery in a foreign land—a free trade in robbery and murder—a deliberate teaching all men to do what they would *not* have others do to them—the

[1] Meaning that for the period beyond six years preceding his death the Statute of Limitations would be a bar.

[2] No legislative action was taken in the matter till 1851, when, as stated elsewhere, the salaries of the Chief Justices were fixed at £8,000 for the Queen's Bench, and £7,000 for the Common Pleas and Exchequer, at which they still remain.

largest accumulation of monstrous evil for the sake of some sordid and doubtful good—the permanent subjection of a whole continent to incurable barbarism, that we may have sugar a halfpenny a pound cheaper. I have never met with *any man* who appears to me to see this question in its true light; but, in answer to Brougham's call, I have sent him a final expression of my sentiments, to be used at his discretion in the Lords this evening. I do hope the Ministry will fail and fall: mischievous as these changes are, they are nothing in comparison to the avowal of a deliberate intention to encourage the Slave Trade of England. If the whole administration were pounced upon at a whitebait dinner at Greenwich, and carried off, by a just retaliation, to work in African mines, by the pirates of Algiers or Barbary, what would be their sufferings compared to those of one cargo of human beings closed packed on the Middle Passage? But these cargoes are counted by tens of thousands.

"As soon as I get home my last daughter[1] leaves the paternal roof—an awful sacrifice, but a subject, on the whole, of rejoicing. All our previous experiments have been successful as to the great essentials of happiness. I am very glad that your son's marriage is near at hand.[2] Your ideas about grandchildren are quite correct—they are the only faultless portion of the human race."

His strong feelings on the ministerial Sugar Duties' Bill, as involving an encouragement to the Slave Trade, appear still more clearly in the following letter, written on August 2, from Chester (the last place on this circuit) to his son, Captain Denman—a letter which also deserves notice for the generous appreciation it contains of the high services to the Slave Trade question of Lord Brougham, on whose political conduct the Captain

[1] Not last in birth, but last married; Anne, Lord Denman's fifth daughter, married, on August 28 1846, Captain Holland, R. N.; his sixth and youngest, Caroline Amelia, had earlier in the same year married the Rev. John George Beresford, so that, including Lady Baynes, three of Denman's daughters were married in 1846.

[2] Sir John Duke Coleridge (now Attorney-General), married in 1846 to a daughter of the Rev. G. T. Seymour, of Faringford Hall, Isle of Wight.

had, it would appear, been making some unfavorable strictures:

"What you say about Brougham is in great part just, and I lament it. But on this subject [Slave Trade] no doubt *can* be entertained as to his perfect sincerity, any more than on his peculiar power to do justice to the cause, having commenced his career by a very able work on the colonies, written at the age of two or three-and-twenty, and having uniformly supported the great principles of justice and humanity under all circumstances with unrivaled vigor and ability. We must take men as we find them. He has damaged himself by indulging personal feelings, and for that reason I am glad he has had the opportunity of citing me, to whom none such can be imputed, in support of his just views. For my own share, I can not allow *any* consideration to interfere with my sense of the duty of standing up for the endangered principle—the very first principle on which society is founded, and which we can not abandon without exposing ourselves, and justly, to the endurance of any amount of oppression. I must seriously lament that my friends have made this [sugar duties] a party question, and given Peel an occasion of making a speech which so effectually condemns them. But when the Whigs rely on such an issue, it is impossible to shrink from some examination of their merits as a ministry and their conduct as a party. I unhappily think it unexampled for meanness, as well as highly unconstitutional; and their obtaining quiet possession of power by the sacrifice of the Africans is one argument more with me against their measures. I have carefully read every word of the debates, and every newspaper that has fallen in my way, with all my original impressions materially strengthened."

From Chester, the next day (August 3), he writes to Lady Denman, while in Court:

"About ten this morning I was actually in hopes of leaving Chester to-day and reaching home to-night, for the entry consisted of three light causes only; but since that time they have entered eleven more, and though six of them are already disposed of, the rest will detain me the whole of to-morrow. Since I have been sitting in Court I have been cheered by a visit here from Richard and Emma [his third son and his wife], making their short trip over (not more than an hour) from Liverpool, and making me very happy by good reports of their children. The thunderstorm seems at length to have produced a small impression on the extreme sultriness, which last night exceeded all I remember. Both courts are very hot. Chester is a crowded and dirty city, a great contrast to the simplicity and charming scenery of Wales which we have just left, still more so to the happy home I am approaching. So Annie has fixed to-morrow fortnight [August 28—for her marriage], by which day I hope to have returned from voting against the iniquitous bill [Sugar Duties' Bill] brought in by ministers.

"If learned counsel will make such long, stupid speeches, learned judges' wives must expect to receive long, stupid letters; but there is a time for all things."

Denman, animated by the generous sentiments of indignation, so strongly expressed in several of the foregoing letters, contrived to reach London from circuit in time to oppose, in the House of Lords, the Government Bill for equalizing the duties on British colonial and slave-produced sugar—a measure which, in his opinion, and that of all the sincere opponents of the Slave Trade, would have a direct tendency alarmingly to increase the accursed traffic.

Lord Clarendon, in introducing the Bill to the House, gave expression to many opinions in the highest degree distasteful and distressing to Lord Denman. He declared, that after struggling for thirty years with unabated courage and energy for the abolition of the Slave Trade, we had succeeded in nothing but making it a smuggling trade; that we had not only not checked, but greatly increased the numbers of slaves torn from their families and country; that we had added infinitely to the horrors of the Middle Passage; that, in order to supply the place of negroes captured by the cruisers, or thrown overboard to avoid them, double the number of slaves were kidnapped in Africa than there had been when the trade was perfectly free.[1]

[1] Hansard, Parl. Deb., third series, vol. lxxxviii. pp. 467–487.

Lord Denman said:

"He felt it an imperative duty to himself, to all with whom he had been connected in political life, and to the people of England, to declare his distinct and irreconcilable hostility to the principles on which this Bill was founded.

"He urged that it must necessarily stimulate and encourage the Slave Trade.

"He thought it utterly impossible to talk of slavery and the Slave Trade with any degree of moderation, or, indeed, with any other feeling than that of the most perfect abhorrence. The noble lord who commenced the discussion, has expressed, in strong terms, his abhorrence of that system; but, it was difficult to suppose that that system could really be regarded with any great abhorrence or disgust by those who proposed a measure directly calculated to aggravate the evil.

"As to the failure of the measures adopted for the suppression of the Slave Trade, it was admitted that last year no less than seventy-five slave ships were captured by British cruisers. It was admitted that both in Cuba and Brazil many persons were desirous of getting rid of their slaves, and were less anxious to protract the system of slavery, because their trade was rendered dangerous by the watchfulness of the British cruisers.

"Yet, the Government had hardly been placed in their seats, when, in July or August, they asked Parliament, suddenly, to legislate on this subject, calling upon it, hastily, to make an inroad upon a mighty scheme for the abolition of the Slave Trade, and for rescuing the human race from a curse and stigma under which they had long labored, and which fostered and maintained a body of men in the practice of piracy of the worst kind.

"It had been said that Free Trade would and must prevail, that there was no means of stopping or checking it in any direction in which it should tend.

"That seemed to him a very alarming doctrine, and he wished the Government would state how they would apply such a principle to the encouragement of bloodshed, murder, and rapine.

"If free trade was this irresistible power which it was in vain to contend against, and to which we must all submit, he wanted to know why that answer should not be given to any of our own subjects who were as disposed to purchase slaves as the Government was to purchase the article produced by slave labor.

"If free trade were to be made the plea for encouraging crime, bloodshed, and all the horrors that took place on the coast of Africa, he did not see why the traffic in slaves should not be directly sanctioned and owned.[1]

Denman's exertions were utterly in vain; "the half-penny a pound less for sugar" was too strong for him; free trade in slaves was beginning to be a cant phrase of the day; and the Government measure, which had been introduced into Parliament with great precipitation late in the session, was hurried through both Houses by sheer force of voting, and received the Royal Assent before the adjournment.

Retiring to the peaceful shades of "woody" Middleton, after the turmoil and vexation of this unsuccessful conflict, he writes thence as follows, on September 17, to his daughter, Lady Baynes:

"I doubt whether I have once written to you in your wedded state, so it is fortunate that a letter falls to be answered on your birthday—a dear and happy day to your parents, and, I am assured, to your husband and all your newly-acquired relations. We are all well here, and a merry party, with the five delightful grandchildren, though our gaiety has been sadly clouded by the loss of so old and familiar a friend as Williams.[2] All are shocked, but to me his loss is from various reasons particularly severe, and that occupation which is often the best recourse against grief, will long renew and embitter mine. But life is a mingled yarn, and the practical lesson is a cheerful one—to take care of ourselves and all who are dear to us, and make one another as happy as we can while life endures. That you and Lambert [Captain Baynes] may enjoy this satisfaction through a long course of happy years is my wish and prayer. Your mother is just come in to add her congratulations and blessings to mine."

[1] Denman's speech is reported, but evidently very imperfectly, in Hansard, Parl. Deb., third series, vol. lxxxviii. pp. 510–514.

[2] Sir John Williams died suddenly, on September 14, 1846, at his seat, Livermore Park, near Bury St. Edmunds, in the seventieth year of his age.

The death of Mr. Justice Williams, adverted to in the above letter, was naturally much felt by Denman. Ever since the Queen's trial in 1820, they had been intimate; had fought together from 1823 to 1826 in the House of Commons against old Eldon and Chancery abuses; and had sat together as Judges in the Court of Queen's Bench for between twelve and thirteen years.

Mr. Justice Williams was succeeded in the Court of Queen's Bench by that admirable Judge, Sir William Erle, who, in November, 1844, had been appointed a Judge of the Common Pleas, of which Court, after a service of nearly thirteen years in the Queen's Bench, he afterwards became Chief Justice, retiring in 1866, after a most distinguished judicial career of twenty-two years' duration. By the unanimous suffrage of the whole legal profession a better judge than Sir William Erle never sat on the Bench—combining in the highest degree learning, diligence, patience, and courtesy. He sat more than three years (from November 1846 to March 1850) in the Court of Queen's Bench while it was presided over by Lord Denman, who had the most thorough appreciation of his valuable qualities, and an affectionate esteem for his high and lovable character.[1]

It was during his vacation weeks at Stony Middleton, in the autumn of 1846, that Denman, indignant at the tone taken by the Press, in regard to the Government Sugar Bill, the Slave Trade, and the Squadron, wrote the verses which he published anonymously in the next year, under the title of "The Slave Trade and the Press." *Facit indignatio versus* is a saying often verified by fact, but the inspiration of wrath is not generally a wise one. Denman's stanzas on this occasion, some of which will be found in the Appendix,[2] hardly seem to atone by the felicity of their execution for the imprudence of their publication. Such, at least, is the present writer's opinion—the reader, if he likes to refer to the Appendix, can judge for himself.

[1] Sir William Erle, born 1793; educated at Winchester and Oxford; D C. L., 1818; called to Bar, 1819; King's Counsel, 1834; Judge of Common Pleas, November, 1844: Queen's Bench, 1846: Chief Judge of Common Pleas, 1859; resigned, November, 1866.

[2] Appendix II

CHAPTER XXXII.

MONTEM SUPPRESSED—ABOLITION OF TRANSPORTATION.

A. D. 1847. ÆT. 68.

IN the spring of the year 1847, Lord Denman presided on the Home Circuit, whence he wrote, from Hertford, the first assize town on that circuit, the following letter to his friend and son-in-law, the Provost of Eton, on the suppression of the too-long tolerated saturnalia of *Montem*, a measure which the Provost (somewhat against the feeling of the Court, and of some old Eton celebrities) was then actively engaged in promoting:

"County Hall, Hertford: March 4, 1847.

"My dear Hodgson,—I don't exactly understand your position. Has the Provost the sole authority? Has it been exercised in union with the Fellows, and with their approbation? I know the head master concurred, but was that only by way of advice, or as exercising some power? Again, what is the Queen's position? Has she power to allow or disallow what the college authority has done, and has Her Majesty added her sanction to their act, or is it only that she makes the holiday by attending at Salt Hill? In the former case, I would advise a memorial, stating, in all their force, the reasons for putting an end to the custom, and appealing for support and protection.

"But if the effect of what has been done is merely to induce Her Majesty to abstain from attending, things would appear to me to be rather different. For then, if she were reluctant to give it up, and if, as you appear to suppose, there be a strong general feeling in favor of its continuance, it may be a strong measure to interfere with people's enjoyment of what they consider a harmless spectacle. In this case it may be better to make a compromise, putting an end to the plunder, and restraining the intemperance, but permitting the gathering, and a subscription from those willing to contribute. I don't pretend to give advice in this uncertainty, but these ideas occur to me as worth consideration."

The evening after the above was written, Denman, having run up from Hertford to London, to be present at the House of Lords, delivered a very powerful speech there, against the abolition of Transportation as a secondary punishment, on the occasion of Lord Grey's Bill for the Custody of Offenders, &c.[1]

While agreeing that the convict establishment of Norfolk Island must be broken up, and transportation to Van Diemen's land suspended, he expressed the strongest possible opinion against the *total abolition* of transportation.

"When he heard it proposed that that great power which consisted in the terrors of Transportation should be abolished, that that great terror should be withdrawn from the minds of those, who, if not actually criminals, might be contemplating crime, he could not but regard such intention with the greatest possible dismay; he could use no lighter word.

"He did not believe, what was sometimes stated, that the punishment of transportation was without the greatest terror for offenders. He had seen examples, not constantly, but on many occasions, of the overwhelming terrors of transportation."

He then dwelt, with great impressiveness, on the topics so frequently adverted to in these discussions—on the great importance of entirely removing from their old haunts and associates the more opulent and influential members of the criminal classes, such as the professional receivers of stolen goods; on the great and serious multiplication of resident criminals, and on the probability that a system of secondary punishment administered in England would never be effectually carried out; finally, on the impossibility of securing for criminals at home what was provided in the colonies, the begin-

[1] Hansard, Parl. Deb., third series, vol. cx. p. 898 et seq.

ning of a new career of life, after their allotted period of punishment had expired.[1]

Had this country alone been concerned in the question of maintaining the system of Colonial Transportation, these arguments would have been unanswerable; but in face of the determined opposition of the Colonies to the continuance of the system, the mother couutry had to give way, and, except on a limited scale to Western Australia, transportation as a secondary punishment has been necessarily abandoned; not, however, without to a great degree, entailing the consequences which the opponents of its abolition foresaw and foretold.

With regard to the terrors of Transportation as a sentence when pronounced by an able judge, and also as giving a notion of some of the qualities that made Denman incomparable as an administrator of the Criminal Law, the present writer may be permitted to relate a circumstance of which he was a witness in the criminal court at Chelmsford, some years before the period now under consideration.

Two men had been convicted before Lord Denman of rape under most aggravated circumstances; they were navigators of the coarsest and roughest order. The Chief Justice, in passing sentence, having commented on the heinous nature of their offense, awarded them fourteen years' transportation. The men stood stolidly insensible; then, after a slight pause, he added, looking fixedly at them, and raising his majestic voice to its full compass, "and do not think *that* a light sentence; so far from it, that I have seen old and hardened offenders—men who, having been sentenced to transportation before, well know what transportation is—I have seen those men sink fainting in the dock before me when it has been my duty to pronounce upon them that dreadful doom."

The effect was electric; the two human brutes in the dock trembled and grew blanched with terror, and many a yet undeveloped member of the criminal classes in the crowded Court, many a one, "who, if not yet criminal, might be contemplating crime," and who had often perhaps talked jestingly of a "trip to Botany Bay," stood

[1] Hansard, Parl. Deb., third series, vol. cx. pp. 936–939.

horror struck at the dreadful nature of a sentence which the law had made second only to death itself, and which, in those days of Norfolk Island, involved sufferings and infamies from which even death itself would have been a release.

The questions stated in his previous letter as to *Montem* having been answered, Denman, who had in the meantime resumed his duties as Judge of Assize, wrote to Hodgson again on the same subject, from Chelmsford, on March 8, as follows:

"After hearing a lecture from the Sheriff's chaplain [on occasion of opening the commission], I sit down to give you a line upon *Montem*. My general opinion is that you should principally rest on the goodness of your case and the actual exercise of authority. If a very powerful counter-demonstration could be procured, it would probably be decisive: but as the greater activity of the other side may obtain a numerical majority, any appeal on your part to that test would be dangerous. Among the Judges you are strong. Shadwell has often expressed to me his anxious desire for the abolition. I called on Coleridge to-day, who has been invested by the enemy, but expresses himself ready to sign a memorial in favor of what has been done by you, if such course should be thought advisable. Of Patteson's feeling in the same way I have no doubt; but we are all out of town [on circuit] for some weeks. I have heavy and shocking work here."

Not long after, the quaint, but of late grossly abused, revelries of *Montem* were suppressed, greatly to the benefit of Eton as a school, but a good deal against the grain of many fine old *laudatores temporis acti*, who never forgave the Provost for laying sacrilegious hands on the revered institution of their boyhood. An exceedingly competent witness, an old Etonian, thoroughly devoted to Eton, thus recently expressed his opinion on *Montem* to the present writer:

"It was a great disgrace to a great school. I was at two celebrations, and they weigh on my mind as two of the dreariest days of my life. Loads of ill-dressed food washed down with bad champagne, the cost to be deducted from the proceeds of that vulgar highway robbery called 'Salt,' reducing what might have been sufficient to start the son of poor parents in life, to a sum barely enough to give him a plethora of pocket money The proof of all this is that the Captain of the School, who was the nominal recipient of the money, was never benefited by it.

"There was of course a furious stand made for the time-*dis*honored abuse, and it required no little courage to abolish it. The Provost showed great firmness, and deserves all the credit, though he doubtless was fortified and assisted by the warm support and approval of Lord Denman."

After the matter had been decided on, Denman wrote to Hodgson, who had been very greatly worried about it, and had gone down to Brighton to refresh himself. The letter alludes also to another vexed Eton question of the time, the Slough and Windsor Branch Railway.

"Cum te Brightoniæ tranquilla refecerit aura,
Care gener, caram, et carâ cum conjuge, prolem,
Vexatum compone animum, tumidoque rebelles
Da pelago curas, atque obliviscere *Montem*.[1]

"I was sorry to hear of Bessie's influenza, but feel strong hope of her complete recovery, and that you will all profit by the fine air of the coast, if you will but throw useless cares behind. This year's Eton meeting can not expect to be highly popular, but it will pass over quietly, or, if the disaffected choose to signalize their ill-humor, they will be the only sufferers. I daresay Hallam would attend, if Dr. Hawtrey desired it, but with us the first day of Trinity Term [May 22] imports the dining together of all the Common-Law Judges. I mentioned your wish to Shadwell, who, however, did not seem eager to attend.

"As to the railway [Slough and Windsor branch] I am required to attend as a *witness*. My evidence is wanted to show that the near approach of steam-engines, &c., to the bathing-places will be injurious to Eton. Do not you think it will? I do with great confidence. Whether

[1] "When, dear son-in-law, the refreshing air of Brighton has set you up—and your wife and children too—you must calm your troubled spirit, give care to the wind and waves, and forget all about *Montem*."

you can avoid a railway, and whether the line proposed may not be the least nuisance compatible with it, I have formed no opinion; still less do I place myself in competition with the college authorities as to the prudence of adopting it, and the satisfactory nature of the precautions promised. This may make my evidence of small value, or even turn it the other way, if on cross-examination I should be convinced that this would be the best of all possible lines. Still, the parties have a right to my opinion."

On this Spring Assizes Lord Denman spent two or three days, between the end of the work at Maidstone and its commencement at Lewes, at Leeds Castle, whence, on March 21, he sent a letter containing the following lines to Lady Denman:

"Contrary to all expectation, we finished our work at Maidstone last night [Saturday], and having postponed the business at Lewes till Tuesday, have the intervening days idle on our hands. Matters might have been better arranged if the necessity for this change of times had been foreseen. We are meanwhile very hospitably entertained by Mr. Wykeham Martin, a great and early friend of Tom's, and have had a delightful ride over a fine open country, and return to this noble castle, formerly the mansion of Lord Fairfax, Cromwell's colleague, whose grim portrait and buff jerkin are carefully preserved. On a sun-bright day, with a kind and unaffected family, everything is genial both within doors and without."

In the spring of 1847, the publication of Prince de Joinville's celebrated *brochure*, and various other circumstances, had given rise to some apprehensions as to the possibility of a successful attack on our coasts by a French fleet, and also to serious doubts as to the immediate efficiency of our own naval defenses. It was considered desirable, in some quarters, to rouse the public feeling on the subject, and Captain Denman, with characteristic ardor, was minded at once to rush into the fray with a pamphlet. His father, whom he had consulted on the policy of this proceeding, sent him some admirable advice in a letter, from which the following are extracts:

"Portland Place: April, 14, 1847.

"Now for your letter [proposed printed letter], of which I have thought a good deal. I distrust myself as an adviser, because, if I were in your position, my feelings would have been exactly the same as your own.

"A great evil is to be prevented, a great good is to be done.

"Those particularly charged with the duty, are not sufficiently alive to its obligation or to the passing exigency, and an individual thinks that he can arouse public opinion, and excite them to the necessary task. This is the thing to be effected by the publication of that individual's views and opinions. Now, consider, in the first place, the probability of making a first impression, The public, as you truly say, is devoted to the love of lucre and the active pursuit of it. ''Tis Avarice all, Ambition is no more.' A most unfavorable disposition for public spirit, or moral rectitude, or any elevated thoughts whatever, and seeking rather an excuse for avoiding them.

"Can there be a stronger presumptive excuse than that the authorities do not seem impressed with the danger? But is it a mere excuse? Is it not something like a good reason? Men in authority, of good understanding, of candid minds, possessed of all the information, with every motive that can actuate any other of the Queen's subjects, in addition to the sense of duty and of character, do not perceive the danger to be imminent. They look out in full day, and through the best glasses, and discern no breakers ahead. Surely the passengers may feel a natural confidence that all is well, and distrust opinions and arguments pointing the other way. For my own part, I fall into this way of thinking, spite of the vigorous proceedings in France. They may be principally the result of apprehension, though not without a secret or professed hope, in De Joinville and his followers, of naval glories. Great means of material mischief have indeed been provided, but there are strong counteracting causes. Both in France and in England the *boutiquier* spirit has taken strong hold of the bulk of the people—peace is evidently the idol of both, and war is held in the greatest horror. I have a notion, too, that public opinion throughout the world would revolt against any unprovoked and wanton injury by either country on the peaceful inhabitants of the other; and further, I believe that in case of real danger the spirit and energy of the people would be roused by the aggression to efforts of which in our unalarmed state we do not fancy either capable."

Adverting to the remedy (impressment) which the Captain wished to propose, and admitting that if the Admiralty continued apathetic, and if an efficient plan could be devised, the temptation to promulgate it would become very strong indeed, he proceeds thus:

"I should say, however, that the efficiency of the proposed plan ought in the first instance to be made manifest to some of the best judges. Some consideration ought also to be given to the probable effect on the projector himself. If offense is given, if the plan is rejected as visionary, positive harm may be added to loss of caste in him. And even if it be reluctantly adopted, he is sometimes ridiculed as having only deprived the superior of his just credit for what he was just going to do.

"These are very crude remarks, very little like "maturer counsel." On one point I think I could feel confident: the propriety of abstaining from any statement of existing dangers that would generally be thought extravagant."

In the Summer Assizes of 1847, Denman, as he had so often done before, traveled the Midland Circuit, soon after his return from which he wrote from Middleton to his friend Coleridge a letter from which the following are extracts:

"Not an hour will I delay answering your kind remembrance and cordial letter, having had no communication with any colleague during the circuit, except on one case of conviction submitted by Wightman for our opinion. Our circuit was a journey of pleasure, occasionally diversified with legal affairs, *rari nantes*. We had too much time everywhere, and for that very reason no leisure, as all was taken up in visiting and travels—the business of the most ordinary kind, and performed accordingly. Like you, I am annoyed at the manner of conducting the criminal business. Few prisoners were defended, scarcely any case opened for the prosecution, though in no instance was I obliged to act as counsel. But the utter carelessness as to the truth coming out, and the habit of slurring over damnatory proofs, required more vigilance in that direction [viz., for the prosecution] than a judge is fond of displaying. I can not help fancying that the Bar is becoming more a stage of transition than a status—an apprenticeship exacted by custom for obtaining some office, such as that of Revising Barrister, County Court Judge, or Commissioner of some sort. I heartily wish the judges were deprived of all patronage of this kind. Towards the end of the assizes the looks of expectation and disappointment are harrowing. With regard to the election,[1] I think Edinburgh[2] a heavy blow and great discouragement to popular reformers. That and Hobhouse's defeat and Hawes' show how little hold the ministry have on public opinion among the middle classes. Their real strength, however—the absence of competition—remains undiminished, or rather increased, and this must make all reasonable men desirous of their acting creditably. Roebuck's absence I heartily lament, as it will secure Weymouth and every other corrupt and unimprovable place from their just doom. I rejoice with you for the emancipation of Gloucester and Monmouth, and am delighted with the manly, spirited, and able exertions of Sir George Grey. Talking of Monmouth, I was saying how inconsistent were our complaints against lodgings anywhere when we never complained there, where they surely are the worst of all. I am glad the cause is removed; perhaps we owe it to Lord Granville Somerset. Let us try our influence at Gloucester with Mr. Grantly Bekeley.

"Erle must have thoroughly enjoyed the Oxford Circuit [on which he had gone this summer with Coleridge]—that fine country, new to him, in company with an old friend, with business enough to excite and amuse him. Your postscript was not the least interesting part of your letter, as I had heard nothing of Patteson before.

[1] The Parliament, which had lasted since August, 1841, had been dissolved on July 23, 1847.

[2] Where Macaulay was unseated.

I trust we shall all meet in Westminster Hall, recruited and refreshed.

"My holiday began here on the 8th [of August], Warwick having come to an end the day before. The music of the axe has been sounding ever since. Days bright and rainy by turns. This morning glorious, but now the birds fly low. The foliage luxuriant beyond example; the harvest, early for us, a-gathering. No study of any kind but French novels, and all the books of the Bakewell Club at once upon the table. No visitors yet but Miss Macaulay. George [now Mr. Justice Denman] expected soon."

CHAPTER XXXIII.

BURON *v.* DENMAN—HAMPDEN'S CASE—HUTT'S COMMITTEE—GREAT SLAVE TRADE SPEECHES OF 1848.

A. D. 1848. ÆT. 69.

THE year 1848 was a busy and exciting one for Denman, too much so indeed, for there can be little doubt that the labor and anxiety he underwent in the course of it, had a great deal to do with undermining his health, and preparing the way for the malady which first openly attacked him in the year following. The intensity, more especially, with which he felt, thought, and worked on the subject of the Slave Trade, produced a strain on the nervous system, which, when added to the continuous brain work imposed upon him by his judicial and other labors, overtasked even his strong powers, and hastened the stroke which finally shattered them. To the suppression of the Slave Trade Denman gave his whole heart, soul, and strength; he regarded the abominable traffic as the monster crime and evil of the whole world; and that vehement hatred of oppression and wrong which throughout life had been a prominent feature in his character, never allowed him to rest or to slumber in what he felt to be the great and sacred cause of trampling out the accursed wickedness from the face of the earth. He firmly believed that the efforts of the squadron, if resolute and firmly directed, not crippled and paralyzed by the captious doubts of lawyers and the timorous over-caution of ministers, were the sole means, under Providence, of finally extinguishing the Slave Trade.

Nothing distressed him more than to see the growing indifference and levity with which, under the influence of able editors and economical doctrinaires, men of cultivation, intelligence, and humanity were disposed to treat the sufferings of the irrepressible "nigger," while they not only questioned the utility of the squadron, but actually represented it as a means by which the area of the slave-hunter's operations had been extended, the horrors of the Middle Passage increased, and the mortality of the slave cargoes more than doubled. Poor, selfish, and half-hearted talk of this kind, drove even the calm and equable temper of Denman beyond the limits of moderation; his earnestness in this work was a life and death earnestness, and it made him mad to hear the parrot prate with which these sciolists of political economy retailed the arguments of the abler and astuter wire-pullers, who had many of them a direct money interest in upholding the iniquitous traffic.

In the early part of this year came on the trial at Bar of *Buron* v. *Denman*, the plaintiff being one of the slave-traders and slave-owners who had a part interest in the barracoon on the Gallinas river, which Captain Denman had destroyed, and the action being a suit for damages against the gallant Captain in respect of the money loss caused by its destruction, and by the liberation of the slaves who had been warehoused in it for export.

The case was tried in the Exchequer on February 14, 15, 16, 1848, before four judges—Barons Parke, Alderson, Rolfe and Platt—and on the last of the three days judgment was given.

The facts already stated (in Chapter 28) as to the destruction of the barracoon and the liberation of the slaves stored in it having been proved to the satisfaction of the jury, the Court held: First, that the plaintiff had *a property in his slaves*, and might maintain trespass for their seizure, *the Slave Trade not being piratical by the law of nations*, and it not appearing that Spain (to which nation the plaintiff belonged) had passed any law abolishing the Slave Trade, pursuant to the treaty embodied in 6 and 7 Wm. IV. c. 6. But they also held:

Secondly: that the ratification of Captain Denman's act by the Ministers of State [in the letters already set forth in Chapter 28] was equivalent to a prior command, and thus rendered it an act of State, for which the Crown alone was responsible.[1]

[1] *Buron* v. *Denman*, 2 Exch. Rep. pp. 167–190. Parke, B., only assented

Thus, in the result, Captain Denman escaped the ignominy of having to pay damages to the slave-owner for having deprived him of his slaves; but in principle the Court affirmed the position that the slave-owner had the right in England to recover damages for his human chattels when taken from him by one of Her Majesty's officers charged and entrusted with the suppression of the Slave Trade; and he only failed so to recover them because that officer's act, having been approved of by the Government, was treated as having been commanded by the Government, so as in the particular case to exonerate him from personal liability.

It is a decision that reflects no honor on the jurisprudence of England: well might Denman say of it, as he did in the House of Lords, that it was the first time the claim of an owner of human beings, made slaves for the purposes of trade, had been recognized in an English Court of Justice.[1] May it be the last!

Shortly before the case of *Buron* v. *Denman* had been decided in the Exchequer, the Queen's Bench had been engaged in the consideration of a matter which, in its day, formed the topic of all dinner parties in London, and of all rectories, curacies, and serious circles throughout the country, the question, viz., whether the Court should or should not issue a mandamus to compel the Archbishop of Canterbury, then Dr. Howley, to allow certain persons to appear and be heard as opposers of the confirmation of Dr. Hampden's election to the Bishopric of Hereford.

The length of learned arguments to which this case gave rise before the courts, may be judged of from the fact that Mr. Jebb's admirable report of the proceedings is a thick and closely-printed volume of 580 pages.[2]

Happily, all that is necessary for the present purpose admits of being stated in comparatively brief compass. A word first as to the antecedents of Dr. Hampden. Dr.

with some hesitation to the second ruling. A bill of exceptions was tendered, but the plaintiff afterwards discontinued his suit, certain terms of settlement of this and similar actions having been agreed to by Government.

[1] On February 22, 1848. Hansard, Parl. Deb., third series, vol. xcvi. p. 1055.

[2] Case of Dr. Hampden, by Richard Jebb, Esq., Barrister-at-law, Benning and Co. 1849.

Renn Dickson Hampden having been, in 1836, appointed by Lord Melbourne Regius Professor of Divinity in the University of Oxford, the University at once assembled in Convocation, and, on the ground of certain alleged unorthodox opinions contained in Dr. Hampden's Bampton Lectures (preached in 1831), and in a pamphlet of later date, entitled "Observations on Religious Dissent," proceeded, by solemn decree, to deprive Dr. Hampden of all they could, viz. certain privileges and emoluments theretofore invariably enjoyed by all persons holding the office of Regius Professor of Divinity. This decree, on motion being made in Convocation to that effect six years afterwards, in 1842, they solemnly refused to repeal, and it remained in full force and effect at the time of the proceedings now to be related.

Dr. Musgrave, Bishop of Hereford, having, late in 1847, been elevated to the Archbishopric of York, an alarming rumor began to spread in ecclesiastical circles that the heretical Regius Professor of Divinity was about to be nominated for the vacant see.

Upon this, thirteen bishops drew up, signed, and transmitted to Lord John Russell, a remonstrance against the appointment, to which Lord John replied, by a communication dated "Chesham Place, December 8, 1847," and which, of all the celebrated letters of its celebrated writer, is perhaps the neatest, the most telling, and the most incisive. What the Chancery lawyers call the charging part of it, is contained in the following paragraphs, the temptation to transcribe which is irresistible:

"In these circumstances, it appears to me that should I withdraw my recommendation of Dr. Hampden, which has been sanctioned by the Queen, I should virtually assent to the doctrine that a decree of the University of Oxford is a perpetual ban of exclusion against a clergyman of eminent learning and irreproachable life; and that, in fact, the supremacy which is now, by law, vested in the Crown, is to be transferred to a majority of the members of one of our Universities.

"Nor should it be forgotten that many of the most prominent among that majority have since joined the communion of the Church of Rome.

"I deeply regret the feeling that is said to be common among the clergy on this subject. But I can not sacrifice the reputation of Dr. Hampden, the rights of the Crown, and what I believe to be the true interests of the Church, to a feeling which I believe to be founded on misapprehension and fomented by prejudice.

"At the same time, I thank your Lordships for an interposition which I believe to be intended for the public benefit.

"I have, &c.,
"J. RUSSELL."

On December 16 the Queen issued her Congé d'Elire and Letters Missive for the election of Dr. Hampden as Bishop of Hereford; on December 28, the election took place, under solemn protest from the Dean, Dr. Mereweather, and nothing further remained to be performed but the *confirmation* of the bishop-elect by the Archbishop of Canterbury.

A royal mandate having been issued to the Archbishop directing him to confirm, he accordingly fixed January 11, 1848, as the time, and St. Mary of the Bow, in Cheapside, as the place, for the confirmation.

It being known that an effort would then and there be made to protest against the confirmation, Dr. Barnaby, the Vicar-General, whose ordinary function it was to act on such occasions for the Archbishop, was in this instance reinforced by the powerful aid of Dr. Lushington and Sir John Dodson, named by the Archbishop as his associates.

The apparitor of the Archbishop's Court having made proclamation, in the old, immemorial form, calling on persons who might object to the confirmation of Dr. Hampden as Bishop of Hereford, to come forward "and make their objections in due form of law, *and they shall be heard*," several objectors, or as the the proper term it seems is, "*opposers*," at once came forward. Hereupon argument was permitted, but on the sole point whether, notwithstanding the plain terms of the proclamation just read, any opposers at all could at this stage of the proceedings appear and be heard. Dr. Lushington (Sir John Dodson entirely agreeing), grounding himself on what had been the invariable practice, from the time of the passing of the statute 25 Henry VIII., to the present day, and on the position that confirmation by the Archbishop was a merely *ministerial, not a judical act*, held clearly that no opposers to the confirmation of Dr. Hampden as Bishop of Hereford could then and there appear or be heard; immediately after which decision the opposers, which seems hard, were, under another old form, accused of contumacy for not appearing; and then the confirmation was solemnly pronounced and published in due form of law.

Three days after, on January 14, 1848, Sir Fitzroy Kelly, in the Court of Queen's Bench, moved for a rule to show cause why a mandamus should not issue to the Archbishop of Canterbury, and Dr. Barnaby, his Vicar-General, commanding them or one of them to allow the opposers of Dr. Hampden's confirmation to appear and be heard before them.

On January 24 and subsequent days, cause was shown by Sir John Jervis and five other learned counsel, in lengthened and able arguments, which were replied to by Sir Fitzroy Kelly and four other learned counel, with equal length and ability; then Sir John Jervis claimed and was allowed to exercise the right of general reply, and finally, after four days of argument, on February 1, 1848, the judges, who were equally divided in opinion (Patteson and Coleridge being in favor of granting the mandamus, and Denman and Erle against it) delivered their judgments *seriatim*.

The judgment of Lord Denman, with which alone the present narrative is concerned, was quite worthy of his great reputation: learned, sagacious, eloquent, and, what was rare with him, enlivened here and there with strokes of grave humor, such as Sir Thomas More on a similar occasion, might not have disdained to employ; and to which the subject matter in some of its aspects almost irresistibly invited. For what could be grosser than the absurdity of first calling on all opposers to appear and be heard, then formally deciding that they could neither appear nor be heard, and then finally recording against them an accusation of contumacy for not appearing, and all this in the course of a solemn function began and ended by prayer! A grave farce gravely carried out in the midst of the nineteenth century, equaling, if not exceeding, in comic drollery any of the quaint inventions with which Rabelais, in his immortal burlesque, sought to cast ridicule on the proceedings of his *Chats Fourrés*, in the old Paris Chamber *des Escomptes*.

In the course of the exhaustive historical investigation with which the judgment opened, the Chief Justice took the opportunity of paying the following graceful tribute to Cranmer, who had been somewhat disparagingly spoken of in the course of the argument, by one of the counsel of the opposers.[1]

One of the counsel for the Crown, with the view of exposing the absurdity of supposing that confirmation by the Archbishop of a bishop's election under the 25 of Henry VIII. was meant to be more than a mere ministerial act, had asked whether such a king as Henry was likely at one and the same moment to deprive the Pope of his vote in the election of bishops and lodge it in the hands of one of his own subjects?

"The only answer [said Lord Denman] to this pertinent question, if I understood it properly, I confess I could not hear without surprise and regret. As I caught it, it was a reflection, and a severe reflection, on that great father of the English Protestant Church—Archbishop Cranmer. I understood the solution of the difficulty to be that 'the King knew how obsequious an Archbishop he had in Cranmer, who would readily conform to any wish the Royal mind might conceive.' Cranmer was not a blameless man—very far from it. Shortly before his death he betrayed a lamentable want of firmness—*not, however, greater than his who was selected from among the apostles as the rock on which was to be built the everlasting Church.* Yet his noble bearing when he met at last the death he had too much feared, might have been expected to protect his memory from general reflections like these."

Upon the solemn mockery of keeping up the old form of calling on all opposers to appear and make their objections to the *Confirmation*, and then not allowing them to appear and be heard, and finally accusing them of

[1] Mr. Badeley.

contumacy for not appearing, and all this accompanied with the solemnity of prayer, Lord Denman pointed out that it was not more absurd than the practice, whose legality no man disputed, of calling on the Dean and Chapter with solemn form of prayer, etc., to *elect* a bishop whom they must elect whether they will or no, and who, as all the world knows, is the nominee of the Crown.

"When [said the Chief Justice] I heard Sir Fitzroy Kelly, with his impressive solemnity of manner, entreat that we would not expose the Archbishop to the mockery of having all the prayers recited for the mere purpose of going through a form and acting a farce, I confess I hardly knew how to meet it. Are the Dean and Chapter to be treated as nothing? Do *they* proceed without prayer and without solemn ceremony? If they are required, notwithstanding all this, under the threat of penal consequences, to elect a particular person and none other—the law which compels them may be an unreasonable, ill-considered, and impious Act of Parliament, that ought to be repealed; but why should there be more objection on account of these mock solemnities being introduced into the presence of the Archbishop than into that of the Dean and Chapter. I forbear, for obvious reasons, from entering more fully into that. The whole matter reminds one of the Roman Augurs, who were said never to meet one another without laughing; and, I think, that if these gentleman had induced us to issue this writ upon considerations of the incredible scandal and impropriety of using a religious solemnity on such an occasion, they would have had some reason to laugh at our expense."

In conclusion, Lord Denman, after having stated at length all his reasons (which appear quite incontrovertible) for the opinion deliberately formed and conscientiously maintained by him, viz., that by the law and practice of England, ever since the statute of 25 Henry VIII., confirmation of the election of a bishop by the Archbishop is purely a *ministerial*, never a judicial act, expressed his conviction that in the due exercise of his discretion he ought to refuse to grant the mandamus.[1]

[1] Where the Court in which a rule is moved is equally divided in opinion, the practice is that the rule is discharged.

"I own that my opinion is so entirely settled, and I must add, so entirely unchanged by all I have heard to-day, that, feeling the utmost disposition to do all that can be done to show my respect for my learned brothers [Patteson and Coleridge], I do not think that I can consent to say, for my part, that this writ ought to go. I think it ought not—I feel confident that if it went, it would be good for nothing—that the return which would be made to it would give it a complete answer. I am satisfied that the only effect of all this would be to keep alive the frightful state of religious, or, rather let me say, theological animosity, which it is impossible not to observe in this country. There would be a delay of at least two years before the return to the writ could be argued—probably four more days would be consumed in argument, and we can not tell how much more when it would come into the Court of Error. The bishopric all that time would be vacant—perhaps other vacancies might occur in other sees, when, no doubt, the example here set would be followed, and in every case I should expect, in the present excited state of men's mind, that the Archbishop would be called upon to summon all mankind to hear whether they had anything to say against the confirmation of the bishop elect and open a Court that would probably never be closed.

"Under all these circumstances, feeling the utmost respect for my learned brethren, and the greatest regret that we do not take the same view, I must own that I feel that some deference is due also to the high person [Archbishop of Canterbury] who is named as the defendant in this rule. Some deference is due to those who certify the fitness of Bishop Hampden for the office to which he is elected. Still, more deference is due to the *peace of the Church and the tranquillity of the State.*

"It seems to me that we should be putting everything to hazard, and leading to consequences which it is impossible to foresee, if we, who are firmly convinced that there is no such law as that upon which these parties seek to act, encouraged the smallest doubt as to its existence. Reserving my opinion on this point, till I had heard all the observations of my learned brothers, and keeping my mind open to the last, and free to say that this is a question which ought to be discussed, I must fairly say, with all respect for my brother Coleridge's admirable argument, that it has confirmed me in the opinion of the danger of exposing the act of Parliament, and the most simple construction of the plainest language, and the most moderate and universal opinion on its effects, to the speculations of those *who will bring their forgotten books down and wipe off the cobwebs from the Decretals and Canons before they can find one argument* for disturbing the settled practice of three hundred years.[1]"

So the rule was discharged, the mandamus refused, and the confirmation of Dr. Hampden's election stood as good and valid in law.

The opponents, indeed, or "opposers" of Dr. Hampden consulted their counsel as to whether they could not carry the case further, but were advised, with undoubted accuracy, by those learned gentlemen that no writ of error or other appeal lay against a *refusal* by the Queen's Bench to grant a mandamus, which it is always discretionary with that Court to grant or not.

So in the Law Courts the matter was at an end: not quite so in Parliament.

In the House of Lords, on February 15, 1848, that famous champion of the Church, the Bishop of Exeter, presented a petition from certain clergymen of the Archdeaconery of Bucks, praying for the repeal of so much of the statute of 25 Henry VIII. as rendered Deans, Chapters, and Bishops liable to the penalties of a *præmunire* in discharge of their respective duties in the election and consecration of bishops in the Christian Church.

The Bishop, in the course of an able speech, spoke of the Act 25 of Henry VIII., which directed Deans and Chapters to proceed with the form of election, accompanied by solemn religious service, and which at the same time compelled them to elect any individual, however unfit they might conscientiously believe him to be, under the penalties of a *præmunire*, as a law of unmixed tyranny.

[1] Jebb's "Report of Bishop Hampden's Case," pp. 495. 496.

He expressed a hope that the opinions of the two learned persons (Patteson and Coleridge) who thought that the confirmation by the Archbishop of the election of a bishop was a *judicial* and not a merely ministerial act, would ultimately prevail as the law of the land.

If the construction put on the statute of Henry by the Chief Justice were allowed to prevail, it would make that Act the "Magna Charter of Tyranny."

Lord Denman said that,

"It did not appear a very proper or convenient course for a judge to enter in discussion in that place respecting his own administration of the laws in a Court of Justice. He could only say of this case that on no occasion to his recollection had he devoted so much time, or bestowed so much inquiry, on any subject that had come before him, nor did he recollect any subject that had caused him greater anxiety. So that if he had erred in any way, it was not without the most careful endeavor to prevent it, and the most diligent search after the truth. He would add that never, on any occasion, had he risen from an inquiry with a more perfect conviction that he had had the good fortune to arrive at the truth.

"He felt the deep responsibility that rested on him when he came to that conclusion, in opposition to opinions which he so justly respected; but, having done so, he, as a judge, was not entitled to withhold it. However great the respect he felt for his learned brethren, and notwithstanding the pain with which, on every occasion, one judge differed from another on questions of great interest and importance—still that judge must pronounce the dictates of his own conscience, and give full effect to his own opinion."

He then gave, in the following short and clear terms, the true ground for refusing the mandamus, viz. that it would make the appointment of bishops rest, not with the Crown, as the law requires, but with the Archbishop, and this on the ground of a mere form, which had been suffered to linger on long after the state of things which had called it into existence had passed away:

"We were asked to grant the madamus on this specific

ground—that, according to the ancient practice, the appearance of objectors having been challenged, before confirmation, the Archbishop was bound to hear any objectors whatever prefer any objections whatever. In other ceremonies such forms had still kept their place, *but merely as a matter of form.* But on the late occasion *the form was sought to be coxverted into a substantive practice, powerful enough to set aside the appointment of a bishop by the Crown.* For, as his noble and learned friend [Lord Lyndhurst] had truly observed, the power of the appointment could not, in fact, be in the Crown if the Archbishop had a power, before confirmation, to call upon all opposers to come forward, to hear their objections, and, should his opinion be in favor of them, to refuse the confirmation and consecration of the person nominated by the Crown.

" The right rev. prelate had called his [Lord Denman's] learned brethren on the Bench who had differed from him, ' the friends of the liberty of the Church.' In his opinion no one who had an opportunity of considering the subject could doubt that his learned brother, Mr. Justice Erle, and himself had conferred a real benefit on the Church by putting a stop to the issue of this writ of mandamus."

Viewing the petition presented by the Bishop of Exeter as merely seeking to put an end to the penalties of *præmunire* as affecting certain of the clergy, Lord Denman expressed it as his opinion that in the case of confirmation the penalty of *præmunire* was wholly unnecessary, the Archbishop being in his judgment imperatively enjoined to confirm the election of a bishop. " Indeed," he added, " the penalty of *præmunire* is in its own nature objectionable, and unworthy of a civilized country. No man ought, for any offense, to be placed out of the protection of the law, and he should gladly see the title of *præmunire* expunged from our code."

Denman then proceed, with that grave and courteous irony of which, though he rarely employed it, he was a master, to suggest to the right rev. prelate a much more effectual remedy in the case than the mere abolition of *præmunire* on failure to elect or to confirm, and that was " the re-enactment of the statute of Edward VI., conferring on the Crown the power, which with regard to Irish bishops it still enjoys, of *the direct appointment of Bishops.*

"He thought an amendment of the 25 Henry VIII., by substituting this simple process for the cumbrous machinery of *Congé d'Elire and Letters Missive* would be a great improvement of the law, and would avoid the scandal and similar questions in Westminster Hall in future. To this extent he should be happy to lend his aid to the right rev. prelate in his endeavors after a reform of the law."

Solvuntur risu tabulæ; the redoubtable Phillpotts had met his match at his own weapons.[1]

A few days after this he wrote the following letter to his friend and son-in-law, Hodgson, who had, it seems, written to the Chief Justice to express his cordial approvement of the judgment in Hampden's case; to congratulate him on Captain Denman's escape, owing to the decision in *Buron* v. *Denman*, from the clutches of the slave-owner; and to communicate his own disappointment in not having been nominated to the recently vacant see of Chester—a preferment for which, perhaps, his exertions for the abolition of *Montem* had not recommended him in high quarters:

"Guildhall: February 19, 1848.

"My dear Hodgson,—Your agreeable and kind letter only disappointed me in not announcing that Her Majesty required your services at Chester. Well, we shall keep you nearer, and see you oftener. Many thanks for your remembrance of my birthday [21st February], which will, I hope, prove auspicious for the commencement of your sanitary visit to Brighton. I am very happy that you approve of my doings in the Hampden case, for it has always been one of the most painful acts of my judicial life to differ with my judicial brethern. But the more I think of it the more I am satisfied of the propriety of our judgment, on the law in the first place, and secondly, in the exercise of our discretion in discharging the rule. Surely the law ought to be altered,

[1] The debate, which is interesting, is well reported in Hansard, Parl. Deb., third series, vol. xcvi. House of Lords, February 15, 1848. Lord Denman's speech extends from pp. 644–647.

but whether any control should be imposed on the Crown, after appointing, seems very doubtful. The Crown, certainly, is not infallible; but who is? I shudder at the very idea of trials for heresy, and a smell of burning comes into my nose. I am wholly ignorant of Hampden's merits or demerits; the best thing arising from the imprudence of appointing him is the name given to our friend, your diocesan [the celebrated prelate, then Bishop of Oxford, late of Winchester] *the Re-tractarian.*[1]

"Joe's case has, indeed, come to a triumphant end for him. I hope a final one."

On February 22, the Earl of Aberdeen, in moving for a return of the number of slave vessels captured by Her Majesty's cruisers during the years 1845, 1846, and 1847, made an able and eloquent speech, in the course of which he spoke, with strong reprobation, of a feeling that seemed to be growing up in favor of recalling the squadron, from a conviction that, so far from diminishing, it increased the loss of life and other horrors of the Middle Passage.[2]

Lord Denman denied that those preventive means had increased the sufferings of the negroes to anything like the extent supposed. He said that

"The torture and misery had always been extreme. He was old enough to remember when a bill was brought into the House of Commons, limiting the number of slaves that should be shipped on board vessels of a certain size and tonnage, *and that bill was vigorously resisted. The very discussion by Parliament whether a wretched captive was to have an inch more or less to lie down in, was treated as an interference with the rights of private property, and an invasion of the principles of Free Trade.*

"Public opinion on this subject appeared to him to have undergone a lamentable and disgraceful change. The treatment of the efforts of our squadron as a mere failure was purely absurd. In fact, some of those who affected to lament its wants of success were only annoyed that it had succeeded too well. They descried the em-

[1] From his having first joined with those who condemned Hampden, and afterwards, having, in the interim, carefully read his books, retracted his former judgment, declaring he could find no heretical pravity in them.

[2] Hansard, Parl. Deb., third series, vol. xcvi. p. 1037.

ployment of our cruisers because it had disappointed the schemes of the slave-traders in Cuba and Brazil, and their allies in other countries."

In the course of this speech Denman reiterated with great emphasis his often avowed opinion that the Slave Trade ought to be regarded and dealt with as being *by the law of nations ipso facto piracy*, and he said that in his opinion it was a great misfortune that Mr. Canning in 1823 did not accept the offer then made by the United States so to declare it. "Had that proposal been accepted," said Denman, "the Slave Trade, I believe, would not now exist."

"His principal reason," he said, "for having thus re-stated on the present occasion his decided opinion on the nature and character of slave-trading, was because he had recently seen the claim of an owner of human beings, made slaves for the purpose of trade, recognized for the first time in an English Court of Justice."[1]

And now the French Revolution of February 24 came, "perplexing kings with fear of change," and profoundly altering in its result the destinies of Europe. Denman, with his brave and cheerful temperament, remained firm and unmoved, sharing neither the exaggerated hopes nor the exaggerated terrors of the times.

He admired as much as any one the magnificent demonstration by which, on the memorable eighth of April, the higher and middle classes of London proved their attachment to the cause of freedom with order; but he had also the moral courage to speak of himself in the House of Lords "as an old friend and well-wisher" to those among the working classes who were seeking for still further measures of political reform; while, though he did not oppose, he by no means gave his unqualified approbation to the Bill introduced by Government (on the ground of the disturbed state of the times, and the numbers of foreign revolutionaries alleged to be flocking into England), for the *Removal of Aliens*. When this last mentioned bill was, on April 13, introduced by Lord Lansdowne into the Upper House, Lord Denman said that,

[1] In allusion to *Buron* v. *Denman*. Lord Denman's speech on this occasion, by no means one of his best, will be found in Hansard, Parl. Deb., third series, vol. xcvi. pp. 1051–1055.

"He could not see a bill of this kind introduced without expressing his very great regret that it was found necessary to give Government a power of such enormous extent—a Bill which would enable any individual to ruin his enemy by secret information to the Secretary of State if he should feel bound to act on the information conveyed to him.

"In former days, when the battle was fought against the Alien Bill year after year in the House of Commons, it was his pride to have been connected with those who contended against it. When, in 1826, that Act was finally repealed, Sir Robert Peel, on whose motion it was abrogated, was received by those who were generally opposed to him, with such shouts of applause as would not soon be forgotten by him."[1]

When, on April 19, Lord Cottenham introduced to the House the "Crown and Government Security Bill," the Duke of Wellington having made some strong observations "on the growing contempt of the people for the law, as shown by the distracted state of the country," Lord Denman, adverting to those observations, said:

"That they might be correct as applicable to those who had made the present Bill necessary, but we would suggest that it was hardly just to the People of England—who had so recently taken into their own hands the vindication of their safety—to assert that there was in the great body of that England a contempt for the law.

"He thought, on the contrary, that when they saw that recent exhibition of peaceful men turning off from the ordinary and needful occupations of life to expose themselves to possible danger and certain inconvenience—he thought there was brought before them the most gratifying proof of attachment to the law, arising from this, that they knew by long experience the benefits of the protection to be derived from it.

"I am sure [said Lord Denman] I can never speak without feelings of the utmost admiration and gratitude, in which all mankind concur, of the conduct of the Noble Duke—his recent conduct in these troubles, and the whole tenor of his life; but I feel that I should be wanting, in some degree, in what is due to the real char-

[1] Hansard, Parl. Deb., third series, vol. xcviii. p. 278.

acter of the English people if I allowed that which looked like a general imputation 'of a growing contempt for the law' to pass without comment."[1]

The Duke explained that he had never meant to impute a growing contempt for law to the English people generally, and that, on the contrary, nobody could admire more than he did the general conduct of the people on occasion of the great demonstration of April 8.

In the course of this summer, Denman received from the United States the following letter from Mr. William Kent, son of the venerable ex-Chancellor, who had recently died, the object of universal respect on both sides of the Atlantic, at the ripe age of eighty-three. Mr. William Kent had been in England three years previously, and been received, as his father's son was sure to be, with cordial hospitality by the English Chief Justice.

"New York, June 6, 1848.

"My Lord,—I venture to request your acceptance of a copy of a discourse recently delivered before the Judiciary and Bar of the State of Norfolk, on the life and character of my father, the late Chancellor Kent.

"It was with deeply gratified feeling that my father received the flattering expression of your opinion of his works and judicial character which ocasionally crossed the Atlantic.

"On my return to America from England, I had the happiness of finding him, though 83 years old, still vigorous in mind and body; and it was an unmingled pleasure to answer his questions about England, and particularly about Westminster Hall, the subject of his meditation and study during so long a period of his life.

"It was his intention, though, I believe, from his unaffected modesty he never carried his intention into effect, to thank you, by letter, for the kindness with which you have so often spoken of him, and for the courtesy shown to his son during his visit in England in 1845.

"I have the honor to be, with the most profound respect.

"Your Lordship's

"Most obedient and most humble servant,

"WILLIAM KENT.

[1] Hansard, Parl. Deb., third series, vol. xcviii. p. 503.

As the summer proceeded it became clear from current conversation, occasional correspondence, and the opinions of the Press, that the evidence taken before Hutt's Committee,[1] then recently published, and as yet unanswered, was producing a very general and strong feeling in a great portion of the public against the policy of keeping up the West African Squadron.

The following letters from the Chief Justice (who presided this summer on the Midland Circuit) to his son, Captain Denman, will show the eager avidity with which he followed the evidence, and the feverish anxiety with which he contemplated the possible result of the inquiry:

"Leicester: July 29, 1848.

"My dearest Joseph,—I have devoured Captain Matson's pamphlet, and not knowing how far his *professional* views may be correct or *bonâ fide*, feel rather pleased with it than otherwise. Do you know him? I should be inclined to make his acquaintance, and if that be not feasible, should be disposed to give him a short letter by the Press. I would accept all his concurrence, lament any difference, show (if it can be done clearly and shortly) that he has misconceived the argument or committed some error, but declare openness to conviction and a wish to conciliate him on the great object common to both, which seems about to be arrested from you by the astuteness of Cliffe,[2] the stupidity of Mr. M—— (who is he?), and the absurd gullibility of Hutt's committee. If the subject takes you, and can be touched with a light hand, it will afford us an opportunity of exposing the evidence of which so much advantage is taken, and the enormous folly of the reaction in public opinion.

[1] So called from Mr. (now the Right Hon. Sir Benjamin) Hutt—its chairman. It was a committee appointed by the House of Commons, in 1847, to consider "of providing for the best means to be adopted for the final extinction of the Slave Trade." The chairman, Mr. Hutt, before the appointment of the committee, had shown what his own conviction was, by declaring in the House of Commons, that, if asked how he would deal with the Slave Trade, he would reply, without doubt or reservation, "Leave the Slave Trade to itself."

[2] Dr. Cliffe—the ablest witness examined before Hutt's committee on the Anti-Squadron and Pro-Slave Trade side: he admitted himself to be a slave-owner.

"The cause has fallen so low that I hardly see a hope of remedy except in its falling still lower. When at zero I do think that if a temperate and effective speech could be made, quietly pointing out the momentary triumph of falsehood in fact, and fallacy in doctrine, and warning them that the Slave Trade is on the eve of a revival ten times more extensive than ever, under England's patronage and for her sordid benefit,—it might be the foundation of good, or at least stop the downward progress from bad to worse."

In a few days he writes again on the same subject:

"Coventry: August 2, 1848.

"My dearest Joe,—I wish I could express half the pleasure it gives me to find myself your fellow-laborer in this good cause, in which great service has already been done if the squadron escapes the Committee.

"I will hope you will find Aberdeen or Brougham accessible to the arguments about treaties; but my points are all on the principle. If Brougham can be persuaded to take up Senhor Cliffe, the exhibition will be truly grand. I think I can do something with him.

"The business of the circuit, very light hitherto, begins to be rather heavy at the last two places, but I have no fear of ending it by Saturday night. Margaret's great affair comes off next week,[1] but even that should not prevent me from coming to town when necessary. When that may be I do not yet collect from the papers. They surely can not mean to whip it through the Lords as in 1846. Who and what is Captain M——? A gentleman who sets out on an adventure to suppress the slave trade and begins his enterprise by discovering that it never can be successful, fortifying that opinion by scraps from all quarters, which he carefully copies in his commonplace book. One thing I will readily concede to him, that for *him*, or such as him, to suppress it is quite as impossible as he thinks it. Perhaps his practice may have contradicted his theory, and doing a noble deed, in nature's spite, his acts may have refuted his opinion. If, on the contrary, he has done nothing, that result may

[1] Second marriage of his fourth daughter, Margaret, with Edward Cropper, Esq., which took place in August, 1848; her first husband, Mr. Macaulay, had died in 1846.

account for his opinion. It is a strange boast for a British naval officer, really bent on the service with which he is intrusted, to find his evidence in all respects perfectly conformable to that of the former slave-trader and present slave-owner [Dr. Cliffe], equally bent on defeating that service. The impudence of the man who imputes the horrors of which he with his fellow slave-owners are the authors, to the attempts of the squadron to prevent them is only unequaled by the perverted ingenuity of him who abounds in refined speculations on remote consequences, overlooking the obvious evils which stare him in the face and defy him."

Denman resolved to make a supreme effort in the House of Lords for the preservation of the squadron, which he regarded as the sole effectual means for the extinction of the Slave Trade. On returning from circuit, he gave notice of motion for August 22, for "an address to the Crown on the subject of the Slave Trade," and having in the interim fully charged his mind with all the mass of evidence, oral and documentary, which at all bore on the subject, he, on the day appointed, appeared in his place, and made the ablest and most powerful speech he ever delivered in either House of Parliament.

The following interesting letter, written to Lady Denman from the House shortly before his great effort was to be made, shows clearly the high-wrought though carefully repressed excitement under which at the moment he was laboring:

"House of Lords: August 22, 1848.
"Half-past two, P. M.

"Dearest Love,—I write to you for the purpose of keeping my mind in a composed state, having filled it as full as it can hold of interesting matter. I hope to carry it through its difficult task with as much steadiness as I raised the last bumper to your health. My journey in the coupé was solitary, but not tedious, for I studied my case thoroughly and found much valuable aid in the Blue Books.

"After breakfast, yesterday, I went to Brougham's, and with him to the House, and we concerted and notified the measures to be taken. I then went with him to Miss

Burdett's[1] to dinner, and met and sat next to the Duke of Wellington, who was remarkably agreeable and good-natured. There was also the Indian Sir Charles Napier (conqueror of Scinde) there, a most agreeable and ready man. Miss Burdett asked much after you. This morning I have been again with Brougham and some knowing people, and now am in the Library to look at all the books and papers that can throw light on my subject.

"I strongly feel the vast responsibility of my task, and what immense consequences may flow from its being well or ill performed. But what can I rest upon with a better chance of securing the needed equanimity, than that kind and affectionate bosom which beats so warmly for everything that is good? All the qualities worth having which I can flatter myself with possessing, are preserved by my being the husband of such a wife, and the father of such children. God bless you.

"Your ever affectionate and faithful husband."

The following brief extracts can, of course, give only a very inadequate notion, though it is hoped they may give some notion, of the merits of this masterly speech:

He began by saying,

"That he must ask their lordships to bear in mind this proposition: that the slave trade was one of the worst of human crimes; the most daring violation of the laws of God and man, prompted by the basest motives, productive of the greatest amount of suffering, and that it more effectually prevented the progress in civilization and happiness of a very large portion of the human race.

"The House of Commons, in full accordance with this principle, had recently appointed a committee 'to consider the best means of providing for the extinction of the Slave Trade.'

"The gentleman who moved the appointment of that committee, and afterward became its chairman (Mr. Hutt), had unfortunately formed a preconceived opinion on one of the most important points to which its inquiries could be directed. He had said, if asked 'What are we to do with the Slave Trade?' he would say,

[1] Baroness Burdett-Coutts.

without reserve, 'Leave the Trade to itself'—*in other words, he assumed, before entering on his function of inquiry, that the squadron ought to be removed from the coast of Africa.*

"Two propositions have been put forward as decidedly conclusive against the continued maintenance of our squadron on the coast of Africa. One of these is that the means employed for the extinction of the traffic have proved ineffectual; the other is, that our attempts to put it down have done more harm than good, and have had the effect of greatly aggravating the horrors of the trade."

Denman then proceeded to the disproof of both these propositions.

As to the first, he proved (*from the evidence taken before Hutt's Committee*) that the vile traffic had been suppressed in the river Quorra, in the Bonny, and also in the Gambia; that instead of the 12,000 negroes formerly exported every year to Cuba, the number had dwindled down to 1,000 in the year 1845; that the exportation to Brazil, also, was being materially and progressively reduced.

"But at the very lowest point of its depression [he said] an unfortunate circumstance had contributed again to increase the traffic. The opinion of the law officers of the Crown had been somewhat unguardedly expressed as to the measures taken in destroying the barracoons; the Foreign Office[1] had communicated those opinions to the Admiralty, the slave-holders had got possession of the letter, and had immediately dispatched it to the coast.

"A report was circulated in Africa that a revolution had taken place in England, that Lord Palmerston had been overthrown, and that the new Government intended to revive the Slave Trade.

"It had been admitted [said Lord Denman] in the evidence, that in 1843 the Slave Trade was considered a losing trade in Brazil, and the evidence of Dr. Cliffe,[2]

[1] In Lord Aberdeen's letter of May 20, 1842, already cited in this volume, chap. xxviii. p. 96.

[2] Senhor José Cliffe, M. D., born in the United States, domiciled in Brazil.

a good authority on the subject, showed that it was abandoned by many persons in despair, *because they thought the Government of England was sincere in the resolution to put it down;* but when they saw reason to doubt the sincerity of the English Government, then it was that the Slave Trade revived with accumulated vigor.

On the second point—viz., that the squadron had made bad worse—Denman produced a prodigious impression on the House and the country by the mode in which he pointed out that the proof before the committee of the squadron's having increased the horrors of the Slave Trade rested mainly on the evidence of Dr. Cliffe, who himself stated that he was still a slave *owner*, and and even admitted further that he had once been a slave *trader*.

"The Committee of the House of Commons [he said] had had before them a person who acknowledged himself to have been a slave trader, and this person the Committee had consulted about the best means of putting down the slave trade! Why, the bare idea of asking a former slave trader, with reference to the means employed for the suppression of the slave trade, seemed to be one of the most preposterous he ever heard of. What! [exclaimed Denman, amid the general laughter of the House] consult the wolf about the best manner of preserving the sheep! The answer, of course, would be, '*Remove the dogs!*'"

Not less effective were his comments on the evidence of the few British officers who, before the Committee, had stated themselves to be opposed to the keeping up of the squadron.

"He was aware that some of the officers employed on that station had expressed an opinion unfavorable to the continuance of the squadron, and he believed that with many the service was unpopular.

"He might refer to the evidence of Captain M——, whom he knew to be a gallant officer—a candid and honorable man—but a gentleman who went out to suppress the slave trade with the conviction that the means used would not be sufficient for the purpose; *who set about an arduous task, requiring all the energies of hope, half disqualified by despair*. This gentleman had actually read to the committee a passage from his memorandum book, copied into it by himself before he left England, embodying that sentiment. Surely it may be suggested without any disrespect either to the Admiralty or to the officer, that men entertaining such an opinion should not be selected for the service."[1]

The effect produced by this vigorous and admirable speech was remarkable; it at once turned the wavering balance of public opinion, and mainly contributed to avert the sacrifice of the squadron.

It was followed up by another speech on August 28, on the same subject, in which Denman was particularly happy in exposing the charge of calumny made against him in the *Morning Chronicle* of August 24:[2]

"Calumny [said Lord Denman] is a strong word, but I do not complain of it, for I perceive the sense in which it is used by the writer. The calumny is not that I stated anything untruly, but that I made strong observations on the evidence of a person who stated himself to have been once a slave trader. If I had incorrectly charged Dr. Cliffe with being a slave trader, I should plead guilty to uttering the worst of calumnies; but when he himself confesses that he has been a slave trader, the character affixed to that crime is not affixed by me, but by the law. The law of England proclaims him, as long as and inasmuch as he was a slave trader, to have been a pirate, a robber, and a felon. So does the law of America, where he was born. So do the public acts of the Brazilian empire, where he was domiciled."

These speeches greatly tended to increase the reputation of Denman as an orator, a matter about which he was comparatively careless; but they accomplished another purpose about which he had been passionately anxious, and which it was the dearest object of his heart to achieve—*they saved the Squadron.*

Not satisfied with his exertions in Parliament alone,

[1] This speech is reported in Hansard, Parl. Deb., third series, vol. ci. pp. 365–371.

[2] This charge of calumny was founded on many very strong observations by Denman on Dr. Cliffe's evidence, which have been omitted in the brief resumé of his speech in the text.

Denman, before this laborious year came to a close, endeavoring to act on public feeling through the press, published a pamphlet entitled "A letter from Lord Denman to Lord Brougham on the Final Extinction of the Slave Trade." This publication necessarily goes over the same ground as his speeches, and presents nothing specially calling for notice here, except, perhaps, the following passage, which explains and justifies the vehemence with which on this question he could not help expressing himself:

"To form a sound judgment on these weighty matters I have studied to divest my mind of every bias. But if any one expects the contemplation of them to awaken no emotion which may find a vent in some vehemence of language, I think he requires correct reasoning from an understanding that must have lost the best security for discerning truth, the moral perception of right and wrong, and a sense of the value of justice and humanity.

CHAPTER XXXIV.

WESTERN SPRING CIRCUIT OF 1849—THE TWO FIRST ATTACKS OF PARALYSIS—RESIGNATION.

A. D. 1849–1850. ÆT. 70–71.

IN the Spring Assizes of 1849, Denman went the Western Circuit with Sir Edward Vaughan Williams, who had been raised to the Bench, as one of the Judges of the Court of Common Pleas, on the transfer of Sir William Erle to the Court of Queen's Bench.[1]

The work on this circuit, especially in its latter stages, was unusually severe, and Denman's health, which had already been shaken by the excitement of the Slave Trade discussions, and the strain of his judicial labors in Westminster Hall, was no doubt unfavorably affected by the protracted sittings, not unfrequently lasting over twelve hours, which occasionally fell to his lot during these assizes.

From a letter written to Lady Denman, from Salisbury, on March 11, the following passage may be extracted, giving a brief account of the reception of himself and his brother judge at Strathfieldsaye by the Duke of Wellington, then in the eightieth year of his age:

"On February 28, on arriving at the Winchfield station, and during the long process of taking the carriage off the truck and putting to the horses, we were assailed by the most bitter snow and rain storm I ever remember. The ground was deeply covered in a moment, but we drove rapidly to Strathfieldsaye, and arrived rather

[1] The Right Hon. Sir Edward Vaughan Williams, called to the Bar, 1823; published his standard work, "On the Law of Executors," in 1832; raised to the Bench, November 1846; retired, 1865, when he was added to the Privy Council.

late, but in time, seeing lights still in the bed-rooms and dressing-rooms. The house was all comfort and brightness, the Duke cordial, easy, good-natured, and his conversation lively and entertaining; my brother Judge 'Boswellized' him. His views of French affairs are encouraging, and accord exactly with my own—viz., that the present Government [the Republic, with Louis Napoleon as President] gives the best security for preserving the peace that can be expected, and that the two Bourbon branches can never bring forth the fruit of good government, enjoying no attachment on the part of France, nor deserving any. He was much amused by the letter in 'Punch' written in his name (offering to give away Jenny Lind to Captain Harris),[1] and he mentioned, incidentally, a practice of his own, which ought to be general, and perhaps may be made so by his example: 'I am always very attentive to ladies on horseback, and always pull up when I meet one.' Then he mentioned having lately met a lady, riding a spirited horse, to whom he offered his company for protection, which she was foolish enough to decline. He rather thought afterwards that it was his new 'daughter,' Jenny Lind. Next morning the hounds met there. I never saw a meet before; it was highly animated."

Sir E. V. Williams has very kindly permitted the publication of his more accurate and graphic account of this visit, containing a very vivid transcript of the sayings and doings of their illustrious host:

"We did not get to Strathfieldsaye till it was so late that the Duke had gone up to dress, and when we met before dinner, he expressed his regret that he had not been in the way to receive us as usual. Nothing could be kinder or more hospitable than his reception. He seemed very well and in excellent spirits. Lord Douro and Lord Charles Wellesley were there, but Lady Douro was in Scotland, and Lady Charles, as I understood, expecting her confinement in London. There was a large party of the county gentlemen of the first

[1] There was a rumor at this time of an intended marriage between the celebrated singer, Jenny Lind (now Madame Goldschmidt), and Captain Harris, a nephew of Mrs. Grote, wife of the celebrated historian of Greece.

distinction. The lady guests were few, and I can not say that they had aristocratical names. Mrs. and Miss Browne and Mrs. Smith (the Brownes are tenants of a house belonging to the Duke in the neighborhood, and Mrs. Smith is the wife of the well-known Assheton Smith);[1] there was also a Miss Walmesley, Mrs. Browne's sister. The Duke led the way to dinner; Lord Denman took Mrs. Smith, and I took Mrs. Browne. Lord Denman sate at the Duke's right hand, and I at his left. The dinner was very superb and good, but the waiting very bad; the display of plate quite magnificent.

"The Duke was most attractive and obliging, and I really think I never knew any one make himself more agreeable. As soon as we had got to the drawing-room, I escaped to my own room and 'Boswellized,' writing down the heads of his talk which I could recollect, and I did the same at breakfast, the next morning, so that I am able to give you pretty exactly some of the things he said.

"The first observations I can recall were with reference to Macaulay's history. He said, 'It is capital, it puts you in the very heart of the society of the time, and makes you live among the people of that day.' Lord Denman said that it was rumored Croker meant to attack it in the 'Quarterly.' The Duke said: 'Well, Croker may say his worst, but he can't make it out anything but a book of great value. It makes you see and feel the motives of the people of those times.' He added, afterwards: 'Macauley has no doubt had great advantages—in Mr. Fox's book, Sir James Mackintosh's, and the French papers. But he has used them very well—*very well indeed.*' Shortly after the Duke said: 'It is curious how the system of a double mission to foreign courts was constantly kept up under the old French Monarchy, one ostensible, the other secret. Even as late as Louis XVI., Mirabeau was sent in that way to Berlin. The English have no notion of this kind of thing, nor of what espoinage there is in every depart-

[1] Schoolfellow at Eton, and former opponent of Denman's at one of his elections for Nottingham; the famous sportsman, rider, and master of hounds.

ment of the public service on the Continent.' Lord Denman said: 'One consequence is that as people write their letters knowing they will be read before they reach their destination, they word them accordingly.' The Duke said: 'Yes, yes, to be sure. I remember when I commanded the army in Spain, I intercepted a vast deal of correspondence. Amongst the rest I used to intercept the letters which a man named Bourke, the Swedish Envoy at Madrid used to send to his court. They used to begin with a regular statement of what the authorities said had taken place, or would take place; but at the end he used to add: *mais il y'a des malveillants* who say so and so; and I soon found out that what he wrote at the begining was false, and what he wished his Government to believe was what the *malveillants* said. I met him many years afterwards in London, and told him what I had suspected, and he said: 'You were quite right, that was our cipher.' Lord Denman observed that he had been told the system of espoinage was never stricter in France than during the first Republic. The Duke said: 'Aye, that was owing to the trouble the secret societies gave, and that was the origin of their strict system of passports. I remember an odd thing about the French system. I was in command of a part of the troops that were employed to help the expedition we sent against Copenhagen, and a gentleman with the *historical* name (this was the Duke's exact expression) of Rosencrantz, who was living thereabouts, asked me to dine. We walked together after dinner, and he told me how much he disliked the French system of police that had been introduced. Said he: 'Do you know, now, I shall have to report all about your having dined with me, and what you said and what I said, and also this very conversation?' I replied to him, 'Well, *we* have not got to quite such a pitch of civilization as that; I shan't have to report anything to my commanding officer unless I like it.'

"Soon after the Duke began to talk about the present state of France, and agreed with Lord Denman that Louis Napoleon had done very well [this was in 1849]. 'I don't know what better they could do than have him,' Lord Denman said. 'Some people think something might be done to steady the French by uniting the two branches of the Bourbon family.' The Duke: 'Oh no! neither of the branches has left a single recollection to make them dear to the people.' He said, 'Carvaignac is a respectable, sensible man. He kept his power as long as it was wanted, and then he could keep it no longer.' He asked Lord Denman if he had been acquainted with Madame de Stael? 'She was' (said the Duke) 'a clever, sensible woman; she told me she thought the old French Republic would have worked well enough if a sucessful soldier had not sprung up. But I think she was wrong. It was tumbling to pieces before; so many of the leading men in it had been found out in such corruptions about money.' He said it was curious how anxious the French nation now were to have the English public opinion favorable to them, and he believed they always looked in their proceedings to what the English would say. 'And it is very strange,' says he, 'the first thing this new Republic did was to tumble on the worst measure England ever took—maintaing able-bodied men at the public expense—and now they are trying the refuse of the English measures (of Spence and Owen), Socialism and that sort of thing.'

"He spoke of Phillpotts, the Bishop, and Lord Denman and the Duke agreed in praising his speeches and his great talents for debate. 'But (said the Duke) he is always at war with somebody, which a bishop ought not to be—he is always in hot water; he can't keep out of hot water. You know what Canning wrote in his letter offering Lyndhurst the Seals: he put in a postscript, *Phillpotto non obstante*.' And this is all I recorded of the dinner talk.

"In the drawing-room the Duke sent Miss Walmesley to the piano to play a chant which he had heard at the Temple Church, and was so much pleased with it that he got them to send him the music. It was for the responses between the Commandments. Later in the evening he begged her to play it again, and it plainly gave him real pleasure to hear it.

"My bed-room was on the ground floor, and was not sumptuously furnished, though there was every possible comfort and a very large bed.

"Next morning at breakfast, in the gallery, the guests were at different tables of four persons for each table—the first being for the Duke and Mrs. Assheton Smith, Lord Denman and myself. The Duke was silent at first, though he seemed in excellent health and spirits, and seemed amused at the conversation that was going on. At last he said: 'So I find I've got a new daughter given me by "Punch"—I've not read it myself, but I am told there is a letter in "Punch." "The Duke of Wellington presents his compliments to Miss Jenny Lind, and will be very happy to act as her father and give her away at her wedding." You know she is going to be married to Captain Harris, Mrs. Grote's nephew? Well, I believe I have given away more young ladies than most men in England, and the last was the prettiest I ever gave away, and that was Lady Ely.'[1] Mrs. Smith said: 'Is it true that Jenny Lind is not going to appear on the stage again?' The Duke said: 'I suppose you think you have a right to ask me, now I am one of the family. Her Majesty (so he always called the Queen) told me she was not going on the stage again, and that Jenny Lind told her so.' He said afterwards, 'I saw Jenny Lind the other day, and did not know her till it was too late, and I'll tell you how it was. I make it a rule, if I see a lady riding before me, never to pass her at a fast pace. I always pull up and pass her quite slowly, that I may not frighten the horse, and if I see a lady whose horse is fidgety and giving her trouble, I always stop and ask her if I can be of any service to her. Well, the other day in the Park I was riding and came up to a lady whose horse was plaguing her, and I stopped and took my hat off and asked her if I could be of any service, and said my horse was quite quiet, and I would ride a little way with her to quiet hers, if she liked it. She knew who I was, and said: "No, your Grace, thank you—I won't trouble you," and rode on. Then it immediately struck me it was Jenny Lind, And her I am sure it was now; and it's very odd I didn't recognize her, for I know her quite well and have often talked to her.' Lord Denman said: 'Your story has not raised

[1] Miss Vere, now the Dowager Marchioness of Ely, married to the third Marquis in 1844.

my opinion of her good sense.' 'Hasn't it,' said the Duke. 'No,' said Lord Denman, 'she ought to have accepted your offer, whether she needed it or not.' The Duke seemed much pleased, and said: 'Oh that's it, is it.'

"After breakfast the hounds met at Strathfieldsaye, and it was a cheerful sight. We left soon after 11 A. M. Nothing could be more cordial in manner than the Duke's adieux. Of course it was mere form—he would have said the same to any other judge who had been his guest; still it was pleasant to be told by such a man that he was very glad to have had the pleasure and the honor of seeing me."

At Winchester the work was heavier than usual, and occupied the greater part of five days. The Judges took the train to Salisbury, and missed the Sheriff, who afterwards, with all his cavalcade, followed the fly in which they drove to their lodgings. The beauty of the cathedral, though he had often seen it before, seems to have struck Denman more than ever on this occasion, and his letter to his wife is enthusiastic on the subject. He tells an odd circumstance connected with one of the eastern windows:

"I must tell you of a curious disfigurement of this noble building; a window at the east end has a wretched painting of a brazen serpent. It was given by the late Lord Radnor, an odd man, who surmounted the painting with his armorial bearings, the Earl's coronet occupying the highest place. The motto or text is unfortunate: 'Thus must the Son of Man be lifted up,' *i. e.* elevated to the dignity of an earldom."

On his way from Dorchester to Exeter, Denman visited for the first time the closely neighboring country-seats of his two sincere friends and highly esteemed judicial brethren, Patteson and Coleridge, then both absent on their respective circuits. He thus mentions his visit to his wife (in a letter of March 18): had his spirits and mental power been what they once were, he would have doubtless thrown more animation into his description.

"Yesterday we turned our faces westward, and visited on our journey both Patteson's and Coleridge's country-seats. I was delighted with their beauty and comfort.

Patteson's (Feniton Court, near Honiton) is really magnificent, with a fine long avenue and a charming undulation of ground. Coleridge's (Heath's Court, Ottery St. Mary) has a delightful garden, close to an ancient church very large and curious. They are about three miles apart, in a fine country."[1]

At Exeter the business was of more than usual importance and difficulty, and he had frequently to sit till a late hour in Court. Writing to Lady Denman, on March 25, from Boconnor, near Bodmin, he says:

"Having done all my duty at Exeter on Saturday night (leaving Court at 10 P.M., after a 13 hours' trial), Tom and I traveled westward, and are now at Mr. Fortescue's, at Boconnor, a very fine park and place, the property of Lady Grenville, who lends it for his residence. He is brother of Lord Fortescue, a most amiable man—his wife a sister of Lord Harrowby's. The house belonged to Sir Bevil Grenville, who maintained the fight for Charles I. in these parts when his cause was desperate everywhere else. I am now writing in the bedroom of that ill-fated king, and am to sleep, I believe, in his bed to-night. We have been twice to church to-day, in two different churches connected with this property, and, it being Lady-Day, have heard two sermons in honor of the Virgin Mary."

On April 1 he writes from Taunton, the last place at the Spring Assizes:

"On Monday, a beautiful sunny day, Mr. Fortescue and Lady Louisa mounted us on ponies, and, with their son, we made a long day's excursion among his woods and plantations, which are of great extent and beauty. The most noble situation among them is called the 'Queen's Bench,' and we mean to hold our Court there occasionally during the Summer Assizes. My work at Bodmin occupied three days, and on the fourth I assisted my brother Williams, and left him in the midst of a long cause, which, I believe, still detains him. We had a pleasant dinner and evening at Plymouth, and yesterday the return journey by the South Devon railway

[1] These two distinguished and excellent judges were brothers-in-law, Patteson having married, as his second wife, Frances Duke, the sister of Mr. Justice Coleridge.

made up for previous disappointments—the sun shining and the sea splashing. At Dawlish, Sir Thomas Acland got into our carriage, and took us for an hour or so to Killerton, his famous and fine place, where we had just time to admire the grounds and take luncheon. At 3 his lady drove us in her pony carriage so as to be just in time for the train which brought us here. I had written to tell the Sheriff not to await us at the station, where we took a fly, with orders to drive to 'the Castle,' whereupon the man took us to a low pot-house of that name. The mistake was soon corrected, and we had a very pleasant *tete-à-tete* evening."

This letter is the last he ever wrote from circuit, and in it, as in those that had immediately preceded it, there is observable, not only an absence of his former life and spirits, but a marked change in his handwriting; instead of the bold, free characters, easily written and easily read, the MS. becomes cramped, feeble, and difficult to decipher. The affection of the cerebral and nervous systems, under which he finally sank, had evidently already commenced its insidious and unnoticed attacks.

"On his return to London [writes his third son, the Honorable Richard Denman], though he appeared to have felt his work more than usual, there was no symptoms that created alarm, until the morning before Easter Term (April 14, 1849), when the power of his right side was suddenly and totally destroyed by a paralytic stroke. By the skill of Sir Benjamin Brodie and Dr. Holland, the blow was averted for a time, and, in a few weeks, the use of his right side was restored to him: but they were very anxious that ample time should be given for complete recovery, and that the mind should be relieved, as far as possible, from the pressure of business and anxiety. It was, however, found impossible to resist his urgent desire to return to his post. He presided in the Court of Queen's Bench during the whole of Trinity Term (May 22 to June 12); twice appeared and spoke in the House of Lords; and when the summer circuits began, he took the business of chamber judge in London.[1] He went during this period to stay

[1] During the Summer Circuit and Long Vacation one of the Common

with Captain Holland, his son-in-law,[1] at Hampstead, as it was hoped that the daily ride to and from London would give him his requisite exercise, and be less fatiguing than going round a circuit. He was not, however, allowed to go through even with the business of chambers, for on July 21, not having been able to resist his desire of again committing his thoughts to paper, on that, to him, most exciting subject, the Slave Trade, he was again attacked by paralysis while in the midst of his writing, and, though the seizure was in its beginning so much more mild and gradual than the first as to give his family ground to hope a more speedy recovery, yet these hopes were soon destroyed; though more slow, it was more complete, and the recovery, which after all was but partial, showed to the end of his life how much his physical power had been shattered."

The first of the two occasions referred to in the above passage, as those on which Denman, after his first stroke of paralysis, addressed the House of Lords, was June 13, 1849, when the then Bishop of Oxford (late of Winchester), in one of the ablest and most eloquent speeches ever pronounced in Parliament, well worthy the son of Wilberforce, proposed an amendment to the Act repealing the Navigation Laws, refusing to the ships of nations actively engaged in the African Slave Trade the privileges proposed to be given by that Act to foreign ships in general. Denman, who heartily supported the amendment, declared in a few emphatic words his firm belief in the final extinction of the Slave Trade: it had been so far repressed that it could be effectually suppressed, nothing being wanted to that end except a firm conviction, on the part of the slave-trading nations, of the sincere determination of England and the other great Powers to put it down.[2]

The second occasion was June 22, 1849, when he spoke at some length and with great ability on moving the second reading of a Bill which had already passed the House of Commons, to enable those persons who

Law Judges always remains in town for conducting the Current business at Judges' Chambers.

[1] Married to Hon. Ann, fifth daughter of Lord Denman.

[2] Hansard, Parl. Deb., third series, vol. cvi. p. 45.

had *religious* scruples against taking an *oath*, to make an affirmation instead.

He pointed out the limited scope of this present Bill as compared with bills of a similar kind which, on three previous occasions, he had brought before the House. "The persons," he said, "whom it was intended to relieve by the present measure, were those who appeared now and then to give evidence in a Court of Justice, and who, on being called on to swear, said, 'On my conscience I believe that the very book on which you ask me to swear prohibits me from taking an oath, and I can not, therefore, take it without sin.'"

He then related with great force and liveliness some scandalous scenes which had recently occurred in Courts of Justice between Judges on the one hand and witnesses on the other, the one seeking to enforce the oath, the other to evade it, and he asked "whether the present state of things was not such as was likely to defeat justice, with no other advantage than the pleasure of sending to gaol a respectable person merely for differing from ourselves on the construction of a doubtful passage?"

His speech, in short, was an able and effective one, but the result of his motion was the same discouraging and direct negative that had attended all his previous efforts on this question in the House of Lords—contents only 10, non-contents 34, a majority of 24 against him in a House of 44.[1]

This measure of simple wisdom and justice, limited, as it was limited in the bill rejected in 1849, to persons objecting, on *religious* grounds, to take an oath, at length became law, five years afterwards, in the year of Denman's death, by virtue of the twentieth clause of the Common Law Procedure Act of 1854, as to Courts of Civil Judicature; and the privilege has been extended, by subsequent legislation, to all Courts, civil or criminal, in the three kingdoms.

One case is still left unprovided for, that of persons objecting to take an oath not on religious grounds at all, but on irreligious grounds, on the ground, namely, of

[1] Hansard, Parl. Deb., third series, vol. cvi.

non-belief in a personal God, and reluctance, therefore, to go through the mockery of invoking Him. As to this case, all that can be said is that every argument applicable to other cases, for substituting affirmations for oaths, applies equally in this, and that the sooner the legislature accords the privilege of affirming instead of swearing to this class of objectors also, the better it will be for the dignity of the Judges, the decorum of the Courts, and the interests of justice and truth.

As soon as Denman could leave town, he went down to Stony Middleton to pass the Long Vacation, remote from the exciting topics of the hour, in a state, as far as possible, of absolute quietude and repose. His removal, however, could not, it was found, safely take place till August 22, before which time, and while still staying with Captain and Mrs. Holland, at Hampstead, he dictated, for he could not write, the following lines to his attached friend and brother Judge, Coleridge:

"Hampstead: August 7, 1849.

"My dear Coleridge,—I am very much obliged for both your letters, both that which arrived on the day I was taken ill, and that which coincides with my slow, but I hope sure, recovery.

"Everything, I believe, has been very prosperous in the course of that progress, but it appears to me extremely gradual. I hope that Talfourd's appointment, every way desirable as it is,[1] will have the effect of removing all difficulties about attending chambers in the vacation; but the more interesting intelligence is that of your wedding,[2] which we rejoice in, hoping to hear that it has gone off perfectly well, and that it unfolds a prospect of everything the most auspicious. I only regret that you were deprived of Patteson's presence [then on Northern Circuit], but I cherish the hope that Wightman [who had also been the Northern Circuit] will bring him to Middleton on his way to Devonshire.

"I enjoy the account of your circuit, and quite agree with you that it would have been much better for me than chambers; but it was not chambers that threw me

[1] Talfourd succeeded Coltman as Judge of the Common Pleas in 1849.
[2] Marriage of a daughter of Mr. Justice Coleridge.

on my back. Pray offer our united congratulations and condolence to Lady Coleridge, and believe me,

"Ever yours truly,

"Δ."[1]

A postscript follows, showing that he was able to amuse himself with literature—"Do you know who wrote 'Friends in Council?'"[2]

On October 1 he again dictated a letter to Coleridge, animated with a delightful spirit of cheerful resignation, even here and there breaking out in playfulness:

"My dear Coleridge,—I will not say that it is worth while to have been so ill for the sake of receiving so much kindness, but a modification of that sentiment might conform pretty exactly to the truth. Perhaps you will not discover by the handwriting that I employ another amanuensis [Lady Denman; on the former occasion Mrs. Holland had probably been scribe]; but I shall make a larger claim on both her patience and on yours than on the last occasion. I think our autumn less advanced than yours, as you describe it. I see a great many trees from my present seat without a single yellow leaf, and we have several real, not China, roses in full blossom, and daily putting forth fresh buds. We are very literary and very idle in our studies. Cholera we have had none, but we are to have a fast on Wednesday (3rd), and I am told a sermon was preached yesterday for the occasion, from which it would appear that our national sins lie chiefly in our ecclesiastical appointments and love of Popery.[3] I hope we shall amend our lives. I hope also that Patteson will not suffer for his ball;[4] that is a dangerous subject in your diocese. I shall be sorry to hear of his occupying the same cell

[1] This mark seems to have been made with his own hand.

[2] Sir Arthur Helps.

[3] A sly hit at the High Church views of Mr. Justice Coleridge. Cholera was prevalent in 1849, and fasts were frequent.

[4] Patteson had sent out invitations for a ball at Feniton Court for September 20; on the 19th a fast was afterwards appointed for the adjoining parish of Ottery St. Mary, and, in consequence, some of the invited stayed away from the dance. The *Western Times* took up the matter, greatly to Patteson's annoyance, as showing the growing influence of the High Church clergy in the diocese of Exeter, and the freedom of the Judge from all "narrow prejudices."

with Mr. Head.[1] I think the unusual warmth of the weather accounts for his feeling more fatigued in the pursuit of partridges, and I am more delighted than I can express to hear of your increasing energy. Now, my dear Coleridge, I must warmly thank you for your practical and most friendly suggestion. My opinion of my own case I mean to scrawl in Greek characters if I can find strength and dexterity for the effort.[2] I am certainly much better than I have been, but sometimes a little dispirited by the slow progress I make. I am, however, by no means desponding, and determined to make the best of everything, notwithstanding the strange alternation of feelings, and the difficulty of distinguishing between power actually acquired and that made more skillful by practice. The expedient you propose may, perhaps, be properly tried, but we are yet nearly a month from term, and a change of circumstances may decide for us otherwise. At all events,

"I am, ever very sincerely yours,

"DENMAN."

This signature, in his own handwriting, has evidently been accomplished with great difficulty, and on the blank leaf of the letter is written twice over (the first attempt having been a comparative failure) the Homeric line descriptive of what he felt to be his precarious condition:

Καὶ νῦν ταῦτά γε πάντα θεῶν ἐν γούνασι κεῖται.[3]

On October 29, he dictated another letter to Coleridge, intended, also, to be seen by Patteson. His two brother Judges had written in the kindest terms, begging him not to think of getting into work before Christmas, and suggesting arrangements by which the business of the Court might, until that time, be carried on in his absence:

"Middleton, October 29, 1849.

"My dear Coleridge,—This is my answer to your

[1] A clerical victim at that time of the episcopal zeal of the fiery prelate, Phillpotts, in whose diocese of Exeter both Patteson and Coleridge had their country seats.

[2] Probably to conceal his view as to his precarious condition from her who acted as his amanuensis.

[3] "And now, in very truth, these things are all in the lap of the gods," *i. e.*, in the hands of Providence.

kind letter to myself and Patteson's to Tom [present Lord Denman]. I agree entirely in your views, and am rejoiced more than I can express, to receive such an assurance of your feelings, but I do think you are a little too indulgent as to the nature of the question. It appears to me that the burden of proving future capacity, lies on the now incapacitated. I understand the Chancellor[1] to have so stated it, and it was that which first occurred to my own mind; if, therefore, the medical opinion is very clear that that capacity can not be expected to return within a reasonable time, I think that the final resolution must now be taken. I offered to go to town to be inspected and examined, but Brodie has kindly offered to make his observation here, and will come to-morrow. Perhaps you will think that I might have delayed writing till the report is made, but I thought it better that you should have my view of the state of the question, and I will write and inform you of his opinion in time for your consultation. I think I may rely on your opinion to that extent in which I agree with its being adopted by our two other brethren [Erle and Wightman], at least supposing Wightman to be in force, but his condition is an important element in the case. I own the difficulty I have most strongly felt has been the postponement till Christmas, but that is entirely removed by what the Chancellor has said, provided you arc unanimous in thinking that the interval may be filled up.

"I can not tell how gladly I hear of Lady Coleridge's improvement in health, trusting, with entire confidence, that it may be very favorable to your own.

"Believe me, my dear brothers,[2]

"Sincerely and affectionately yours.

"DENMAN."

Sir Benjamin Brodie came down to Middleton, and his opinion then was that if Lord Denman abstained from judicial work till after the ensuing Christmas, there was a sufficient possibility of his then being able permanently to resume his judicial duties to justify him in postponing his resignation.

His brother Judges, with the most active kindness and

[1] Lord Cottenham. [2] Coleridge and Patteson.

consideration, made every arrangement, regardless of the additional labor thus imposed on themselves, for carrying on without him the business of the Queen's Bench, both in Banc and at Nisi Prius, till the Christmas Vacation, he supplying them, from time to time, with all needful information upon motions for new trials in cases which had been tried before him on the assizes and during the sittings before his attack.

Several letters communicating such information have been preserved, but are naturally not of sufficient interest to justify insertion. The last of the series (written to Coleridge) was commenced on December 22, and continued on the 25th. It is in his own hand, the writing very shaky, and evidently the result of considerable labor, but still a great improvement on his previous attempts. Omitting a reference to a case of *Reg.* v. *Hay*, of no interest, except, as the newspapers say, to the parties concerned, the letter runs thus:

"Middleton : December 22, 1849.

"My dear Coleridge,—I sit down to thank you after a sunny drive and a visit to the monster lily at Chatsworth, covering the water of a tank twenty feet square.

"Christmas Day.

"Many happy years to you and yours! I did not believe a word in the papers about you [as to intended retirement], and hope you do me the same justice. Spite of paragraphs *nothing* has passed. My plan is to take my seat on the first day of Hilary Term (January 11, 1850), finish off all I must take part in, and then decide. What the doctors will say I know not, but my opinion wholly agrees with that expresed by you and Patteson two months ago. I have no respect for the doctrine ot the 'safe side' carried to excess. 'Had these children stayed at home,' &c. But at the present moment I can form no resolution, for my wife has had a dangerous illness,[1] and keeps me very anxious. With kindest brotherly remembrances,

"I am, most truly and affectionately,

"My dear Coleridge, yours,

"DENMAN."

His family and those constantly about him, knowing

[1] Bright's disease.

how unfit he really was to resume work, were alarmed at his apparently firm resolution and expressed intention to do so. His best friends took the view that the time for his retirement had definitely come—a view which Brougham expressed with characteristic energy as follows:

"Cannes: December 18, 1849.

"My dear friend,—Since I last wrote, two months ago, my eye has been kept on Middleton and B. R. [Bancum Reginæ, Queen's Bench], and I must now declare the clear and unhesitating conclusion to which I have arrived, that it is a duty to yourself, your family, your friends, your own comfort, your precious life—I will add your fame, your enduring fame—that you should not hesitate a moment about retiring at once from office. You have been seventeen years Chief Justice—Ellenborough was sixteen, Tenterden fourteen, Kenyon being eighteen—so that you have well earned your ease, and you will enjoy it. You can read, can write, can legislate, can sit in the Privy Council and House of Lords. In short you should on no account whatever complain. Observe, I don't regard this, after all I have said, as optional. I am putting it as though you had the choice. I am quite certain you have no such thing. You have had two attacks, and the third would be fatal, or worse. Attend to the fact;—you would get excited and nervous—one risk for a nervous malady. You would get suspicious of yourself; this would make you uneasy and irritable—another risk. Some ass of a witness, or fop of a counsel, would put you out, throw you off your guard—more excitement and more risk. So I really can not quite leave you the 'month for your decision.' I almost object to your jurisdiction. I still must object very peremptorily to the opinions you will get from colleagues, &c.; they will tell you one thing and to themselves another thing. I take the question into my own hands, and pray you only to affirm my decision and excuse this. I wish you were in this noble climate, the finest sunshine and the air quite bracing. My belief is you would be much the better for it.

"Yours ever,

"BROUGHAM."

The day before the above letter was written from Cannes, Patteson, as Senior Puisne Judge of the Queen's Bench, had written on behalf of himself and his brother judges to Sir Benjamin Brodie in order to obtain his opinion, in consultation with Dr. Holland,[1] as to the probability of Lord Denman's being able to resume his seat without risk to his health, and in full possession of his faculties, mental and bodily, on the first day of the ensuing Hilary Term (January 11) or at any proximately subsequent period. In the course of his note to Sir B. Brodie Mr. Justice Patteson says:

"We can legally continue to conduct the business of the Court, as we have during the last term, and without personal inconvenience to ourselves; but obviously not with the same efficiency and satisfaction to the public as if we had our head with us, and especially such a head as Lord Denman, whose absence is a serious loss to the public service.

"I am quite confident that Lord Denman is the last man in the world who would permit such a state of things to continue any longer, unless there was a very strong probability and almost a moral certainty that it would be put an end to by his resumption within a short time of his seat, without fear of consequences."

Adverting to a suggestion that had apparently been made in the course of correspondence, Patteson adds:

"I think it hardly practicable that a Judge should sit in Court, having notes of what passes in legal arguments taken by some one for him because he is unable to take them himself, from a permanent bodily infirmity, though his mind be not affected; and if it were even practicable it would be anything but desirable or decorous."

Lord Denman's son George (now Mr. Justice Denman), who had then for some few years been called to the Bar, and had thus an opportunity of knowing the feeling on the subject in Westminster Hall, was very anxious to get from Sir Benjamin Brodie a decided opinion, which might be shown to his father, as to the probability or

[1] Now Sir Henry Holland, Bart., born 1788; Physician-in-Ordinary to the Queen, 1852; the accomplished author of "Medical Notes and Reflections," "Recollections of a Past Life," &c.

otherwise of his being able within a reasonable period, to resume his seat.

Sir Benjamin's letter in answer was written on Christmas Day, 1849, and though expressed with great caution and the nicest care to avoid any language capable of wounding the susceptibilities of his illustrious friend and relative, it yet clearly conveyed the joint opinion of Dr. Holland and himself—1st. That it would be impossible to fix on any definite period at which Lord Denman could resume his duties of Chief Justice; 2nd. That, under the whole circumstances of the case, it had become their duty to suggest that he should lose no time in resigning his office.

This communication and Brougham's letter no doubt produced a strong effect, but Denman still insisted on putting off his final decision till after his return to town and a consultation with some physician less likely to be influenced by extra-professional feelings than he perhaps imagined might be the case with his old friend, Dr. Holland, and his still older friend and first cousin, Sir Benjamin Brodie.

He received many kind letters about this time from his judicial brethren, among which room must be found for the following characteristic lines from his good, simple-hearted, and altogether excellent colleague, Wightman.

"Hampton, December 31, 1849.

"My dear Lord,—I can not suffer the old year to pass away, or date a letter 1849, for the last time, without sending our best and warmest hopes and wishes for the coming and many future years to you and yours. I am sitting, as I daresay you are, in the midst of children and grandchildren, which is as happy a state as can be wished for on the last day of 1849, by one who was born some years before the end of the present century;[1] but, after all, I am not so old as my years would indicate, for I was young enough, on Friday last, the 29th instant, at the instigation of my youngest daughter, to go with her to Vauxhall to see the effects of the prodigious tide, which, we were assured by the philosophers, would take

[1] Mr. Justice Wightman was born in 1785, and was now, therefore, in his sixty-fifth year.

place on that day. But it did so happen that the tide, instead of being higher, was rather lower than usual, leaving the philosophers no other consolation than the belief that their theory was right, and that it ought to have been higher. Of our brethren I know nothing, as I believe they are all out of town; a conclusion at which I have arrived from the applications that have been made to me here, on the ground that there was no other Judge in London, Hampton being considered within the metropolitan district. I can well imagine Middleton in its winter garb, from my knowledge of it in its summer clothing, and can fancy the appearance of the hills when covered with snow, different, but picturesque as ever, and on a fine day as beautiful as in summer. But how do you manage for the air and exercise I know you delight in? Is it not too cold for open carriages of any sort? But I believe that any kind of going out into the air is better than sitting with nose and knees over the fire, reading the 'Memories of Mrs. Hannah More,' as I have been doing all the morning. We all send our best and kindest regards and wishes to Lady Denman, the Marshal, and Mrs. Denman [present Lord and his first wife], and every one of the family now with you; and

"Believe me ever, my dear Lord,

"Yours, most sincerely,

"WILLIAM WIGHTMAN."[1]

Upon his return to town, on January 19, 1850, Denman, who had meanwhile been induced, owing, in great measure, to the serious illness of Lady Denman, to forego his intention of taking his seat in Court on the first day of Hilary Term, submitted his case to the celebrated physician, Dr. Thomas Watson,[2] from whom he received the following clear, able, and decisive opinion:

"16 Henrietta Street, Cavendish Square,
"January 22, 1850.

"My dear Lord Denman,—The task you have assigned me, though a painful, is not a difficult one.

[1] To those who knew Mr. Justice Wightman, the little good-natured sneer at the philosophers, and the trait of spending a winter's day, "nose and knees" over the fire, reading "Hannah More's Memoirs," will be delicious.

[2] Born 1792; created a Baronet, A. D. 1866; President of the College of Physicians, 1862; Chief Physician-in-Ordinary to the Queen, 1870.

"It is painful to me to disappoint what I know to be your own hope and desire, but, in contributing my opinion on a question so important, I am bound to make your safety the paramount object of my regard.

"I think it would be very imprudent and very unsafe for your Lordship to again exercise your judicial functions.

"A portion of your nervous system, the source of voluntary power over the right side of the body, has more than once suffered damage, is still, though recovering, in a hurt, infirm, and unsound condition. Each indication of mischief has been more strongly marked, and more slowly and imperfectly repaired, than the former. Hitherto, that neighboring portion of the same nervous system which ministers to the intellect is happily intact. But the failure which has already happened to the limbs is only too plain an index of the ruin which the slightest act of imprudence might determine to the mental faculties, and even to life. Under ordinary care there is nothing in your Lordship's present state to forbid the hope of years yet to come of physical comfort, and of mental integrity and enjoyment. But these, in my humble judgment, would be put in jeopardy by every occasion of great intellectual effort, of excitement of mind or of unusual bodily exertion, fatigue, or exposure.

"Upon these grounds I am as clear in dehorting your Lordship from attendance in Court to deliver a single judgment, as from continuing to subject your brain to the pressure and hazard of the duties belonging to your high judicial office.

"Your Lordship will, I am sure, believe that I come to this conclusion conscientiously and reluctantly, and that it would have been much more agreeable to me, had I dared, to give you counsel more in accordance with your own wishes.

"I remain, my dear Lord, with the greatest respect and esteem, and with every good wish,

"Your obliged and faithful servant,

"THOMAS WATSON."

This opinion was decisive, and he at once determined to resign. Before, however, actually sending in his resignation, and thus depriving himself of all further power of judicial action, he felt it incumbent on him to hold long and anxious consultations with his colleagues on the judgments it would be fitting to pass in certain difficult and important cases which had been argued before himself and them while he was still presiding in the Court of Queen's Bench, and which yet awaited a final decision. In one of these cases, especially, that of *Russell* v. *Phillips*, he took a great interest, feeling that it involved a gross attempt on the part of the defendant to defeat justice by technicalities of law. In this case it was not till after long and anxious arguments that he succeeded in convincing his brother judges that they had a discretion in the matter, and were not absolutely bound down by the rigid rules of the Common Law to allow further resistance to a just claim, which would have involved the claimant in vexatious and costly, perhaps ruinously costly, litigation. Having at length brought them round, judgment was given in accordance with his views. This was on February 26.

This act of justice, the last in which he took part as a judge, having been accomplished, he felt that his work was finished: he had nothing further to wait for, and, on February 28 he placed his formal resignation in the hands of the Prime Minister (Lord John Russell).

During the period that had elapsed between his determination to resign and his actual resignation, he had been engaged in an unpleasant correspondence with the Prime Minister on the subject of his successor, who, greatly to his surprise and vexation, was, he found, to be Lord Campbell.

Campbell, by his whole conduct of the case of *Stockdale* v. *Hansard*, and of the controversies thence arising, had given considerable annoyance to Denman; but he had still more aroused his indignation by insinuating in some of his subsequent publications,[1] that the Chief Justice of the Court of Queen's Bench, by his proceedings in *Stockdale* v. *Hansard*, had not only wantonly hazarded the bringing about a collision between rival authorities in the State, but had, moreover, set aside

[1] As in "Lives of the Chief Justices," vol. ii. pp. 134, 148–164, and 166 (Holt's Life), and "Lives of the Chancellors," vol. i. p. 373.

legal doctrines which had been revered for ages, for the mere purpose of securing popularity by a clap-trap display of uncalled-for heroism.

That the passages in Campbell's books relied upon as involving these imputations, were indiscreet, offensive, and in exceedingly bad taste, may readily be admitted, but it appears very questionable whether Denman's protest was not, to say the least of it, almost equally ill-advised. Had not the illness under which he was laboring somewhat clouded the clearness of his judgment, and increased to a morbid extent his nervous irritability, he would probably not have permitted himself to take a step which, though called forth by strong provocation, and dictated by a high and imperious sense of duty, was certainly not characterized by that fine tact and dignified self-respect which had generally been shown so conspicuously throughout the whole course of his judicial career.

It would have been more pleasing to have passed over this incident altogether without notice, but as that would hardly be consistent with the duty of presenting an impartial record of his life, the next best course seems to be to dismiss it with little more than the simple statement that such a remonstrance was made, and made in effectually.

The line taken by Lord John Russell is stated and explained in a letter written by him after the receipt of Denman's first protest, which contained an intimation that he was preparing, and would soon send, as he afterwards did, a fuller and more detailed statement of his reasons for objecting to the appointment. This letter of the Prime Minister, which appears to be as judicious in sentiment as it is kindly and appreciative in tone, runs thus:

"Downing Street; January 29, 1850.

"My dear Lord Denman,—The Lord Chancellor told me on Saturday, in answer to a question of mine, what had passed between you and him. He had previously given me his opinion that, in the event of your being unable to resume your seat on the Bench, Lord Campbell would be the fittest person to succeed you.

"I mentioned to the Queen this opinion, supporting

it by my own, but of course have not taken any formal steps.

"Since your conversation with the Chancellor I have referred to the life of Lord Holt [in Campbell's "Lives of the Chief Justices"] which I had not previously read.

"I do not think that the passages you refer to are written in a becoming spirit towards the Judges of the Queen's Bench. No one can be more persuaded than I am that in the decisions given on Privilege, as on all other cases, none but a conscientious sense of duty was allowed to prevail. I wish, therefore, Lord Campbell had not expressed himself in a manner that may be considered offensive by the present Judges of the Queen's Bench.

"At the same time, writings as well as speeches[1] may be ill-advised and yet not of weight enough to counterbalance superior merit.

"You may consider, therefore, that it is unnecessary to make a more full statement of your views on the subject of Lord Campbell.

"Especially, I should say, if you would allow me to do so, that your name stands already high among all classes in this country as a model of uprightness and independence in the judicial office. If, as I infer, you are about to resign, it would surely be better to carry an undivided homage with you in your retirement than to raise a question as to your successor, in which many may think you right, but many others may think you wrong.

"I have written this letter in full confidence in your attributing it to no other than good motives and a sincere regard for yourself.

"I remain, my dear Lord Denman,
"Very truly yours,
J. RUSSELL."

The fact is that the real objections to Lord Campbell as a successor to Lord Denman were of a kind not very easy for the latter to state. They were not so much his

[1] Denman in his letter had only complained of "*writings*," the additional word "*speeches*," introduced by Lord John, no doubt conveyed a covert allusion—*more noto Johannis nostri*—to Denman's own speeches on the Queen's trial, which had been justly held no bar to his appointment as Chief Justice.

indulgence in a few offensive insinuations in his books, or sneers in his conversation. They were rather these: that he had always been a self-seeker; that the tone of his character was wanting in elevation, and his bearing deficient in that lofty self-respect and dignified courtesy which had so graced his predecessor. But these objections, though neither trifling nor unfounded, could not seriously be put in competition against Campbell's overpoweringly strong claims on the Whig party, or against those qualities which nobody denied him to possess, and with which the litigants in his Court were more immediately and practically concerned—extensive legal learning, ready acuteness, sound judgment, and indefatigable industry.[1]

The formal resignation, which, as already stated, had been sent in to the Premier on February 28, was accepted by him on March 1—on which day, after a service of seventeen years and nearly four months, Lord Denman ceased to be Chief Justice of England.

[1] It should be recorded to the credit of Lord Campbell that, immediately on Lord Denman's resignation, he offered to continue the eldest son in the lucrative office of Marshal and Associate—an offer that was not accepted. The note making the offer was written from Stratheden House, March 3, 1850, and ran thus:—

"Dear Mr. Denman—I beg the favor of you to continue in the office of Marshal and Associate. If you kindly consent to do so, perhaps you will have the goodness to call here, that we may make some arrangements for the circuit.

"Yours, very faithfully,
"CAMPBELL."

CHAPTER XXXV.

ADDRESSES ON RESIGNATION AND CORRESPONDENCE.

A. D. 1850. ÆT. 71.

NO sooner was Lord Denman's retirement made generally known than he became the object of one of those national demonstrations which are rare in England, and are only accorded to those who in their public career have called forth, not only the respect and veneration, but also the love of their countrymen.

The homage paid to him was, in the happy phrase of Lord John Russell's lately cited letter, an "undivided homage."

The Press was unanimous in doing justice to his great qualities, in tributes whose eloquence and warmth of feeling were worthy of the illustrious magistrate they honored; and all those orders and associations of men with whom, in the exercise of his high functions, he had been more or less connected, vied one with another in presenting to him addresses, which were not merely formal tokens of respect, but the genuine expression of real and deep sentiments of reverence and regard.

The Bar of Westminster Hall, represented by the Attorney-General, then Sir John Jervis,[1] the Bars of the Midland and Home Circuits, the Judges of the Court of Queen's Bench, the Corporation of the City of London (whose freedom had been presented to him at the close of the Queen's trial, and with which he had been so honorably connected as Common Ser-

[1] A singularly able man, who, in the opinion of many, ought to have succeeded Lord Denman as Chief Justice of England. He became, before the close of 1850, Chief Justice of the Common Pleas, but died prematurely six years afterwards: born 1802; called to the Bar, 1824; Solicitor and Attorney-General, 1846; Chief Justice of the Common Pleas, 1850; died. 1856.

geant); the Corporation of Nottingham (the borough he had so long represented in Parliament), the Grand Jury of his native county of Derby, and those of the counties of Northampton, Nottingham, Lincoln, Leicester, Warwick, and Kent, not to mention many others of all orders and classes, were among those who, on this occasion, forwarded addresses to him.

The greater part of these addresses, together with Lord Denman's replies, will be found collected in the Appendix;[1] those of the Attorney-General, of the gentlemen of his native county, of the City of London, and of his brother Judges of the Court of Queen's Bench, may be selected for insertion here.

Owing to Lord Denman's having already sent in his resignation, and being, therefore, unable to appear in Court, the address of the Attorney-General was not oral, but written. It ran thus:

"Temple: March 1, 1850.

"My Lord,—I should have desired in open Court, before the profession and the public, to give utterance to the regret of the Bar that illness compels your Lordship to resign the high office you have so long filled with distinguished honor to yourself and eminent advantage to your country.

"I may thus, however, be allowed to convey the expression of our feelings, and to assure your Lordship that the learning, the impartiality, the high sense of honor, the firmness and the dignity which marked and ennobled your administration of justice, have always commanded admiration and respect; while every practitioner in your Lordship's court bears grateful testimony to the kindness and the courtesy that endeared you to us all.

"We are sensible that failing health and advancing years entitle your Lordship to lay aside the arduous duties of the judge; but we pray that you may be blessed with vigor to enjoy the leisure you have justly earned, and to devote to the public service the patriotism and the eloquence already so conspicuous in the annals of Parliament.

"In the evening of an eventful life, your Lordship

[1] See Appendix VI.

will carry with you into retirement the affectionate sympathies of every member of the profession, and will reap some reward for your labors in the knowledge that you will long live in their memory, an example to applaud and emulate.

"I have the honor to be, my Lord, with sentiments of sincere respect and affection,

"Your Lordship's faithful servant,

"JOHN JERVIS."

Lord Denman's reply was as follows:

"38 Portland Place: March 1, 1850.

"Dear Mr. Attorney,—I receive, with the highest satisfaction, your kind letter, expressing your own sentiments, and those of the Bar in general, on my retirement from office.

"If I have merited in any degree your valuable approbation, I am conscious that mainly it must be ascribed to the learning, liberality, and candor, by which you and your brethren rendered the performance of my laborious duties during so many years both easy and delightful.

"Fully aware of my many deficiencies in other respects, I yet will not disclaim the praise of a constant and earnest endeavor to discover truth and promote justice; and, it is my pride to feel, that, with the assistance of my excellent colleagues, I have not failed in my anxious wish to sustain and even elevate the character of the English Bar.

"Among the many consolations which support me in taking this painful step, none will be more effectual than to witness the increasing prosperity and honor of the profession, which you so worthily represent.

"With every feeling of esteem and respect towards yourself,

"I remain, my dear Mr. Attorney,

"Your faithful and obedient servant.

"DENMAN."

The address from the gentlemen serving on the Grand Jury of his native county of Derby, was in these words:

"*To the Right Hon. Thomas, Lord Denman.*

"Grand Jury Room, Derby: March 21, 1850.

"We, the High Sheriff and Grand Jurors of the County

of Derby, beg to express to your Lordship our deep regret that the state of your health should have compelled you to resign your high office of Chief Justice of England.

"By those who are capable of appreciating the importance of a wise, just, and dignified administration of the law, such a resignation will be considered a great national loss; but every manly and generous mind must be gratified by the reflection that your retirement is accompanied by all the consolations that a good man can desire—the consciousness of having discharged all the duties of this great trust with the strictest integrity, and the full assurance that a grateful public will do justice to a merit so distinguished.

"The earlier part of your professional life, my Lord, is remembered by some of us. In every step of it your talents and acquirements, graced by eloquence of the highest order, cast a luster about you that never failed to charm; but it was by your sterling integrity, your unflinching determination to do your duty on all occasions, and the noble and manly sentiments ever animating you, that you won the respect and admiration of all.

"Your Lordship's life presents a valuable history, which can not be too closely and attentively read.

"It will stimulate the preparations of the young for the career they are about to run, it will encourage the exertions of those who have commenced the race, and, though very few can hope to reach your success, all will be the better for thinking upon and studying your great example.

"Permit us, my Lord, to say that it is no small source of gratification and pride to us that you belong to our native county.

"We beg to add our most earnest wishes for the continuance of a life so justly dear and still so highly valuable to the people of this great country.

"ROBERT ARKWRIGHT, High Sheriff,
"HENRY S. WILMOT, Foreman,
"And twenty-two other names."

Lord Denman returned the following genial and kindly reply:

"Gentlemen,—I wish I could think myself deserving

of the very high praise bestowed upon me by your partiality.

"I am so proud of belonging to your county that I can not refrain from introducing another fact which seems to give the finish and a real value to my history.

"Near a hundred years have elapsed since my father left his native town, in very humble circumstances, and with slender means. By his exertions, during a long course of years, he was enabled to afford me the education which advanced me; and he instilled those principles, habits, and tastes, which have led to your favorable estimate of my services.

"It is delightful to know that the same process is at this moment going on in thousands of English families, and that, though the high honors must be confined to few, the exertions made in order to obtain them, will be as useful and honorable to the aspirants as valuable to the public.

"Much of the remainder of my life will be passed, gentlemen, among you, and nothing can be more agreeable to the grateful object of your kindness than his own warm appreciation of it, and his indulgence in similar sentiments towards yourselves.

"I remain, most respectfully,

"Your obliged and faithful servant,

"DENMAN."

The following was the address from the Common Council of the City of London:

"*To the Right Hon. Thomas, Lord Denman, late Lord Chief Justice of England.*

"My Lord,—The Lord Mayor,[1] Aldermen and Commons of the City of London, in Common Council assembled, respectfully desire to express to your Lordship their regret that the state of your health has induced your Lordship to resign the high office of Lord Chief Justice of England.

"Many years have now elapsed since the citizens of London, through their representatives in the Common Council, had the great satisfaction of offering to your

[1] Farncomb.

Lordship their congratulations upon your advancement to that great office.

"From a long experience of your estimable qualities during the period of your connection with the City in the office of Common Sergeant, and from the interest which they had thence been led to take in your Lordship's welfare, the most favorable anticipations and ardent wishes were then expressed that you might be able to discharge your duties as Chief Justice with honor to yourself and with benefit to the country.

"That these wishes and anticipations have, through the long period during which you have presided over the administration of justice, been most fully realized is, we rejoice to find, the general feeling of the nation, while to us it has proved a source of the most heartfelt satisfaction.

"Truly, my Lord, do we feel that highly as the office of Chief Justice of England has ever been esteemed, it has acquired fresh honor and distinction from the manner in which you have discharged its duties and sustained its dignity, faithfully and courageously asserting the supremacy of the law, and the independence and purity of its administration, on all occasions and in every emergency.

"Some there are, my Lord, still amongst us who have witnessed with pride your Lordship's progress, from the time of your first connection with the City of London, and from a much earlier period, and all of us now unite in the expression of regret for a cause which deprives the country of your valuable services, and in an earnest wish that through a lengthened period of improved health your Lordship may enjoy the satisfaction arising from the remembrance of duties of the highest importance ably and faithfully discharged.

"MEREWETHER."

To this address Lord Denman returned a reply, in the course of which, referring to his illustrious predecessor as a City Judge and Chief Justice, Lord Holt, he said:

"I felt that I could only hope to emulate his fame by following his example, and forced against my will, into circumstances closely resembling those in which he was placed, I found in his conduct a perfect precedent for my own. Like him, I asserted the majesty of the law, and the sacred principles of constitutional freedom, happier in this alone, that, whereas he had the misfortune to differ from his brother judges, I had the satisfaction of receiving the unanimous concurrence of judges as learned and conscientious as ever adorned the bench of Westminster Hall."

Lord Denman, in a separate reply to the Lord Mayor and Aldermen, who, in a Court held on March 26, had separately passed a resolution to his honor, again refers to what he always considered—as in this reply he calls it—the most important event of his life, the course he took in the case of *Stockdale* v. *Hansard*. As this reply is very much to the same purpose as that to the Common Council, and has the advantage of being expressed with more terseness and energy, it will be as well to reprint it here, leaving the other to the Appendix.

"*To the Lord Mayor and Aldermen of London.*

"My Lord and Gentlemen,—From the moment when I first had the honor of sitting as a judge beside the magistrates of London, to the present, when I have to acknowledge the approbation with which you crown my last labors, I have experienced the utmost kindness from you. I beg leave to offer my cordial thanks for this and every other instance of it.

"The judicial offices which your corporation has the privilege of appointing impose a severe burden upon the holders.

"In former times the eminent men who have occupied the highest stations of the law had previously acted as City judges.

"The most virtuous of Chancellors, Sir Thomas More, was Common Sergeant of London. Sir Edward Coke and others performed, as Recorders of London, some part of the duties of Chief Justice before they filled that office.

"The greatest of them all, in my opinion, was Chief Justice Holt, your Recorder, and by his great example I always endeavored to regulate my judicial course.

"I have the satisfaction of knowing that the most important decision in which I have taken part was in exact accordance to his declared opinion: from that opinion, indeed, his brethren dissented, but the majority of the judges and a great majority of the Lords, with Lord Somers at their head, established his doctrine as true.

"I had the good fortune to assert the same doctrine with the full concurrence of my brethren, and, with every disposition to cavil at our judgment, that judgment was never questioned in a Court of Error.

"Forgive my alluding to this, the most important event of my life, and the most nearly affecting my judicial reputation.

"I beseech you to accept my sincere wishes for your prosperity and welfare as individuals, and that, under your guardianship, the honor and happiness of the inhabitants of this great metropolis may ever be secured and advanced.

"I have the honor to remain, my Lord and gentlemen, your attached and grateful servant,

"DENMAN.

"March 28, 1850."

The following letter from the Judges of the Queen's Bench (in the well-known handwriting of his friend Patteson) must have given Denman the sincerest gratification:

"Dear Lord Denman,—We trust you will accept the accompanying token of our regard,[1] which has its principal value in the affectionate sincerity with which it is offered.

"It has given us much pleasure to see you receiving, from time to time since your retirement, repeated testimonials of the love and respect which you have justly earned by your discharge for so many years of the high and difficult duties of your great office. Perhaps you will think that no persons can estimate so accurately as ourselves how well you have deserved them. And we *do* desire to bear sincere and considerate testimony to the learning, good sense and ability, the industry and uprightness, the candor, patience, dignity and good

[1] An inkstand, with a choice inscription (auctore Coleridge): three years afterwards this valuable heirloom was stolen from Lord Denman's study at Stony Middleton, but, to his great joy, after some weeks recovered again.

temper, with which you have adorned the Bench on which we have had the happines to sit as your assistants.

"But we are bound to add to this, our gratitude for the uniform kindness which individually we have experienced at your hands; the hearty acceptance which you have ever given to such assistance as it was our duty and in our power to afford you; and the delightful friendliness, without change or diminution at any time, which has shed a peculiar charm on our private intercourse. By these we have been made, we trust, more useful servants to the public, as, we are sure, we have been able to enjoy our few leisure hours more perfectly.

"You may well believe how deeply we regret that we are no longer to labor together. Long may you be spared, peacefully and happily to adorn and enjoy the leisure which you have so well earned; and may we be permitted still, from time to time, the pleasure of our old friendly intercourse; and at all times may we retain that place in your affection with which we venture to believe you have hitherto honored us.

"We remain, dear Lord Denman,

"With the sincerest esteem and regard,

"Your affectionate friends,

"J. PATTESON. WM. WIGHTMAN.

"J. T. COLERIDGE. W. ERLE.

"April 15, 1850."

Denman's reply was as follows:

"My dear Coleridge,—I have received, with feelings that defy expression, the precious gift you have presented to me for yourself and my other late colleagues of the Court of Queen's Bench.

"This testimony is far more valuable than any other can possibly be, not only for the reason given by yourselves—your greater opportunity of observing my judicial conduct—but from your own superior power of forming a true judgment. Much must, indeed, be allowed for your partiality, but that partiality itself confers the highest honor. Such a testimony, borne by such men, after an intimate connection of many years in the discharge of the duties we have performed together, is the most valuable tribute that can be paid to a retiring judge.

"I will not affect now to offer any apology for the many occasional shortcomings and defects of which I have been too painfully conscious. As these have left no impression on your minds, they ought not to disturb in mine the perfect satisfaction that your kind words impart. But I should be wanting in gratitude and justice if I omitted to avow my great obligation to your able, strenuous, and ever-ready exertions. Without such co-operation, I am convinced, that in our busy and arduous time, scarcely any man could have adequately sustained the character of Chief Justice of England. For me, I am quite sure, the task would have been too heavy, and I well know how much of the public approbation I have had the good fortune to enjoy is to be ascribed to yourselves.

"The cordiality and cheerfulness with which the assistance was rendered, prompted, as it was, by the sense of duty, was, perhaps, even more the fruit of that friendship which it has ever been my care to cultivate, and my happiness to secure. I, with you, feel confident that it will continue during our lives; the remainder of mine would, indeed, be a blank without it.

"I have delayed this letter for some hours, because I wished my eldest son to be my amanuensis. He has, also, often experienced your kindness, and will preserve this token as the most valuable possession of the family. Its classical beauty is its smallest merit, and the gracious and kind inscription is still surpassed by the admirable letter that accompanies it.

"Your grateful and affectionate friend and brother,

"DENMAN."

It was not only from the Judges of his own Court that Denman at this time received many valuable assurances of regard and affection.

Mr. Baron Parke (afterwards Lord Wensleydale), was at this time the senior Judge on the Midland Circuit, and, as such, became the medium of forwarding several of the addresses from the Grand Juries of the Midland Counties; in forwarding that from Lincoln, he expressed himself as follows:

"Lincoln: March 12, 1850.

"My dear Lord,—When I was discharging the Grand

Jury to-day, the foreman announced that they had unanimously resolved to address you, and he read the address, and requested me to forward it to you.

"I promised to do so, and added that I concurred most cordially in every sentiment that it expressed, and I told the truth.

"It must be a great satisfaction to you to close your most distinguished career as an advocate and a judge with so many testimonies of respect and affection.

"Long may you live to enjoy your deserved reputation.

"I received your message and saw your letter to Whitehurst.[1] You say too much of our sincere praise.

"Believe me, my dear Lord,
"Most sincerely yours,
"JAMES PARKE."

Mr. Justice Talfourd,[2] then on the Western Circuit, expressed his feelings characteristically in a sonnet, afterwards inserted in the first number of "Household Words," and inclosed in the following letter:

"Salisbury: March 12, 1850.

"My dear Lord Denman,--I should have ventured before this to express my share in the universal sentiment which attends your parting from the seat which never can be so graced again, if I had not wished to try and embody it in the concise form which a sonnet gives; and I have found the subject so utterly beyond such a space, that I have thought of it and tried it, till I found it best to send you anything rather than be any longer silent.

"It is a very feeble attempt to embody feelings to which all words are inadequate; and I can only commend it to your old indulgence, and assure you, in all the sincerity of prose, that I remain,

"My dear Lord Denman,
"With fondest wishes for your happiness,
"Most respectfully and truly yours,
"T. N. TALFOURD."

[1] In answer to an address of the Bar of the Midland Circuit, of which Mr. Whitehurst, Q. C., was then the leader.

[2] Sir Thomas Noon Talfourd; born 1795; called to Bar, 1821; Sergeant, 1833; M. P. for Reading, 1835, in which year the drama of "Ion" was acted; Judge of Common Pleas, 1849: died of apoplexy while charging the Grand Jury of Stafford, March 13, 1854. Denman was a warm admirer of Talfourd's oratorical and dramatic talents.

"P.S.—If you do not forbid me, I think I shall send the lines to our friend Dickens for his first number of "Household Words'—for which I own I tremble."

The sonnet, not by any means one of Talfourd's happiest efforts, runs thus:

"*To Lord Denman, retiring from the Chief Justiceship of England.*

"There is a solemn rapture in the hail
With which a nation blesses thy repose,
In sense that it is deathless; that the close
Of man's extremest age whose boyhood glows
While pondering o'er thy lineaments, shall fail
To delegate to cold historic tale
What Denman was; for dignity that flows
Not in the moulds of compliment extern,
But from a generous spirit's purest urn
Springs vital; Justice softened, yet unswayed
By beautiful affections; thoughts that burn
With noblest fire—for men who never saw
Thy form, shall take its likeness, as they learn
In vision clear, the majesty of law."

Denman's reply was as follows:

"London: March 14, 1850.

"My Dear Talfourd,—Tenterden said to John Williams, on receiving some of his Greek compositions,

"Si quali cuperem referre possem
Græco carmine gratias referrem.

"I wish I could return an answer worthy of your beautiful and genial sonnet. I would express the pleasure that an old man who has meant well must feel when he leaves active life in seeing others following in the track who will preserve and extend whatever has been praiseworthy in his own principles and conduct. The additional pleasure of receiving from them exalted praise for his endeavors is too much to be expected, but can not be too highly prized.

"I, like you, feel a little nervous when our friend Dickens quits the scenes with which he is so happily familiar;[1] but if he thinks your sonnet and the subject will be well placed in his new publication, it will only

[1] The apprehensions of Lord Denman and Talfourd were, as all the world knows, without adequate foundation: "Household Words" was a great success.

give me pleasure to see my name united with his and yours. "Ever very sincerely yours,

"DENMAN."

Wightman, writing from Norwich, on April 7, 1850, sums up, with characteristic clearness and accuracy, the effect and value of the universal testimony.

"My dear Lord,—However deeply we and all who know you, as well as the public, feel our loss in your retirement, I am not sure but that, for your sake, we ought to rejoice at it, for otherwise you yourself would never have known how great and universal was the love and respect entertained for you. Chief Justices have retired before now, but I am not aware of any instance in which so much and such universal regret and sympathy have been shown."

Denman was much gratified by a letter written about this time to his son George (now Mr. Justice Denman) by that accomplished scholar, Mr. John Leycester Adolphus, who, in conjunction with the late Thomas Flower Ellis, had for a period of many years been legal reporter in the Court of Queen's Bench.[1] Mr. Adolphus was a Tory of the old school, and his testimony, on that very account, and also owing to the singularly reticent and undemonstrative nature of the writer, was regarded by Lord Denman as additionally valuable. The occasion of the letter being written is explained in the letter itself:

"16 Montague Place: April 23, 1850.

"My dear Denman,—I am very much obliged, should say flattered, if it did not seem formal, by your sending me a copy of the Home Circuit poem.[2] It does much honor to the circuit and justice to Lord Denman. The lines at the beginning of p. 6 are a portrait to be treasured up: the electrical, instinctive righteousness which they describe was, in many instances which I remember, as beneficial to public justice as it was noble in its momentary effect.

[1] Born 1793; Newdegate prize poem, subject, "Niobe," Oxford, 1814; second class classics, 1815; writer, in 1820, of a much talked of pamphlet proving Scott to be the author of the Waverley Novels; Reporter in Court of Queen's Bench for many years and County Court Judge; died 1868.

[2] Printed in Appendix at end of the addresses.

"Mine is the testimony of a Tory, and there may be an expression or two in the verses which I flinch from—but, on the whole, I should perhaps have made the panegyric stronger rather than weaker, even with reference to the subject of politics. On the question of the 'Senate,' I agree in thinking that he had the dignity of being not only bold, but thoroughly in the right.

"Perhaps a dissentient as to general politics may feel more strongly than the writer of these lines, who has hardly particularized it enough, *the unblemished purity from all tincture of party which was so great a characteristic of Lord Denman's Chief Justiceship.* Ready enough I should have been to mark any fault in that respect, and sorry enough I was, from political prepossession, when Sir Thomas Denman was placed at the head of our Court. This may be said without scruple, even to you, when I can add that I was still more sorry when he was obliged to leave it.

"I do not personally know the writer of the lines, but envy him the opportunity and ability, and join him heartily in the prayer with which he concludes. And will you let me convey through you, most warmly and respectfully, the same good wishes to Lord Denman himself, whenever you can conveniently mention them.

"Believe me, dear Denman,

"Very truly yours,

"J. L. ADOLPHUS."

It was not in England only that Lord Denman, on his retirement, received the "undivided homage" of all orders of men; in America, also, his distinguished career had been watched with the highest interest by the many eminent jurists who then adorned the Bar and the Bench in the United States. The venerable Chancellor Kent, Mr. Justice Story, and many other celebrated American lawyers, had, as has been seen, from time to time communicated to him valuable expressions of sympathy and regard, and now he had the gratification of receiving from the accomplished diplomatist, writer, and orator, Mr. Edward Everett, late Minister of the United States at the Court of St. James', the following graceful tribute of national esteem and personal affection :

"Cambridge, U. S.: May 14, 1850.

"My dear Lord Denman,—I can not deny myself the satisfaction of recalling myself to your recollection, for the sake of tendering you, from this side of the Atlantic, that tribute of respect which has been so largely paid you at home on the occasion of your retirement.

"You know so well the professional community that exists between the two countries, that you will not be surprised to learn that we watch the movements of persons like yourself with scarcely less interest than if they were our countrymen; while, for reasons not necessary to be stated, your own course as a statesman and a magistrate, and, in both capacities, as a great assertor of liberal principles, has probably commanded a more unanimous sympathy in the United States than even in your own England.

"The personal obligation I owe to you and Lady Denman for the numerous friendly attentions with which you honored us during our residence in England makes me peculiarly desirous of expressing to you, on this occasion, my warm feelings of respectful attachment, and my fervent wishes that your long and honored career of active duty may be crowned with many years of serene and happy age.

"My dutiful compliments to Lady Denman, in which Mrs. Everett begs to join me.

"I remain, my dear Lord Denman,
"Most faithfully yours,
"EDWARD EVERETT."

Lord Denman's answer was as follows:

"London: June 3, 1850.

"My dear Mr. Everett,—Your letter demands my warmest thanks, evincing the greatest kindness, and exciting the liveliest satisfaction.

"That the approbation of my judicial career, so favorably viewed by my own countrymen, should be echoed on the other side of the Atlantic by your enlightened Bar, that my general public conduct should be so kindly appreciated in the United States, and that the judgments should receive your sanction, biased, perhaps, by your friendship, which is, however, itself a distinguished honor,—this combination confers on your letter an inestimable value in my eyes.

"I hope that you may be called upon to return to this country, where no one will rejoice more than myself in renewing a friendly intercourse with you and your family.

"Lady Denman desires to join in these sentiments

"With your obliged and faithful servant,

"DENMAN."

The force and freshness, the grace and variety of the answers dictated by Lord Denman to the great and almost embarrassing mass of the letters and addresses he at this time received, showed that the disease which had so severely shaken his bodily powers had left his mental faculties comparatively untouched. He had not sufficiently recovered the use of his hand to be able to *write* any of the answers which he composed with so much felicity and ease; rest and repose were still most needful to him, and after a brief sojourn in London, he retired for the summer and autumn to solace himself among his plantations and improvements in Stony Middleton, with the pleasures of literature and the affectionate society of his wife, children and grandchildren.

In this calm and cheerful retreat he made steady progress towards a temporary recovery, and gradually regained the command of his pen, though the act of writing continued throughout the whole of this year to be a work of labor and difficulty—a circumstance which sufficiently accounts for the rarity of his correspondence.

On October 18, 1850, the forty-sixth anniversary of his wedding-day, he wrote with his own hand the following verses to his wife, which have been preserved by the pious care of his daughter, Lady Baynes, to whom he gave them after her mother's death. They possess a simple and touching pathos, which will probably speak to the hearts of all:

"October 18, 1850.

"Full six and forty years have flown
Since first I claimed you for my own;
You trusted then your youthful charms
To an adoring husband's arms.
Well saw he with those charms combined
The upright, generous, feeling mind;

The noble nature's inborn grace,
The soul, e'en lovelier than the face.
Well did you keep Affection's vow,
Precious when made, far dearer now.
In that long maze of varied years,
Of joys and sorrows, hopes and fears,
Though oft a cloud perplexed the view,
Love never failed to guide us through.
Downward we pace, but hand-in-hand—
Hope tells us of that happy land
Where tumults, pain, and sorrow cease,
That land of harmony and peace—
A house not made with hands, endeared
By all we cherished or revered;—
The aged, who sunk in ripe decay,
The buds in childhood plucked away,
The future haven to receive
The dear ones we on earth must leave—
Where Friendship rears a hallowed shrine.
And Love is endless and divine."

The following letter, written a little earlier, and in a firmer hand, to his old friend Coleridge, will show how actively he kept alive his interest in the profession of which he had so long been the chief ornament:

"Middleton: September, 2, 1850.

"My dear Coleridge,—Thanks for your account of your circuit, so well and wisely closed. I traced it when the papers enabled me, and thought, with you, the libel jury, at Exeter, wrong. The case curiously illustrates Fox's distinction (when he introduced the Libel Act) between 'meaning' and 'importing' the one 'intent of man,' the other 'signification of word.' Had not we a similar question from Liverpool, *coram* Erle?

"I have not seen the 'Prelude'[1] or 'Eldorado,' and am a very bad and scratchy reader.

"The first I heard of the astonishing appointment[2] was from Wilde's own letter to Brougham, which B. sent to me announcing it. My astonishment was great, but momentary.

"Nothing will persuade me that poor dear Shadwell was not killed by his son's lamentable death, co-operating with every derangement of the system, and insuring

[1] Wordsworth's Prelude to the "Excursion."

[2] Wilde's appointment as Lord Chancellor in succession to Lord Cottenham, on July 15, 1850, when he was created Lord Truro.

the victory to bronchitis in its contest with life. I had quite recently a very affectionate letter from him.[1]

"Wonderful changes in this short time; but is it not more wonderful to see so little change in others as old or older and as much worked?[2]

"The greatest change is in the law itself, by the last County Courts' Act, and is irrational. If the experience of small sums justifies the £50, it justifies any amount, and Westminster Hall is superfluous. What information have we of the effect of examining parties—is it to be done in criminal cases too?

"We see what you say of Lady Coleridge with great pleasure, and congratulate your grand-paternity; but I observe also what you say of yourself, and exhort you as an old and sincere friend, and still more as attached to the profession and concerned for the public, to husband your powers, and preserve your activity and usefulness by all prudent means as long as possible. The same I say through you to Patteson, and request also some partridges of his shooting, if they can be spared, and he will secure their safe arrival by *not* paying carriage.

"We are gradually improving—have had the Provost [Hodgson] a short time, and set him up. Richard, with his wife and three of his five children, is with us now. Gurney seems to deserve his good fortune.[3] Jervis is highly esteemed on this circuit.[4]

"Ever yours,

"DENMAN."

A later letter of the same year to the same old friend, is in the handwriting either of Lady Denman or one of his daughters:

"December, 17, 1850.

"My dear Coleridge,—I am always happy to hear from you, even on so slender an occasion as Hetley's reports. I proceed to offer you a little medical advice.

[1] Vice-Chancellor Shadwell died on August 10, 1850, in his seventy-second year; he had not very long before lost his eldest son by drowning, and never got over the shock.

[2] Lyndhurst (then seventy-eight) was seven years older than Denman and Shadwell; Brougham and Campbell each one year older.

[3] Russell Gurney, Q.C., recently appointed Recorder of London.

[4] Sir John Jervis, who had been appointed Chief Justice of the Common Pleas on July 15, 1850 (on the promotion of Sir Thomas Wilde to the Chancellorship), went the Midland as his first judicial circuit.

"I think your case decidedly nervous, and recommend that you make a point of considering your judicial business as the only occupation of your life; everything else should be calculated for your comfort and relaxation, and as much of your work as you can properly suffer to be done by others should be thrown on your younger brethren. Remember that you are very *emeritus* [Mr. J. Coleridge had at this time been more than fifteen years on the Bench], but may reasonably expect five years, at least, added to your time, according to the happy experience of our three brethren.

"I am really sorry for what you tell me of the Chancellor [Wilde], having hoped he would compel himself to decide. How will he like the elevation of Lord Cranworth?[1] I think he is a very nice little peer.

"I agree with you in condemning any slight, much more any breach of faith, towards Parke. I think his crotchets really awful, but I doubt whether any of us have taken more pains to be right. His learning would be highly useful, and his eccentricity sufficiently kept under in the House of Lords;[2] an honor conferred on him would be really an homage done to the legal profession.

"I know you will be glad to hear that Lady Denman's health is such as to release me from all anxiety; and that I am pursuing my recovery with the same slow, but unremitting and undeviating, tortoise process.

"We are now made very happy by the presence of our children, and mean to spend a merry Christmas in this cool land. Remember us kindly to Lady Coleridge, who will, I think, approve of my advice to you, and remind you of it when necessary.

"Yours, ever,

"DENMAN."

The signature is in Lord Denman's handwriting, and so is the following:

"P. S. — Excuse an amanuensis; writing rather fatigues—"

[1] Sir Robert Mounsey Rolfe, appointed Vice-Chancellor on Nov. 2, 1850, and raised to the Peerage, as Lord Cranworth, in December, 1850.

[2] He was made a Peer, as Lord Wensleydale, in 1856; at first, as is well known, for life, but eventually with the usual descent to heirs male, which in his case was inoperative.

—a circumstance sufficiently obvious from the evident difficulty with which even those few words have been framed.

It is a pleasing proof, both of his cheerfulness at that time, and of his kindly nature at all times, that on Christmas Day, 1850, he made shift to write with his own feeble and unsteady hand, the following note to his grandson, Henry Denman Macaulay, the eldest son of his fourth daughter and of Lord Macaulay's brother, then a child of a little over seven years:

"Middleton: Christmas Day, 1850.

"My dear Harry,—I am very glad to receive a letter all of your own writing. You write the word '*righting*.' This is a mistake, for *righting* means a different thing from *writing*. But even the mistake proves that you have made some progress in learning, for you spell *right* rightly.

"I hope you will go on from well to better, and be a *right* good scholar, a *right* good son, a *right* good brother, and, in short, a *right* good man.

"I shall *write* no more at present, except my good wishes to yourself and all at both houses on the Dingle Bank, for a *right* merry Christmas and a *right* happy new year, and many of them.

"Your *right* loving grandfather,

"DENMAN."

CHAPTER XXXVI.

LAW AMENDMENT.—LETTERS FROM BROUGHAM.

A.D. 1851, 1852. ÆT. 72, 73.

IN the year 1851, and the earlier part of 1852, Lord Denman's health considerably improved, and he was able to a great extent to resume his active interest in the questions of the day, and especially in all matters relating to the reform of the law.

To the success of one very important measure for amending the English law of Evidence—that by which parties to suits were made competent and compellable to give evidence—he was enabled, though no longer in a position to support it in the House of Lords, very materially to contribute, by a most able letter, which, on April 15, 1851, he sent to the "Law Review," the principal organ of the supporters of Law Reform.

The Bill embodying this great improvement in English procedure was prepared by that eminent law reformer, Mr. Pitt Taylor, and submitted to Lord Denman for his approval. After some little hesitation in the first instance, Denman, on full and mature consideration, gave the proposed bill his entire sanction and approval. Being unable himself to take charge of it in the House of Lords, the conduct of it there was intrusted to Lord Brougham, from which circumstance it came to be known as Lord Brougham's Act.[1] But though Lord Denman was thus deprived of the honors of its Parliamentary parentage, it may be doubted whether any one circumstance so greatly contributed to insure its safe passage through both Houses as Denman's very interesting and able letter, published in the "Law Review," which at

[1] It received the royal assent in August, 1851, and is cited as the 14 and 15 Vic. c. 99. See "Taylor on Evidence," section 1216, p. 1167, ed. 1868.

once arrested the attention and commanded the assent of all persons of candid mind, both in the legislature and in the legal profession.

The length of this admirable letter precludes insertion of the whole of it, but the following passage with reference to the general aversion of the Judges of the Superior Courts to changes in the law, is so valuable, as conveying the result of Denman's long experience in his relations, as a steady and veteran law reformer, with those learned persons, that it ought to be given without abridgment. It should be studied by all who rely on the aid of the judicature as a body for the encouragement and active promotion of Law Reform.

"To form schemes for altering the law is no part of the judge's vocation. They have sometimes to my knowledge felt somewhat aggrieved by being expected to have done so, or required to perform that task.

"The lines of Horace, hackneyed by frequent quotation on account of their true and felicitous description of a certain phase of human nature, are much more applicable to judges than to literary or theatrical censors,—

> "'——Clament periisse pudorem
> Cuncti pœne patres, eà cum reprehendere coner,
> Quæ gravis Æsopus quæ doctus Roscius egit;
> Vel quia nil rectum nisi quod placuit sibi ducunt;
> Vel quia turpe putant parere minoribus, et quæ
> Imberbes didicere, senes perdenda fateri.'

"Besides the constant occupation of their minds in their important functions, and the necessity for the undisturbed enjoyment of their hard-earned leisure, there are feelings in the Judges which must ever strengthen the reluctance to assent to alteration. They have administered the law as they found it, with implicit confidence, and even veneration, which unite in them with all the obvious and instinctive motives for abhorring change. It is painful to condemn the past and present. Even if they concur in the projected improvement, they had rather that others should be the persons to counsel it. What has satisfied mankind so long may be suffered to remain during their time, alas! too short at the best.

"Some of the chiefs in our Superior Courts are advanced to the Peerage, in the expectation, possibly, that in Parliament they will propose a remedy for defects made apparent to them while presiding over the administration of the law. My own activity in such legislation has not been excessive: I rather blush for the little I have attempted, and the less I have been able to do. But I confess I have felt discouragement, regret, and even humiliation, at receiving the answer of some of my contemporaries to points which I have thought it my duty to lay before them. 'The principle is perfectly right; I can not answer your reasoning, and I see the objection to the present state of the law, and none to the change, except that it is a change; yet *I can not bring myself* to concur in it.' It is a fact on record, which will startle existing judges, most of whom probably never heard of it (as I am now traveling forty years back), that Lord Ellenborough *announced in the House of Lords the unanimous opinion of his eleven brother judges, that it would be wrong to repeal the law which punished with death a larceny to the amount of five shillings in a shop!* The oracle had not been consulted, it solemnly volunteered this fearful edict. Perhaps, also, every member of the present Parliament will be astonished to hear that the bill was for that time rejected.

"I can not forget one particular fallacy which I have frequently observed, and which tends to increase the aversion of some judges to change. The system which they find they believe to have been established on full deliberation by the wisdom of former ages; and hence impute to all innovators the arrogance of reversing a decision; *whereas in truth the existing system is for the most part the neglected growth of time and accident;* circumstances have prevented the revision that is now taking place, and the existing defect is only left uncured because no deliberation has ever been had upon it."

Passing from this to consider the principle on which the old law of exclusion was founded, viz. that the evidence of interested witnesses "can never induce any rational belief," Lord Denman proceeds to ask:

"On what ground is the assertion warranted that no man, speaking with the bias of interest on his mind, can speak the truth? Made with respect to ourselves or any individual of our acquaintance, it is an imputation as false as insulting, and would be rejected with just indignation. The earlier part of Mr. Amos's treatise furnishes a simple and lucid narrative of the various causes which, under his own observation, have insured the triumph of candor and veracity over the principle of self interest, and I have seldom read a defense for mankind from one of the charges most commonly brought against it more ingenious or more just than that contained in those pages. I must also bear witness, as far as opinion goes, that, notwithstanding the frequent contrarieties of testimony observable in courts of justice, the amount of willful falsehood, undoubtedly great, is far less than is generally supposed.

"'Ask no questions, and you will hear no lies,' is a vernacular caution often administered to inconvenient inquisitiveness. It seems to me to comprise the whole argument in opposition to this bill. But no one will advise us to prefer darkness to light because the latter must sometimes reveal unsightly objects; still less will prudence suggest an entire abstinence from food, though that is the only perfect security against swallowing poison.

"With these views, which I merely state, leaving the argument in abler hands, I give in my adhesion to the principle of Lord Brougham's Bill, and respectfully thus tender my vote for its further progress.

"I remain, dear Sir, very truly yours,

"DENMAN.

"Parsloes: April 21, 1851."[1]

This was not the only contribution of the kind that Denman made in his retirement to the cause which, from his first entry into professional life, he always had so much at heart—the cause of Law Reform. In the year 1852, while the Common Law Procedure Act of that year was in its passage through Parliament, the late Chief Justice, who was exceedingly pleased by the boldness and thoroughness of that excellent measure, lent it efficient aid by a series of short letters which he wrote, from time to time, on various points as they suggested

[1] Parsloes was a place near Dagenham, in Essex, then occupied by his third son, Richard, with whom Denman was at this time staying.

themselves, and afterwards collected in a small pamphlet, which he published in 1852, under the title of "Letters to the Lord Chancellor on Law Reform."

The amendments of the law for the promotion of which these letters were written have, with few exceptions, been since carried into effect, and the discussions on points of technical procedure with which they are principally occupied would have no interest for the general reader, and only a retrospective and historical interest for the professional reader. Their general tone, which, as might be expected, was in the highest degree liberal and enlightened, may be adequately judged of by the following passage from the concluding letter of the series:

"The present crisis can not fail to suggest considerations of the highest importance. There are appearances of an attempt to establish order on absolute power, and to teach mankind the lesson that the will of one may be most safely intrusted with the interests of all. But if there be truth in moral reasoning, or in long experience, we know that without the basis of law no solid fabric of order can possibly be reared, or any security be given for the rights which even the best meant and best devised decrees may pretend to confer. It appears to be the peculiar mission of England to exhibit to the nations of the world a steady government, a peaceful—because contented—people. *And that content must not be looked for, since it can not and ought not to exist where a Press is free and the people but moderately enlightened, while a single grievance is willfully retained after exposure.*"

So impressed was Denman with the ability and success with which the accomplished Commissioners had conceived and carried out their important work, that on May 27, 1852, he, for the first time since his second paralytic seizure, and for the last time in his life, rose in his place and addressed the House of Lords, on the occasion of Lord Truro's moving the third reading of the Common Law Procedure Bill of 1852, in high commendation of the bill and of its learned authors. In a few emphatic words he expressed "the happiness he felt at bearing his humble testimony to the truth of his noble and learned friend's (the Chancellor's) statement with respect both to the merits of the measure, and of the Commissioners by whom it had been prepared. They were men of the highest ability, and they had performed the duties intrusted to them in a manner creditable to themselves and most advantageous for the country."

After suggesting one or two trifling amendments, he sat down—his latest utterance in Parliament, like so many of his earliest, having for its subject the great cause of the Amendment of the Law.

In his exertions for the progress of Law Reform, in the years 1851 and 1852, his most vigorous and able coadjutor was his old friend and ally, Henry Brougham, many of whose letters to him during this period have been preserved among his papers. They are very characteristic letters, but are frequently not very quotable, being many of them filled with complaints, not expressed in the most courtly language, at the lukewarmness as a law reformer of "Jonathan Wilde" (as Brougham always persisted in calling the then Chancellor, Lord Truro, formerly Sir Thomas Wilde), and with vehement insinuations against the alleged jobbery of the Princess his wife.[1] That Lord Truro was a somewhat slow and reluctant law reformer was true enough; the other imputations were utterly non-proven, and in all probability quite baseless.

Brougham's letters show, among other things, his own eagerness to obtain place and promotion for those who had served the public objects he had most at heart, and they are all instinct with the morbid restlessness of a mind which could only exist in the excitement and turmoil of an incessant activity. It is not improbable that the feverish fussiness of Brougham, by urging Denman to exertions for which he was not fitted, may have in some degree contributed to accelerate the attack which, at the close of 1852, finally prostrated him.

Among Brougham's letters from Cannes there are a few passages relating to contemporary French politics which are not without interest. The following, too,

[1] Augusta Emma d'Este, daughter of the Duke of Sussex and Lady Augusta Murray. Wilde won the lady by the singular zeal and ability with which he sought (though in vain) to establish her and her brother's legitimacy before the House of Lords, in the famous case of the Sussex peerage.

written from Walmer Castle, in the early summer of 1851, gives a pleasant picture of the Great Duke and of his affection and esteem for Denman:

"I received your letter the day I left town for Brockett Hall, and delayed writing till now that I might be able to give you my report of the Duke's health, which I can do most satisfactorily, having passed the whole of last evening alone with him (there is only Lady Charles Wellesley here). I certainly never saw him better, and seldom so well in all respects. I am sure very small parties agree best with him, though his extreme good-nature makes him often submit to go into larger ones, I mean dinners, for evening parties he always liked and likes. Of all the evenings I ever passed with him I really think this was the most interesting, and on all subjects. He asked much and kindly, and with the greatest interest, after you, and when I told him I should tell you, and that it would gratify you, he begged me to do so, and to say everything most kind. I told him how you valued him privately and personally, as well as publicly, and that no time ever would erase from your mind the sense of his gallant and friendly conduct in your instance [in the matter of the silk gown in 1828]. He seemed much pleased, and also expressed himself most becomingly on the topic, and I really think as amicably as becomingly. He spoke with pleasure of Middleton, where he said he had been to see you from Chatsworth, and what a nice place he thought it."

Brougham's impressions of the *coup d'état* of December 2, 1851, and its probable issues, are thus given in letters written from Cannes, within a few days and weeks after its occurrence. On December 8, 1851, he writes:

"I did not expect a *coup d'état* now, hardly even in the spring, but I believe the general fear, the general desire of *la paix à tout prix* (on which I had reckoned), will certainly now prevent any serious or wide-spreading mischief. Louis Napoleon is quite sure to succeed for the present. But his uncle depended on an army and generals; he must depend after a while on an assembly and debaters, and he has not one that anybody ever heard of."

On the 23rd, after referring to certain excesses of the Reds and the Socialists, he writes;

"These things, and the atrocities elsewhere, have completely played Louis Napoleon's game, and he is safe for a while. All feel that he alone can now prevent the worst mischiefs, and so they will support him till he has an opportunity of giving good measures and wise laws, and then I think he will both get a better grounded support and deserve it. His grand difficuly is that he can not, like his uncle, govern by the army alone; he must have an assembly, and the two together will be very difficult to rule by. He has shown the greatest talents for affairs in my judgment; but that he had a right so to act will depend on his case. He must prove the conspiracy against himself, as well as that of the Reds against society."

On January 13, 1852, he writes, still from Cannes, on the same subject;

"We are fated to witness a retrograde movement in Europe under the fatal influence of fear. Here we have France entirely under that influence, and Louis Napoleon owes to it his eight millions of votes vesting in him absolute power. The vile revolution of 1848 no doubt is the remote cause, but the immediate is fear of mob rule; and a most just fear, too, only that it is going to make the whole country in love with military despotism. I find many reasonable people prepared to take peace and quiet and security at that or at any price. He is resolved, it seems, to put down Parliamentary Government and the Press. He regards himself as a sort of Providence to effect these changes; and as the factions in Parliament, the follies of the mob agitators, and the insolence of the Press, have made liberal government for the moment unpopular, he expects to succeed. Of course he had the good wishes of the Continental governments, and I should apprehend of the upper classes as well. I fear he has something of the same sympathy among ourselves."

The same letter contains the following passage on the enforced retirement of Lord Palmerston from the Foreign Office, in December, 1851, and on the satisfaction it caused among the Continental absolutists:

"I find there is very great delight everywhere at Palmerston's overthrow, which was inevitable after his Kossuth insanity; but the mode and manner of it has been, I understand, most offensive, and such as he is not likely to forgive.[1] I find it was a surprise on almost all his colleagues. Grey had no hand whatever in it. The 'Letter-Writer' [Lord John Russell] seems to have done it all himself,[2] and he is much mistaken if he reckons on Stanley [Lord Derby] as no longer capable of forming a Government, or on any Reform cry as being sufficient to carry him through. As to 'No Popery,' it it is more likely to tell against than for him."

Writing from Boulogne, on his way to London, on January 28, 1852, he says:

"The state of France is such as to fill men with sorrow, even more than alarm. Absolute despotism, worse than Oriental, because the man thinks he has the whole people with him, except the reflecting and respectable classes, of whom he makes no account. The *coup d'état* had really been not only justifiable, but useful. Then came the votes, which seemed to have turned his head, and now it seems as if he were capable of anything. This Orleans' confiscation is in all respects abominable; but the distribution of the spoil has disgusted me far more than the robbery itself. Meanwhile I can see no use in our Press raving against him, and I hope Parliament will not join in the useless and hurtful chorus, though I admit it is not easy to avoid it. Of war I have no great fear, but preparation is all right. The risk is not of his knowingly and willfully making war, but, without the *scienter*, doing some other violent act that may lead to it."

Soon after Brougham's arrival in England, on February 20, 1852, Palmerston's revenge was taken; Lord John Russell resigned on the Militia Bill, and Lord Derby, on the 23rd, succeeded in forming a ministry which held together till the next December. Brougham writes thus:

[1] He did not; but, biding his time, in February, 1852, he upset Lord John Russell's ministry on the Militia Bill, and brought in the Tories.

[2] Moved thereto, as afterwards explained in Parliament, by the Queen and Prince Albert.

"So you see they are out. A more unhappy moment for a crisis, and especially for a dissolution,[1] could not have been chosen; but I entirely admit that a feeble government at such a time was not desirable. And now, instead of Jonathan, we shall have Sugden to remit all law amendment, but I daresay with Jonathan's assistance. I must say I think J. Russell's treatment of his colleagues too bad. He writes Durham letters, and sends them to the papers before he even lets one of his colleagues see them. And he announces that the Government is at an end, twice a year ago, and now, before he has seen *one* of them—thus proving it was either a preconcerted move, or that he acted without asking their opinion—out of this dilemma he has no escape. And now we are under one of the cleverest and lightest and most ill-furnished heads in England, with a great many good qualities more or less unavailing."

[1] The dissolution did not take place till July 1.

CHAPTER XXXVII.

LADY DENMAN'S DEATH—NICE—THIRD AND FINAL STROKE OF PARALYSIS.

A. D., 1852. ÆT. 73.

IN the summer of 1852 there came upon Denman the saddest bereavement that ever befel him, in the loss of her whose loving companionship, through a period of nearly half a century, had been the joy and delight of his youth, the crowning blessedness of his manhood, the unspeakable solace of his decline.

Lady Denman, who had for some years been in a feeble state of health, had spent several months with her husband, in the spring and early summer of 1852, at Parsloes, near Dagenham, in Essex, a country-house then occupied by her third son, Richard, his wife and family.

The eldest daughter of Mr. and Mrs. Richard Denman, a lovely child of nine years of age, of most angelic goodness and sweetness of nature, named after her grandmother, Theodosia Anne, had died, after a short illness, on June 3, while Lady Denman was in the house. She was herself then very ill; [1] the death of her favorite granddaughter deeply affected her; the unfavorable symptoms increased, violent and frequent hemorrhages set in, and she died from the consequent exhaustion, on June 28, in the seventy-third year of her age.

The following hasty lines, giving an account of her last hours, were written by Denman, with trembling and unsteady hand, to his eldest daughter, Mrs. Wright:

"During the whole of yesterday she was often unconscious, and had but short intervals of disturbed

[1] Suffering under that insidious and dangerous malady known as Bright's disease.

sleep. She could hardly articulate, but continued to express her warm affection for those about her. Her smiles across the looks of suffering were most beautiful. When I kissed and wished her good-night she returned the pressure with an animation that gave me for a moment strong hopes of reaction and recovery. To the last faint struggle her heart was overflowing with love and her lips with blessing."

The shock of this separation, after after a union of eight-and-forty years passed in uninterrupted tenderness and affection, was such as might be expected from the deep and sensitive nature of Denman. He never got over it, but, though surrounded with the loving attentions of children as deeply devoted as ever gathered round the declining years of a father, he yet always felt, though he rarely if ever expressed it, that abiding sense of a "hidden want" which saps the springs of life and poisons the sources of enjoyment.

The remains of the wife and the grandchild lie buried side by side in Dagenham Churchyard, and the following simple and touching inscription, written by Denman himself, was placed above their grave:

IN MEMORY OF
THEODOSIA ANNE, THE WIFE OF THOMAS, LORD DENMAN,
CHIEF JUSTICE OF ENGLAND.
BORN 21ST NOVEMBER, 1779; DIED JUNE 28TH, 1852.
AND OF HER
GRAND- AND GOD-CHILD, THEODOSIA ANNE, THE ELDEST
DAUGHTER OF RICHARD AND EMMA DENMAN.
BORN JUNE 26TH, 1843: DIED 3RD JUNE, 1852.

THE STONE WHICH RECORDS THEIR DEATH MAY TELL IN THE
SAME LANGUAGE OF THE VIRTUES OF WHICH ONE GAVE EARLY PROOF,
AND BY WHICH THE OTHER WAS, THROUGH A LONG LIFE
ENDEARED TO ALL WHO KNEW HER.
INNOCENT, PIOUS, GENTLE, AND AFFECTIONATE:
WELL PREPARED FOR THAT BLISS WHICH THEIR BEREAVED FRIENDS
HUMBLY TRUST THEY ARE NOW ENJOYING TOGETHER.

Everything was done that could be done to lighten the burden of his sorrow. They took him for change of air and scene to Scarborough, and in the late autumn he accompanied Mr. and Mrs. Richard Denman and their remaining children to Nice, where his son had been advised by his medical attendants to pass the winter.

One subject, and one subject only, beyond the limits of his private grief, had still power to move him deeply —too deeply for his happiness and peace—and that was the terrible, ever-haunting subject of Slavery and the Slave Trade. By this time Mrs. Stowe's master work had taken by storm the attention of all the world. Knowing the effect it would have on their father, his children at first tried to keep it from him, but this, in the case of one not absolutely secluded from society, was, of course, impossible. He read it, and with what result is easy to conceive. It moved him not only with pity and horror, but filled him also with bitterness and wrath, under the inspiration of which, coupled, no doubt, with a mistaken sense of over-mastering duty, he was led to perpetrate the most ill-advised and regretable action of his life—the publication, namely, in the late autumn of 1852, first separately in newspapers, afterwards collectively as a pamphlet, of certain "Letters on 'Uncle Tom's Cabin,' 'Bleak House,' 'Slavery and the Slave Trade,'" in which he permitted himself to make the most unwarrantable and rancorous attacks on Dickens, whom he charged with having, in "Bleak House" (by his inimitable caricature of philanthropy run mad, in the person of Mrs. Jellaby), and also in certain articles in "Household Words," "taken pains to discourage the efforts then making to put down Slavery and the Slave Trade," and thus "having done his best to replunge the world into barbarism."

Strictures such as these, directed in terms of the bitterest invective against Charles Dickens, Denman's old friend and steady admirer—the incomparable satirist and humorist who in "Martin Chuzzlewit" and "American Notes" had done more than any other writer, not even excepting Mrs. Stowe, to keep alive in England a horror and detestation of slavery as practiced in the United States—were indeed sad and unjustifiable. The subject, though its mention in any truthful record of Denman's life was unavoidable, is too painful a one to dwell upon. *Non ragionam di lor.*

Some members of the family soon became not unnaturally anxious to excuse as far as possible, on the ground of morbid excitement and overwrought feeling, this unfortunate indulgence in "letter writing," and Mrs. Cropper[1] inclosed to Dickens a communication in this sense, drawn up with great tact and kindliness by her brother George, the present Mr. Justice Denman.

The reply of Dickens—a reply strongly marked by proper self-respect, good sense and good feeling—was as follows:—

"Tavistock House, January 21, 1853.

"Dear Mrs. Cropper,—I think it best on full consideration to send you the inclosed letter back without reading it. I have set forth to you the truth of the subject, and have utterly dismissed Lord Denman's part in it from my mind. What he has written and what I have done, nothing can change. The only one thing in abeyance is the question whether injudicious partisanship will awaken reaction against the Slave. That we shall all see for ourselves—too soon, I think—and the perusal of your brother's letter could assist none of us. I say again I have cleared my mind of Lord Denman's last opinions of me. I know I deserve his former and wiser judgment, and I cancel the rest for ever.

"My dear Mrs. Cropper,

"Faithfully yours,

"CHARLES DICKENS."

It is pleasant to pass from this sad business and see Denman, before he left England, again under the influence of a kindlier and better mood, a mood that was native and natural to him—of high admiration and sympathy for all that was really good and for all that was truly great.

The Great Duke died on September 16, 1852, and Denman, who had always entertained the highest veneration for his great qualities; who, on private grounds, moreover, had occasion to be deeply grateful to him; and who, like all the world, was much impressed by his death, endeavored to give expression to his feelings on

[1] Denman's fourth daughter, Margaret.

the occasion in the following quatrain, by no means the worst among the many metrical effusions which the death of the great Captain called forth :—

> In youth and age, in peace and war the same,
> With many tasks, but still one only aim,
> For England's weal with single heart he stood,
> Best of the great, and greatest of the good.

It was early in November when Denman, with his son and daughter-in-law, arrived in Nice, where he soon found several persons whom it was pleasant to know; amongst others Sir George Napier (brother of the heroic conqueror of Scinde) and his wife, with whom he soon grew into terms of intimacy. But it was the old story; in changing sky and climate he had not changed the current of his thoughts, and the black shadow of that infinite anguish and wickedness in the far lands and seas, which he was so powerless to mitigate, darkened over his spirit as much by the shores of the Mediterranean as among the hills of Derbyshire. Whatever might for a time occupy the foreground, this brooding presence ever lowered in the background of his mind.

While in this state of overcharged and morbid predisposition for perilous excitement, there came to him from Mrs. Stowe (who wrote, of course, in the most utter ignorance of the shattered state of his nervous system) an impassioned and most eloquent letter, which was certainly not calculated to allay the fever of the mind under which he labored. It was written in answer to a letter which Denman had sent to her from England, containing, in language poured forth warmly from the heart, the expressions of his gratitude and admiration for her memorable book, and his deep sense of the service which it had already rendered, and was destined to render still more thereafter, to the progress of the great cause. Mrs. Stowe's reply was in these terms:

"My Lord,—Could anything flatter me into an unwarrantable estimate of myself, it would be commendation from such sources as your Lordship. But I am utterly incredulous of all that is said; it passes by me like a dream. I can only see that when a higher Being has purposes to be accomplished he can make even a grain of mustard seed the means.

"I wrote what I did because as a woman, as a mother, I was oppressed and heartbroken with the sorrows and injustice I saw; because as a Christian I felt the dishonor to Christianity; because as a lover of my country I trembled at the coming day of wrath.

"It is no merit in the sorrowful that they weep, or to the oppressed and smothering that they gasp and struggle, nor to me that I must speak for the oppressed who can not speak for themselves.

"My Lord, such men as your Lordship have great power. You can do much. The expression of your opinion is of great weight. So does this horrible evil paralyze public sentiment here, that we who stand for liberty must look for aid to the public sentiment of nations, and in that sentiment none are so powerful as the great minds of England. The hope, therefore, which I conceive from seeing such men in England as Archbishop Whately, the Earls of Carlisle and Shaftesbury, Arthur Helps, Kingsley, and your Lordship, interested in our movements, is great.

"All men of any distinction in England have weight with a certain circle of minds here, and by their distance from the evil, and entire disconnection, can present it in a light very different from that in which any native-born American can.

"Any one here can be hustled down, for all the capital, all the political power, and much of the ecclesiastical, is against the agitation of this subject; but you can force them to agitate.

"In your reviews, in your literature, you can notice and hold up before the world those awful facts which, but for you, they would go on scornfully denying as they have done.

"Furthermore, there are men in the Slave States, repressed and kept under, who are more glad than they dare to say at what you do. They hope that you will keep on, and bring about such a state of things as they can take advantage of to accomplish emancipation.

"I have now nearly through the press[1] a volume entitled 'Key to Uncle Tom's Cabin.' It contains documentary and attested evidence to show that if my rep

[1] Published in 1852

resentations have erred anywhere, it is by being under rather than over-colored. Oh, my Lord! never was such an awful story told under the sun. I have written it with perfect horror. One-third of the book is taken up with legal documents, statute laws, decisions of courts, reports of trials. It is worse than I supposed or dreamed.

"My Lord, I am conscious that this is not my work, for mine is another field; but I have been forced to it by the unblushing denials and most impudent representations with regard to what I said in my book as to slave law.

"It seems to me that this tremendous story can not be told in the civilized world without forcing attention. On the whole, there is hope, there is movement, there is evidently 'a stirring of bones in this valley of vision.' Standing as I do between the living and the dead, feeble in health and often very sorrowful, I have little realization of anything personal in this matter further than the consciousness of struggle and labor. I thank your Lordship, therefore, more for the noble and hearty interest which you feel in this sacred and suffering cause, than even for the very kind opinion you have been kind enough to express of me. It has done much good. All that the book has done might have been crushed but for the reinforcement and support of your country. May God bless it and you, is the prayer of

"Yours, very gratefully,
"H. B. STOWE."

It may have been only a coincidence, not a consequence, that, very shortly after the receipt of this letter, Denman was prostrated by the terrible final stroke of paralysis, which, for the remainder of his days, made his tongue incapable of articulate speech and his hand of self-originated writing.

What is certain is this, that his last seizure took place on the very day he had inclosed to his daughter, Mrs. Cropper, his reply to Mrs. Stowe's letter, requesting her to forward it to the great American authoress, whose correct address he did not know, and who (as will be seen above) had given no address in her letter to him. The very last words he ever wrote, *except as a copy of words written for him by others*, were Mrs. Cropper's name and address on the above-mentioned envelope.

It was on December 2, 1852, that this strange and terrible affliction befell him; strange as well as terrible, for it had this peculiarity about it, that while he retained his intellectual and emotional faculties almost unimpaired, his powers of communication with others by writing as well as by speech were absolutely and entirely taken from him. That speech, indeed, should go was quite in the ordinary course of paralytic seizures, but it does not, it is believed, always, or indeed often, follow, to the extent that it did in Denman's case, that the power of self-originated writing should be so totally extinguished. He could frame written letters with a pen, he could readily distinguish one ivory letter from another when arranged in lines before him; but to form these letters into words, or words into sentences, was utterly beyond his powers, unless the words and sentences were written, or put together as a model for him to copy from. When he had received letters—and many kind correspondents, knowing the delight he felt in perusing them, were constant in writing to him—the only way he could acknowledge them was by copying in a sort of formal print-hand any passage in them that had particularly pleased him, and causing that to be sent to the writers, in token that he had read and been pleased by their communications.

The state to which he was now reduced may be judged of by the following, passage from a brief account drawn up by his son, Richard, of the days that he passed at Nice, between his attack in December and his return to England in the spring.

"The sore infliction of dumbness he bore with wonderful patience. It was the more heavy to him, because he had always taken great pains to express his meaning with clearness, and the sudden discovery that he could not make himself understood puzzled and annoyed him. Dr. Travis [then practicing at Nice], who attended him with the utmost skill and care, entertained the hope (which, alas! proved fallacious) that as the severity of the stroke wore off, the power of speech would return, and in the meantime various attempts were made to assist him to make himself understood by giving him ivory letters, which he might form into words, or by encouraging him to write his wishes with his left hand now that the right was completely paralyzed. He soon wrote very tolerably with the left hand, but it was found that he could *originate nothing*, and when some deeds were sent from England for his signature he could only sign his name by seeing it written out and copying it.

"And yet his mind was as clear as ever to receive impressions. He could read, and could clearly understand everything that was either read or said to him. Law reports, debates in Parliament, &c., interested him as much as ever, and he showed by his countenance and by signs that he not only appreciated fine passages, but that he perfectly understood controverted points, and could he have expressed himself was as capable as ever of deciding them.

"But all power of expression was lost, the magnificent voice, which had been all his life raised for justice and liberty, was never to utter another word. He was like a casket full of precious jewels which no earthly power could unlock, and those who were near and dear to him were never again to hear from his lips the words of wisdom and honor!"

Mrs. Cropper writes to the same effect:

"With loss of speech he lost also the power of writing letters, or expressing himself in any way, and he never learned again to sign his own name except by copying it from print. His mind was clear to the last, his memory appeared to be perfect, but so entirely destroyed was his power of *expression in any way*, that his mode of replying to the frequent letters from his family friends was by simply copying them out and sending his own copies."

Many of these touching mementoes of his love and interest in all that belonged to him have been preserved with pious care by the various members of his family—melancholy fragments of a noble ruin.

CHAPTER XXXVIII.

DENMAN'S LONG INFIRMITY—HIS WONDERFUL PATIENCE UNDER IT—HIS DEATH.

A. D. 1853, 1854. ÆT. 74 TO 75.

AS it was evident that no benefit was to be hoped for from a prolonged residence abroad, Denman, under the care of his son and daughter-in-law, left Nice for England in April, 1853, and returned to his well-loved home at Stony Middleton, then in the occupation of his second daughter, Mrs. Hodgson, and her children.

Mrs. Hodgson had become a widow during her father's absence in Italy, the Provost having sunk under the effects of a severe attack of influenza, on December 29, 1852, only a few weeks after the final stroke of paralysis which had prostrated his old friend and father-in-law. The end of Francis Hodgson had been painless and peaceful. As he lay rapidly sinking from exhaustion, he faintly exclaimed "How beautiful!" and in reply to a question from his wife, who had asked, "What, dear, is so beautiful?" his answer was, "The mercy of God," and so he passed away.[1]

Denman had immediately acceded to a suggestion that the widow and children, who were left rather slenderly provided for, should thenceforth make their home at Stony Middleton, where, accordingly, he found them on his return.

Mrs. Cropper, who had gone over to Stony Middleton to meet her father, thus describes the interview:—

"I remember, very well, going to see my father on his return from Nice, after the blow which had deprived

[1] Hodgson was about three years younger than Denman, having been born on November 16, 1781 (Denman in February, 1779): he was a little over seventy-one at the time of his death.

him of speech. The widow and children of the Provost, Hodgson (who had died during my father's absence from England), were at the moment gathered round him. It was his first meeting with them after their sad and irreparable loss. My little boy, Joseph, was with me. He was a very lively, bright child, and unconscious of any sorrow. He went merrily into the room, and at the sight of him something touched my dear father, and he then wept freely, tears not having come before from him in the course of this sorrowful meeting."

For nearly a year after his return to England, Denman remained at Stony Middleton, amid the woods which in happier days his right hand had planted, and the lawns and gardens he had made so beautiful for himself—tenderly waited on and soothed by his sons and daughters, his sons-in-law and daughters-in-law, and their children, some of whom were always with him—Admiral and Lady Baynes, or some other members of his numerous family supplying the place of Mrs. Hodgson, during her brief absences at Brighton or elsewhere.

Mrs. Hodgson's account of her father's bearing under his sore affliction is very interesting; "We all of us," she writes, "loved and reverenced him before as deeply as we thought it possible; but his noble constancy, his uniform good humor, his unwearied and heroic patience under suffering, filled us with a new sentiment of the profoundest veneration."

He found his chief solace in reading and being read to. The Bible was his constant study; never a day passed without his reading in it: he also took great delight in the dramatists, not only in Shakespeare, but in the two great masters of the French drama, Corneille and Racine—the grand Roman roll of the one, and the exquisitely tender pathos of the other, giving him infinite pleasure. One day, a little before his death, feeling no doubt the rapid decay of his strength, he pointed out to his eldest son that grand line of Corneille,—

"J' attends la mort sans l'espoir ni la crainte."

But what he most enjoyed was being read to; and here occasionally (it was the only point in which he was so) he was a little exacting. To read the *Times* newspaper to him daily, omitting nothing that was of interest or importance, was the loving labor for many months of those who watched over him. If anything was omitted, he was quick to find it out, giving the reader by an expressive look an intimation that he or she "had been skipping."

Mrs. Hodgson tells a story of one of their readings which shows he had not lost his once keen power of being amused, or what Mr. Carlyle would call "his healthy faculty" of hearty laughter.

The reader on the occasion in question, was one of Mrs. Hodgson's daughters, then quite a little girl, and the book was the life of Theodore Hook, in a particular portion of which—that relating to the Berners Street story—the word "*hoax*" repeatedly occurs. This the child, whenever she came to it, uniformly pronounced as a dissyllable, "*ho-ax*," which so amused Denman that when Mrs. Hodgson came into the room she found him roaring with laughter, which he could only explain by causing the book to be brought to him, pointing out the word, and making the child read it again, which, to his great delight, she immediately did in the same manner as before.

His courteous observance of all polite usages where ladies were concerned was not at all diminished by his state of infirmity: every day at Middleton he caused himself to be dressed for the family dinner as carefully as though he had been going to Holland House or Chatsworth.

He delighted in his daily drives in the neighborhood; and in being wheeled slowly about the garden in a bath-chair. He had preserved quite unimpaired his fondness for scenery, his delight in pictures, and his passion for flowers.

On the whole, owing to his admirable self-restraint, patience and gentleness, aided by the loving care of a family who vied with one another in gratifying his every wish and anticipating his every want, he was enabled to pass, with subdued but tolerable cheerfulness, through a state of severe trial, that by many would have been converted into a period of protracted torment both to themselves and all around them.

In the spring of 1854, Mrs. Hodgson having been obliged to leave Stony Middleton, Denman went to reside with his eldest son and his eldest son's first wife, at Stoke Albany, in Northampton, where his brother-in-law, Vevers, had once been rector. There he remained till his death, the object of as holy and tender a solicitude and affection as were ever bestowed on a beloved parent. Denman had once said to that eldest son, that "he was afraid to tell him how much he loved him:" it was now the son's turn to prove to the father the priceless worth and solace of true filial devotion.

It was known that Denman liked to be written to; and many letters, which he has preserved, from Patteson, Coleridge, and others of his old friends, show how amiably and solicitously they, in this respect, endeavored to contribute to his gratification. Among the letters of this class, and they were many, which Denman received through his long illness, three must have given him peculiar pleasure—two from the venerable Samuel Rogers, then long past his 80th year, and one from the good and amiable Duke of Devonshire, whose kindness to Denman and his family survived through all chances and changes to the end.

On March 24, 1853, Rogers writes, in his small, exquisitely delicate "Italian hand," showing no sign of age or shakiness:

"My dear Friend,—How can I thank you for your many kind inquiries after me, and for the little book, which I have read with great delight? Your friendship and your benevolence never sleep night or day. As for me, I am as well as I can hope to be, and you are always in my thoughts. I can never forget you, here or hereafter.

"SAMUEL ROGERS.

"22 St. James's Place: March 14, 1853."

The next is of some six months' later date:

"September 28, 1854.

"My dear Friend,—I need not say with what delight I have read your letter from Stony Middleton.[1]

"Pray give my love to one and all there. As I am not with you, and must be elsewhere, I am here consol-

[1] Written for him by Mrs. Hodgson, he having read and approved of it.

ing myself by the seaside, and wishing you were all with me, not omitting the young voices[1] that are rejoicing you all day long.

"I am as well as I can hope to be, but should be better if I could transport myself where you are; for so great a pleasure I would resign the waves of this beautiful sea, and the thousand 'Ladyes' on horseback who are passing before me.

"Ever most affectionately yours,

"SAMUEL ROGERS.

"I can not say how much I think myself obliged to her who has written your charming letter.

"79 Marine Parade, Brighton."

The letter from the Duke of Devonshire, written in the winter of 1854, is also from Brighton, and contains a reference to the venerable poet:

"Brighton: February 17, 1854.

"My dear Lord,—You can not think how much I am delighted with the lines you send me,[2] and by your having written them out yourself for me. I think them most beautiful and touching; and, besides, as they are copied in your hand, I shall always keep and consider them as a great treasure.

"I must add, besides, that you have been the means of my having a great satisfaction—that of giving pleasure to poor Rogers on seeing him to-day. I read the verses out loud to him, and it appeared to me that he admired and liked them very much indeed. *When he saw your handwriting, he kissed it.*

"I called afterwards, in hopes of showing my acquisition to Mrs. Hodgson,[3] but she was out, and I found afterwards had called on me with James [novelist], who is to be shown my bird's-nest of a house one of these days.

"Receive a thousand thanks from me, my dear Lord Denman, And believe me,

"Your faithful and most attached servant,

"DEVONSHIRE."

[1] Of Mrs. Hodgson's children.

[2] Copying verses that struck him in reading, and sending them, when copied, was one of Denman's substitutes for correspondence. What the lines here alluded to were, is not known.

[3] Denman was now at Stoke Albany and Mrs. Hodgson at Brighton.

There is one more letter of this last period which must still be added: it is from Mrs. Stowe, who, in the spring of the year 1853, had come over to Europe, and been received by the flower of the English matronhood with the homage which was her due: but who, greatly to her sorrow, had been unable to see Lord Denman, then secluded from the world under the dark cloud of affliction and disease. Soon after her return to America she sent him the following very beautiful letter, which reached him, probably, towards the close of 1853, or in the early part of 1854:[1]

"Dear and venerated Friend,—It was the hope of my heart, when I left America for England, that I should have the honor and pleasure of an interview with your Lordship. How was my heart saddened when on my arrival I found that the heavy hand of disease had been laid upon you, and that I could not hope for that pleasure! But I trust, my Lord, that you have learned that the pressure of this sore affliction is after all but the weight of a Father's hand, and that the privation which secludes you from human intercourse and society is but the overshadowing of the wings of the Almighty, bringing your soul nearer to God.

"My Lord, may it console and bless you to think that you have to the last and latest extent given your noble powers to a most worthy and sacred cause, a cause dear to the heart of that Saviour who came to bring liberty to the captive and the opening of the prison to those who are bound.

"No great good is ever gained to man without the suffering of the good. Jesus Himself, the Captain of our Salvation, was made perfect only through suffering; and may you, my Lord, be among those who count it blessedness to endure affliction.

"May that Redeemer whose consolations are nearer and more intimate than those of earthly friendship, bless you. May the Holy Comforter dwell with you; and may all this light affliction, which endureth but for

[1] Mrs. Stowe arrived at Liverpool from the United States on April 11. 1853, and left England, on her return, on September 7

a moment, work out for you a far more exceeding and eternal weight of glory.

"With affectionate veneration,

"Your sincere admirer and friend,

"H. B. STOWE."

There is a tone of holy and religious thought about that beautiful letter, like a strain of solemn music, that harmonizes with the close of this long and eventful life-drama.

For now the end was drawing very near. It came at last, as often happens, somewhat unexpectedly; but not so suddenly as to prevent the assemblage round his death-bed of all the principal members of his large and deeply attached family. Consciousness remained to the last. Looks expressive of a yearning love and tenderness, kisses, and close embraces were not wanting. At length, as though the bonds of speech were burst suddenly asunder by the pressure of thoughts struggling for utterance, he lifted up his voice with a loud cry, and in the effort breathed out his life.

Lord Denman died on September 22, 1854, aged a little over seventy-five years and seven months.

He lies buried in Stoke Albany churchyard, where a stone with a short and plain inscription was placed over his grave by his eldest son, in record of the last resting place "of the great and good Lord Denman."

His fourth daughter, the Hon. Mrs. Cropper, with the co-operation of several other members of the family, and of some of the most distinguished of his old friends and brother Judges, among whom may be mentioned Lord Brougham, Lord Wensleydale, Sir John Taylor Coleridge, and Chief Justice Erle, caused a memorial window and monument to be set up in remembrance of him, in the Church of Penshurst in Kent, the parish in which, "Swaylands," the country residence of Mr. and Mrs. Cropper, is situated.

In the inscription on the brass plate beneath the window are the two following sentences, which fitly commemorate his public and his private virtues:—

"In discharging the duties of his high office, without ever losing sight of the civil or religious liberties of the people, he was vigilant to maintain the dignity of the constituted authorities and the law of the land.

"In private life, he was a dutiful son, a tender husband, an affectionate father, a delightful companion, a faithful friend, and a sincere Christian."

There was a strain of high and antique nobleness in Denman's character that well entitled him to such a memento within the precincts of that venerable mansion and those ancient groves, that are so inseparably associated with the name of him who fell at Zutphen—that "gentle mirror of true and perfect chivalry"—Sir Philip Sidney.

But there was that also in his career which might seem not unjustly to have earned for him some monumental record among the national worthies of England. Had his death followed closely on his resignation, it is not improbable that such a commemoration might have been accorded; but the four years of disease and decay which intervened, had withdrawn him from the observation of the public, and when he passed away, amid the excitement of the Crimean War, the mind of the nation was set on other things.

Nearly twenty years have gone by since then, but it may well be doubted whether in all that interval any higher minded citizen or better man has descended into the grave. Is it too late to repair the long omission? Is there any good reason why, by the contributions of those—and they must be numerous—who admire his character and career, a memorial bust might not even now be placed in Westminster Abbey, which might perpetuate in marble, for the veneration of posterity, the noble lineaments of the "good and great" Chief Justice?

APPENDIX.

Selections from Lord Denman's Verses

I. TRANSLATIONS.

The Lament of Danae.[1]

(*From Simonides*, 7, 1, 121.)

When the wind, resounding high,
Blustered from the northern sky;
When the waves in stronger tide
Dashed against the vessel's side;
Her careworn cheeks with tears bedewed,
Her sleeping infant Danae viewed;
And trembling still with new alarms
Around him cast a mother's arms.
"My child! what woes does Danae weep,
But thy young limbs are wrapt in sleep.
In that poor nook, all sad and dark,
While lightnings play about our bark,
Thy quiet bosom only knows
The heavy sigh of deep repose.
"The howling wind, the raging sea,
No terror can excite in thee;
The angry surges wake no care
That burst above thy long deep hair:
But couldst thou feel what I deplore,
Then would I bid thee sleep the more!
Sleep on, sweet boy, still be the deep!
Oh, could I lull my woes to sleep!
Jove, let thy mighty hand o'erthrow
The baffled malice of my foe;
And may this child, in future years,
Avenge his mother's wrongs and tears."

Anthology, p. 360. Ed. 1813.

Ode to the Athenian Patriots.

(*From Callistratus*, *Scol.* 7, 1, 155.)

I'll wreathe my sword in myrtle bough,
The sword that laid the tyrant low,
When patriots, burning to be free,
To Athens gave equality.

[1] These lines were written while Lord Denman was still at Eton.

Harmodius, hail! tho' reft of breath,
Thou ne'er shalt feel the stroke of death:
The Heroes' happy isles shall be
The bright abode allotted thee.

I'll wreathe the sword in myrtle bough,
The sword that laid Hipparchus low,
When at Minerva's adverse fane
He knelt, and never rose again.

While Freedom's name is understood,
You shall delight the wise and good;
You dared to set your country free
And gave her laws equality.

Anthology, p. 122.

ANOTHER TRANSLATION OF THE SAME.[1]

In myrtle my sword will I wreathe,
Like our patriots, the noble and brave,
Who devoted the tyrant to death,
And to Athens equality gave!

Loved Harmodius, thou never shalt die!
The poets exultingly tell
That thine is the fullness of joy
Where Achilles and Diomed dwell.

In myrtle my sword will I wreathe,
Like our patriots, the noble and brave
Who devoted Hipparchus to death,
And buried his pride in the grave.

At the altar the tyrant they seized,
While Minerva he vainly implored;
And the Goddess of Wisdom was pleased
With the victim of Liberty's sword.

May your bliss be immortal on high
Among men as your glory shall be:
Ye doomed the usurper to die,
And bade our dear country be free.

Anthology, p. 123, 124.

CHORUS FROM THE ANDROMACHE OF EURIPIDES

To lofty Ilion when the Spartan dame
Was led, all blooming, by her shepherd boy,
Majestic to the princely couch she came,
No consort, but a curse to him and Troy.
For her, O Troy! against thy menaced town
Greece brought her thousand ships, her fire and sword,
Her rapid vengeance mow'd thy bulwarks down,
And slew thy best defense, my dear loved lord.

[1] This is the translation which Byron so much admired. See note to twentieth stanza of the third canto of "Childe Harold."

Yes—round those walls the savage conqueror bore,
  Bound to his car, the body of the brave:
Torn from my bride-bed to a hostile shore,
  I live to feel what 'tis to be a slave.
While round the awful form the Goddess rears,
  Driv'n by hard threats, my suppliant arms are thrown,
I melt, dissolving in perpetual tears,
  Like drops that tremble from a roof of stone.

Anthology, p. 261.

TRANSLATION FROM MILTON'S SIXTH ITALIAN SONNET.

A simple youth, a lover most sincere,
  Since now, alas! your converse I must leave,
  To you, fair maid, my true heart let me give,
A parting present, which through many a year
Faithful, intrepid, constant, I have known,
  Courteous, and mild, and kind in every thought:
  Amid the great world's tumults tempest-fraught,
It seeks for succor in itself alone.
Far above Fortune's power and Envy base
  The hopes and fears that vulgar minds abuse,
Genius and Honor and Song's soothing art
  It dearly prizes, and adores the Muse.
'Tis only somewhat softer in that place
Which Love has wounded with his cureless dart.

The above are all youthful compositions. In the later years of his life Lord Denman recurred, as one of the favorite amusements of his leisure, to his early habit of translation, especially from Horace. The following are some of those which have been preserved among his papers:—

HORAC. BOOK I, ODE 3.

Sic te Diva potens Cypri.

So may the potent Cyprian queen
So Helen's brothers, stars of silvery sheen,
And he of winds the lord and sire,
Only Iapyx suffering to respire,
Guide thee, O ship, intrusted to convey
The dearer portion of my life away!
Preserve thy sacred charge and land
My Virgil safely on the Athenian strand.
  A breast of oak and brass had he,
Who first committed to the ruthless sea
His fragile bark; nor feared the roar
Of gales fierce struggling from the Libyan shore,
With tempests from the north; nor showers
Of the sad Hyads, nor the raging powers
Of Him who with a master's pride
Swells Adria's waves or bids their wrath subside.

What death could daunt his soul with awe,
Who with dry eyes the wallowing monsters saw,
The turgid main with ruin spread,
And th' Acroceraunian crags lowering like Fate ahead? 11
In vain wise Jove has planned
The severing ocean to part land from land,
If impious ships may freely dare
To leap across the gulfs by him established there.
Braving Heav'n's wrath, the audacious mind
Thro' each forbidden outrage drags mankind.
Prometheus, bolder than his sire,
Purloined for Man the elemental Fire;
From Fire brought down to Man, a birth
Of Plague and Fever brooded over Earth;
And to Death's erst remote abode
Necessity cut short the lingering road.
With wings for mortals never made
Did Dædalus the void of air invade;
Hell's barrier Hercules laid low;
To Heaven itself our mad desires would go;
Nor suffer Jove, through our rebellious pride,
To lay his angry thunderbolts aside.

BOOK I. ODE 9. (November, 1849.)

Vides ut alta stet nive candidum
Soracte.

Dost thou not see Soracte's height
With depth of snow is dazzling white?
The woods no more their weight sustain,
The streams are bound in icy chain.

Dissolve the cold, while on the dogs
With lavish hand you fling the logs,
And, Thaliarchus, from your store
The four years' wine more freely pour.

Trust with the gods the rest, whose will
Can bid the warring winds be still,
Cypress and ancient ash tree cease
Their strife, and lift their heads in peace.

Seek not the morrow to foresee,
And each fresh day, whate'er it be,
Deem so much gained, nor, madly wise,
Oh, Boy, the dame of love despise.

Ere hoary Age, morose, uncouth,
Check the free sports of blooming youth,
Let gentle whispers, low yet clear,
Breathe in soft Twilight's secret ear;

While shrilling forth from darkened shade
The laugh betrays the lurking maid,
Then from white arms be bracelets torn,
From fingers rings too loosely worn.

Book I. Ode 14.

O navis, referent in mare te novi
Fluctus?

Oh ship, the boiling waves again
Would drive thee to the stormy main;
What dost thou? see thy naked side
With oars yet unsupplied.

Thy bowsprit sprung, thy stately mast
Split with wild Afric's furious blast;
No ropes, thy threatened keel to save,
Lashed by the tyrant wave;

No sails entire—no gods to hear
The cry of thy distress and fear,
O gallant daughter of the wood
On the proud hill that stood,

The frowning guard of Pontus' coast,
Thy name, thy race, an empty boast;
The wretched seaman, vexed with storms,
Mocks at the noblest forms.

The winds make sport of thee—Beware!
My fear, my wearying burden of sad care!
Oh, may you fly the fierce tide's dangerous shocks
'Mid the Cycladean rocks.

Book I. Ode 22.

Integer vitæ, scelerisque purus.

The honest man, whose life is pure,
Needs not the javelin of the Moor,
Nor bow, nor quiver teeming with the darts
Whose poison reaches hearts.

Whether through Syrte's eddying sands he go,
Or wild Caucasian mountain heaped with snow,
Or the far realms where, fabled in old song,
Hydaspes rolls along.

For late, when in the Sabine grove,
I, careless wandering, sang my love—
My Lalage—a wolf, the shepherd's dread,
Saw me unarmed—and fled.

A monster, whose portentous jaw
Exceeds whatever Daunia saw,
Or, nurse of lions—Juba's land,
Bred in her arid sand.

Place me in those dull fields whose trees
Are freshened by no summer breeze,
The region ever doomed to bear
Foul fogs and filthy air.

Or, where the houseless desert feels
Too near the hot sun's burning wheels,
E'en there will I in Lalage rejoice—
Sweet smile, and sweeter voice.

Book I. Ode 24.

Quis desiderio sit pudor aut modus.

Why blush to weep, why check the tear
For one so honored and so dear,
Mourn, O Melpomene, to whom the Sire
Gave melting voice and lyre.

In endless sleep Quinctilius lies—
Modesty, Truth without disguise,
Sister to Justice, Honor clear,
When shall they find his peer?

Bewailed by all the good his fall,
By thee, my Virgil, most of all;
Pious in vain thy prayers ascend
To ask of Heaven thy friend.

Could'st thou, like Orpheus, move the trees,
And even with sweeter melodies,
The life blood could no more pervade
The disembodied shade

Which Hermes, with relentless wand
Once drives among his sable band—
Hard Fate! but Patience, though it can not cure,
Yet soothes what men endure

Book II. Ode 6.

Septimi, Gades aditure mecum, et.

Dear fellow traveler to that land
Unconquered still by Roman hand;
To Gades, and the fretful shores
Where still the Moorish whirlpool roars.

Let Tibur be my final rest,
My weary age's quiet nest;
That peaceful haven let me gain,
From war, from travel, and the main.

If Fate forbids, I'll seek the brink
Of sweet Galesas' stream, where drink
The fleecy flocks that haunt the plain,
Laconian Phalantus' reign.

That nook of earth, that lovely coast,
Smiles on my captive fancy most:
Whose honey not to Hybla yields,
Nor olive to Venafran fields.

Clime favored by the Heavenly King,
With winter mild, and lengthened spring,
Where friendly Aalon bids the vine
Richly pour forth Falernian wine.

That spot beloved, those towers, attend
My presence not without my friend;
And of the bard you now hold dear
The ashes there shall claim your tear.

Book II. Ode 10.

Rectius vives, Licini, neque altum.

Wisely Licinius live, nor urge
The open ocean's furious surge;
Nor, whilst you fear the tempest's roar,
Too closely hug the treacherous shore.

The lover of the golden mean
Is not in sordid dwelling seen,
Nor wakes the envy that will fall
On him who boasts his pompous hall.

The loftiest pine that scorns the vale
Must quiver in the wintry gale;
High towers with heavier ruin break;
The lightnings smite the highest peak.

In minds well schooled, a fate severe
Destroys not hope—a kind fate, fear.
Great Jove, who bids the tempest rage,
Will smooth with halcyon smiles the wave.

Ill fortune, changing, may relent;
Not always Phœbus' bow is bent;
His happier mood may strike e'er long
The lyre, and wake the Muse to song.

Bold be your spirit when the blow
Of Fortune seeks to lay you low,
And wisely reef the sails that swell
When prosperous gales too fast impel.

Book 3. Ode 6.

Delicta majorum immeritus lues.

The evils wrought in other times,
O Roman! thy forefathers' crimes,
 'Tis thine to suffer and deplore,
Till all the images divine,
And every godhead's crumbling shrine,
 Thy pious penitence restore.

The power to rule on Earth is given
By that o'erruling power in Heaven,
 The Sovereign Arbiter of fate,

Whose favor, sought, thy greatness wills;
Neglected, showers ten thousand ills
  On sad Hesperia's ruined state.

Twice did Moneses and the band
Of Pacoris our assaults withstand,
  (Efforts how vain, by Heaven unblest!)
And on their swelling bosom wore
The very necklace which before
  Had glittered on a Roman breast.

Dacian, who hurls his darts afar,
And Ethiop, fierce in ocean war,
  Glorying had seen their prostrate prey
By faction weakened and debased,
Wellnigh had laid our city waste,
  And swept her name from Earth away.

For Vice at first had dared despise
Connubial rites, domestic ties,
  The cherished sanctity of Home,
And, rushing from that turbid source
Disaster whelmed with torrent force
  Imperial and corrupted Rome.

Oh, never from such parents sprung
The Roman youths, when Rome was young,
  Who dyed with Punic blood the wave,
Who the dire Hannibal laid low,
And Pyrrhus and each mighty foe
  Armed for our fall, to ruin gave.

No! but a manly offspring born
Of warrior peasants, taught at morn
  To delve with Sabine spades the land,
In vigorous sport to wield at eve
The massy cudgel, and receive
  War's weapons from a mother's hand.

When Sol now pointed to the East
The mountain shadows—man and beast
  Ceased work, with daylong toil oppressed;
And his departing chariot's flight
Brought on the friendly hour of night,
  The hour of darkness and of rest.[1]

Book III. Ode 9.

Donec gratus eram tibi.

HORACE.

While I was loved by thee, as now
  Is loved that favored youth who flings
His arms around thy neck of snow,
  I lived more blest than Persian kings.

[1] The sixth, seventh, eighth, and last stanzas of the original have been left untranslated by Lord Denman.

LYDIA.

Ere Chloe was to me preferred,
  Ere thou hadst felt her warmer flame,
Then Lydia's high renown was heard,
  Surpassing Ilia's honored name.

HORACE.

Now Cretan Chloe is my care,
  Skilled in soft lute and airs divine;
Her cherished life, if Fate would spare,
  I, fearless, could my own resign.

LYDIA.

The youthful Calais stirs my breast,
  The Thurian's son, with mutual fire;
Twice would I die to save him, blest
  In double anguish to expire.

HORACE.

What if our ancient love return
  And join the hearts that now are twain;
If I the gold-haired Chloe spurn,
  And woo my Lydia once again.

LYDIA.

Though he be fairer than a star,
  Thou light as cork, and than the sea
On Adria's shore more stormy far,
  With thee I'll live, I'll die with thee.

Book III. Ode 29.

Tyrrhena regum progenies, tibi.

Sprung from Etruria's royal line,
  Mæcenas! at thy friend's abode
There is a cask of virgin wine.
  Roses, and perfume that has flowed
'Erst o'er thy locks—no more delay.
  Let Œsula's soft-sloping brow,
And Tibur bathed in constant spray,
  For other scenes release thee now;
Thy glut of grandeur leave awhile,
  The massive wall and cloud-capped dome,
Nor flatter, with unceasing smile,
  The smoke, and wealth, and noise of Rome.

Change, not unpleasing to the great,
  A poor man's scant but cleanly fare,
With no proud pomp of purple state,
  May smooth the anxious brow of care.
The sun glares forth with scorching eye,
  The dog-star burns the sultry plain,
The lion rages in the sky,
  The summer days are come again;

The weary swain to welcome shades
  Drives his faint flock to streams and groves—
While not one wandering breath invades
  The silence of the bank he loves.

Guarding the safety of the State,
  'Tis thine to watch with prudent mind
What China, Persia meditate,
  What Tanais, what remotest Ind.

The God who all Fate's secret knows,
  Yet wisely shrouds from human sight,
But laughs, when mortals would expose
  What he enwraps in darkest night.
Rule thou the present, all the rest
  Moves like a stream—now peaceful flowing
To sink in Ocean's tranquil breast,
  Now trees and rocks in whirlpools throwing,
Flocks, herds, the peasants ruined dwelling,
  Rolling along with thundering sound.

When the chafed stream with floods is swelling;
  And woods and mountains roar around,
He of himself is lord and king
  Who with each setting sun can say,
"To morrow calm or storm may bring,
  It recks not, I have lived to-day!"

That Power which brightens all the sky,
  Or with loud whirlwinds shakes the Pole—
The deeds once done—the time gone by—
  Has fixed beyond his own control.

With insolent and mocking glee
  Fortune her wayward game will play;
And now to others, now to me,
  Her ever-shifting smiles display.
I praise her while the turn is mine,
  But, if her nimble wings she ply,
All that she gave me I resign,
  And cling to virtuous poverty.

'Tis not for me, when groans the mast,
  With furious storms from Afric's shore,
With prayers and vows to woo the blast
  Lest one rich Tyrian cargo more
Increase the greedy ocean's prey—
  Me through the vexed Ægean seas
Shall then my two-oared skiff convey,
  With kind twin-stars and favoring breeze.

Book IV. Ode 3.

Quem tu Melpomene semel.

Melpomene, celestial maid,
Whom at his birth thy favoring eye surveyed,

Him never Isthmian toils shall bring
The applauded conqueror from the battle's ring;
Nor fiery steeds his chariot place
First at the goal, the winner of the race:
Nor War his brows with Delian laurels deck
For trampling on the vanquished tyrant's neck.

But streams thro' fertile Tibur gliding,
And groves, in leafy shade their votary hiding,
Shall in Æolian verse proclaim
To distant ages his ennobled name.

Of princely Rome the general voice
Has ranked me with her much-loved bards, the choice
Of Envy for a while denied,
Now in low murmurs all her taunts subside.

Oh thou who temperest the full swell
Of sounds that echo from the golden shell,
Who e'en from voiceless fish could'st pour
The swan's soft music in his dying hour!
'Tis thy sole bounty that I see
The passer-by's raised finger point out me,
And to that glorious style aspire—
The favorite minstrel of the Roman lyre,
That I can sing—oh power benign!—
And that I please (if that I please) is thine.

Book iv. Ode 9.

Ne forte credas interitura, quæ.

Oh! think not that the verse will die
Which tempered to the harmonious string,
With art of new-tried minstrelsy,
Here by my native stream I sing.

Though Homer fill the highest throne,
Lord of an universal reign,
Is Pindar's daring flight unknown;
Or bold Alcæus' threatening strain?

The measures by Anacreon played
Enchant us still; and warm and young
The raptures of the Æolian maid
As when her lips her passion sung.

Not first did Sparta's beauteous queen
The adulterer's garb and curls admire—
His glittering train and princely mien—
Till glowed her breast with guilty fire.

Not Teucer bent Cydonian bow
First, nor the brave old Cretan king
With his stout sire assailed the foe
In wars the Muse would gladly sing.

Not once was sacked imperial Troy,
  Nor Hector and his brethren brave,
For the chaste wife and nursling boy,
  Deep scars in fight received and gave.

'Ere Agamemnon left his coast
  Full many a hero fought and fell—
Their names are gone—their memory lost;
  They had no bard their fame to tell.

Little is manly virtue raised
  Above the grave of coward sloth,
If all unhonored and unpraised
  Oblivion's night encircle both.

Thy name, thy toils to serve the State,
  Shall, Lollius, by my lays be told—
Thy soul erect in every fate,
  Prudent and valiant—wise yet bold.

Consul, not only for the year
  Distinguished by the illustrious name,
But through all time to warm and cheer
  The bright example and the fame.

Oft as the faithful and the good,
  The Judge, sworn foe to fraud and wrong,
Firm in that dangerous gap has stood
  That parts the feeble and the strong.

Who spurns the Expedient for the Right,
  Scorns money's all-attractive charms,
And through mean crowds that clogged his fight
  Has nobly cleared his conquering arms.

Oh, never call that mortal blessed
  Who, boastful of his treasured store,
And of the much, too much, possessed,
  Yet, inly murmuring, pines for more.

More justly is that title given
  To him who, wisely grateful, shares
The large benevolence of Heaven,
  Yet poverty with patience bears.

Who shrinks from crime, and fears disgrace
  Far worse than death, that conquers all,
And Death himself can fearless face
  At friendship's or his country's call.

Book IV. Ode 12.

Jam veris comites, quæ mare temperant.

The Thracian airs that wait on Spring
Impel the vessel's canvas wing,
The brooks from wintry snows are freed,
  From hardening frost the mead.

The bird whose tuneful strains bewail
Cecropian horrors—dreadful tale!
Now with the expectant mother's care,
  Does her soft nest prepare.

While sheep on tender herbage graze,
Their guardian pipes his rustic lays,
Charming the deity that loves
  The Arcadian fields and groves.

Virgil, the times to thirst incline,
But would you taste my Chian wine,
Thou client of the rich and great,
  With nard must earn the treat.

A little box, no more I ask,
Shall from its cellar lift the cask,
Potent to kindle hope's bright ray,
  And wash foul care away.

Such pleasures if thou haste to share,
Come, but thy ransom with thee bear,
My flowing cups unbought I can not give,
  Wealth's proud prerogative.

Delays and love of gain suspend,
Think of the gloomy pyre, and blend
A little folly, sweet if rare,
  With the grave thoughts of care.

The two following translations, from Catullus and Beranger, were also made in his later years.

CATULLUS. ODE IV.

Phaselus ille quem videtis hospites.

Friends! this pinnace that you see
Says that none so fleet as she
Ever swam the waves—had force
To o'ertake her rapid course,
Taking flight from shore to shore,
Winged with sail, or urged by oar;
Says that Adria's dangerous coast,
And the Cyclads vouch her boast,
Rhodes, erect in noble pride,
Fierce Propontis' onward tide,
Wild, inhospitable Thrace,
And that gulf, her native place,
Where, though pinnace now, of yore
On the crest of high Cytore,
A leafy grove, she oft consigned
Whispers to the passing wind.
You, Amastris, Pontic Queen,
You, Cytore, with box-trees green,
Says our pinnace, long ago,
Well her history knew, and know

That she crowned your heights, her oars
First dipped in waves that wash your shores,
And through raging storms abhorred,
Thence in safety bore her lord.
Right or left the gales might blow,
Or with both Jove aid the prow,
Never did her crew assuage
With weak vows the sea-god's rage.
From the sea she earliest knew
To this lake,[1] so bright and blue.
Now all is past. No more she floats,
But, in age, to you devotes,
Earned by toil, her peaceful sleep,
Kind twin stars that rule the deep.

BERANGER. LA BONNE VIEILLE.

Vous vieillerez, o ma belle maitresse!

You must grow old, my beauteous wife!
  And time for me shall be no more,
The ebbing sands of shortened life,
  Escape with twice their speed of yore!
Survive me, but in wintry age
  Think of the joys that blessed our spring,
By the calm fire sad cares assuage,
  And sing the songs I used to sing.

Maidens and youths shall love to trace
  The fading lines where beauty dwelt,
With fond regard admire your face,
  No wonder at the flame I felt.
They'll ask you of this much-wept lover,
  Tell them my love, its warmth, its pains,
By the kind fire, oh talk me over,
  And sing again my favorite strains.

"Say was he kind?" oh, then confess,
  Without a blush, "I loved him ever,"
"Could gain or guile his soul possess?"
Proudly you'll answer, "Never, never!"
Tell, how he touched, with feeling true,
  To tenderer notes, a joyous string;
By the calm fire old thoughts renew,
  And sing the songs I used to sing.

I taught *your* tears for France to stream,
  Tell our brave youth. a patriot band,
That hope and glory were my theme,
  When prostrate lay our native land;
Tell how the furious northern blast
  Whelmed the fair bays of many a spring;
In the bright future plunge the past,
  And sing the songs I used to sing.

[1] The Lake of Como, where he dedicated the pinnace to Castor and Pollux.

Belovèd one, when my poor fame
  Claims in lone age your sorrowing hours,
When your weak hands my portrait frame
  With brightest wreaths of vernal flowers,
Think we shall meet in happier sphere;
  Joy has no end there, love no wing;
Bid hope your latest sunset cheer,
  And sing the songs I used to sing.

II. ORIGINAL VERSES.

Of the three following pieces, the first was written at Winterslow, A. D. 1796 (æt. 17); the two following, at Cambridge, A. D. 1799–1800 (æt. 20, 21).

Lines on Thorney Down,

A high hill, crowned with wood, rising over Salisbury Plain.

A. D. 1796, ÆT. 17.

Genius of that romantic hill, whose sod
Has often by my pilgrim feet been trod,
Hail, rough old sire, who lift'st thy head so high,
The monarch of this bleak sterility!
Hail to thy mossy venerable oaks,
Which never trembled at the woodman's strokes,
Where strongly working fancy can retrace
Religious fury on the Druid's face.
Hail to thy hoary thorns which downward grow,
Like the last wild locks on an old man's brow.
Thy yews amid the festal hollies green,
Which add the last gloom to this dreary scene,
To me this dreary scene more joy affords
Than the gay parks which please the pride of lords.

Say—for the dread Egyptians often find
In thy recesses shelter from the wind,
And oft the vagrant whom long wanderings tire
Borrows from thee a solitary fire—
To me when anxious with more just alarms,
Wilt thou unfold thy hospitable arms?
Wilt thou receive and comfort one poor guest,
Who flies the world and looks to thee for rest?

For oh! this world, where the raw lad aspires
To reach the glittering aim of his desires,
Whose path the artless girl would fain behold,
All strewed with roses and all paved with gold.
Surely this world, in solemn mockery drest,
Can give few pleasures to the generous breast,
And, far from common ill, for private good
The honest man would fly to solitude.

It must not be, and man would ill espouse
This partial plan, which reason disavows;
Whate'er his passions or desires may be,
Man's scene of action is society;
Sunk by calamity, involved in strife,
These are the only real terms of life,
In *equal portions* gratefully to share
Joy's honied drop, and the crude draught of care.

Yet sure, if aught such suffering can abate,
And set the soul beyond the reach of fate,
This precious balm with kindliest aid will fall
At some serene and peaceful interval,
When, to sublimely tempered thought inclined,
It leaves the bustle of the world behind.

Then up to view all nations would I call,
Their grandeur and subjection, rise and fall,
While history's page, extended to my eye,
Still more endears my native liberty.
Then Science might her varied gifts impart
Instruct the reason and amend the heart;
In every bud while moral maxims spring,
"Sermons in stones and good in everything."

The passions hushed, the temper mildly even,
While views of nature lift the soul to Heaven.
Oft as on this my rambling fancies turn,
I think of thee, old desolated bourn,
The quiet harbor, where my skiff may moor
When the winds whistle, and the thunders roar,
Where I, at ease, may all my tackling trim,
  Then tempt the wave once more, to sink or swim.

To the above may be added the following "Verses on the Slave Trade and the Press," written in 1846, published in 1847, and referred to in Chap. XXXI.

Hail to the Press, whose pitying care
  The friendless pauper's doom displayed,
The loathsome toil, the sordid fare,
  The swift disease, the lingering aid!
Hail to the Press, who dared to face
  The power austere and dimly seen,
Which, tow'ring in its pride of place,
  Contending factions[1] joined to screen!
Rebuke from thee the mighty found,
  The lowliest comfort and redress—
For such high service, freely sound
  Thy own just praises, generous Press!

[1] The abominations imputed to most persons concerned in administering the Poor Law in the Andover Union are alluded to.

O joyful thought!—For all the ills
  That injured men from men endure,
A power which can whate'er it wills,
  Proclaims a vengeance and a cure.
Well sang the bard of Hope—" Where'er
  Degraded nature groans or pines,
Scorched by hot Guinea's flagrant air
  Chill'd in Siberia's dreary mines,
Truth shall pervade the darkness there,
  With newly-wakened smiles to bless
The dreadful features of Despair," [1]
  Her guide, her guard, the glorious Press.

No respite for her noble rage,
  No idle sloth will guilt allow,
New battles daily called to wage,
  And weave fresh laurels for her brow.
Ev'n now o'er Afric's wasted soil
  The tide of savage war is rolled
That captive men, war's only spoil,
  By Christians may be bought and sold.
From home and country fiercely torn,
  The wife's embrace, the babe's caress,
Dragged to the fatal coast, in scorn
  Of Heav'n, of Nature, of the Press.

What hurrying ship escaped from view,
  Swift o'er the Atlantic waters ran?
Her ruling force a ruffian few,
  Her crowded cargo pinion'd man.
One only sight, one sound, to cheer
  The drooping, stifled, heart-struck slave,
To see a brother's death and hear
  His body plunge beneath the wave.[2]
Awake, arise! from death alone
  His bursting bosom hopes redress.
On earth, too, be some pity shown,
  Plead for the victims, Christian Press!

Not one, not ten—a hundred sail
  Skulking from many a creek and bay,
Hundreds in every floating jail,
  To life-long slavery bear away.
No crime has yoked the sable neck,
  And sunk young manhood in despair,
The ruthless jailors pace the deck,
  The worst, the only, culprits there.

[1] Campbell's "Pleasures of Hope."

"Where'er degraded nature groans or pines,
On Guinea's shore, in Sibir's dreary mines.
Truth shall pervade the unfathom'd darkness there,
And light the dreadful features of Despair," &c.

[2] Lord Brougham's speech on the Sugar Bill in the House of Lords, and Lord George Bentinck's in the House of Commons.

The guiltless on a foreign soil
  Condemned to till a burning field,
Waste wretched life in baneful toil,
  And feel the lash they ought to wield.

And dares the Legion fiend of Gold,
  Untired, inflexible, so long
By England baffled, shamed, controll'd,
  Hope for her recreant aid to Wrong?
And shall the slanderous demon say
  She has so soon the memory lost
Of deeds that gild her brightest day,
  Except to count and grudge their cost?
Nay, that her huckstering sons prepare,
  In loss and profit versed too well,
The thief to urge—his spoil to share?
  Indignant Press, the taunt repel!

What? tongue-tied all? at such a time
  Forget your triumph and your boast,
Champion of weakness, foe to crime,
  Slumbers the guard on SUCH a post?
If England tamely standing by,
  The just, the generous, and the free,
Can hear the tale with tearless eye,
  'Tis that she deems it can not be.
She knows thy tender sympathy,
  Thy pitying care for deep distress,
She waits the true alarm from thee,
  Her warning from the watchful Press.

The oracle adjured to speak
  Its high behest to worlds around,
Slow comes the answer, faint and weak,
  And mixed with many a vulgar sound.
"Unseen to us, the scourge, the rack,
  The mangled flesh, the torturing thong,
The slaves are 'distant,' they are 'black,'[1]
  Theirs is 'imaginary' wrong.
Unheard by us the piercing cries,
  Life's desperate struggle, latest groan,
On other heads the evil lies,
  The shameful gain is all our own.

"Impatient sufferers, quell your fears!
  Left to itself hard slavery breeds
Its own defeat in three score years;[2]
  Perhaps in five! May bloody deeds
Prompt bloodier vengeance! Hard the fate,
  Bitter the insults bondsmen feel,
Give your sad lives a shorter date,
  Fix in your tyrants' hearts the steel;
Approving England, calm and mute,
  Shall sip her cheapened sweets, and see

[1] "Times."

[2] "Daily News."

The man degraded to a brute,
  The slave by hate and crime set free!

"And sage philosophy declares,[1]
  From curious reasonings well combined,
That, dealing in whatever wares,
  Trade must range free and unconfined.
Free to make jest of scruples dry,
  The pirate's wages free to pay,
Deal in the war-won skulls,[2] and buy
  From the fell Thug his blood-stained prey.
This forcing hotbed Nature made,
  That Christian men to full success
May drive the sails of prosperous trade—
  Teach the true doctrine, liberal Press!

"*Can British fabrics find their gold*
  But from the toil of suffering slaves?[3]
Must care for Afric's woes withhold
  The least indulgence luxury craves?
Though outraged faith and honor chide,
  Though Nature shrink, though mercy weep,
Whatever ills mankind betide,
  WE SWEAR TO HAVE OUR SUGAR CHEAP!
Thus may the lowly peasant gain
  Luxurious meals before unknown,
And we, the great, no loss sustain,
  Except of our good name alone.

"The hypocrite[4] and saint may prate
  Of holy writ, and nature's law;
The ascendant star that sways our fate
  And keeps the spell-bound world in awe:
CONSISTENCY—the pride of Peel[5]
  The guiding light of Russell's course,[6]
Which braves the call of patriot zeal,
  But shrinks from clamor, yields to force.
Consistency demands that you,
  Britons, to whom some errors fall,

[1] "Morning Chronicle."

[2] Cannibalism was encouraged by Europeans in New Zealand, that the skulls of the slain might be made a subject of merchandise. The article was well known at the Custom House.

[3] Resolutions of the Anti-Slavery Committee in 1841 and 1846. At the latter period, though not at the former, they distinctly "deny that the Government measure will have any tendency to increase the Slave Trade!"

[4] "Spectator," &c.

[5] Catholic Emancipation; Government Plan of Education; Protection and Tariff; Sliding Scale and Free Trade; Income Tax; Mr. Cobden in 1843 and in 1846. Compare also the proem with the peroration, the argument with the vote of Sir Robert Peel on the sugar-duty question.

[6] Fixed Duty or Free Trade; Income Tax, Coercion Bill; Irish Arms' Bill, &c. Compare the slave measures of 1833 and 1838 with those of 1841 and 1846.

No base, no vicious aim eschew,
  But foster and promote them all.

"Let the stol'n negro pine a slave,
  Let ruthless Trade her curses shower,
Or I reject the boon you gave,
  And fling away this short-lived power."
The frigid Premier speaks the threat,
  To senators' enraptured ears,
A promise that their power shall yet
  Live to the end of sev'n long years.
In varying strains the skillful Press,
  Low reasoning or declaiming loud,
Hails the bold wrong, beyond redress
  Decreed, established, and avowed.

O great and venerable name,
  Albion ! illumed by Gospel light;
Boasting to build a deathless fame
  On the deep-rooted rock of Right,
Proud in Opinion's golden chain
  The admiring nation's hearts to bind,
And holding forth thy moral reign
  A faultless model for mankind—
How shall that triple bond outlast
  The dark resolve, the fatal hour
Which sees thee yield thy glorious Past
  To sordid Wealth, or baser Power?

O Thou whose equal eye surveys
  Unhappy Afric's realms undone,
From that abyss of misery raise
  These brethren of thy only Son ! [1]
O Thou, all wise, all just, all good,
  Deign to suppress thy wrath divine,
Forbear to visit, for the blood
  By Moloch poured on Mammon's shrine
Quench not the blush of honest shame,
  Touch reckless hearts with love again,
Let Christians still deserve their name,
  And men remember they are men !

[1] "Forasmuch as ye did it TO THE LEAST OF THESE, MY BRETHREN, ye did it unto me."

INDEX.

www.ingramcontent.com/pod-product-compliance
Lightning Source LLC
LaVergne TN
LVHW010159110826
845151LV00002B/555

* 9 7 8 1 4 2 5 5 3 6 2 4 4 *